COMPOSITIONAL DATA OBJECTS

The IMC/IMCL

Reference Manual

COMPOSITIONAL DATA OBJECTS

The IMC/IMCL

Reference Manual

Reiner Durchholz and **Gernot Richter**
Gesellschaft für Mathematik und Datenverarbeitung (GMD), Germany

JOHN WILEY & SONS
Chichester · New York · Brisbane · Toronto · Singapore

Other Wiley Editorial Offices

John Wiley & Sons, Inc., 605 Third Avenue,
New York, NY 10158-0012, USA

Jacaranda Wiley Ltd, G.P.O. Box 859, Brisbane,
Queensland 4001, Australia

John Wiley & Sons (Canada) Ltd, 22 Worcester Road,
Rexdale, Ontario M9W 1L1, Canada

John Wiley & Sons (SEA) Pte Ltd, 37 Jalan Pemimpin # 05-04,
Black B, Union Industrial Building, Singapore 2057

Library of Congress Cataloging-in-Publication Data

Durchholz, Reiner.
Compositional data objects : the IMC/IMCL reference manual /
Reiner Durchholz and Gernot Richter.
p. cm.
Includes bibliographical references (p.) and index.
ISBN 0 471 93470 4
1. Data structures (Computer science) 2. Object-oriented
programming (Computer science) I. Richter, Gernot II. Title.
QA76.9.D35D87 1992
005.7'3—dc20 92-25262
CIP

British Library Cataloguing in Publication Data

A catalogue record for this book is available from the British Library

ISBN 0 471 93470 4

Produced from camera-ready copy supplied by the authors
Printed and bound in Great Britain by Bookcraft (Bath) Ltd.

Contents

Preface

With the advent of database systems in the late sixties and early seventies, "data structures" came to the fore as objects in their own right, separate from the programs for their processing. Thus, in the past two decades, the issue of data structures has been of particular concern in the database world. With the growing conceptual autonomy of data structures evidence increased that the data in a database represent information about an application world, or, more precisely, formal models of pieces of information about this world. Applications in business and administration predominated. To capture the information structures typically found in these areas, various data models were proposed. They were usually seen as belonging to one of three classes: the hierarchical, the network or the relational model class. To maintain a survey of proposed models and to understand similarities and differences was not easy. Some efforts were made to clarify the relationship between model classes (e.g., [Wolf74], [Earn74], [StHe75]). Others attempted direct comparison of single models (e.g., [KeKlTs77]). Quite soon, the variety of data models required a systematic compilation and comparison of their features [CODA73b]. It was then that the need for a comparative formal description of the various approaches to information structure modelling based on a common conceptual system became apparent. Recent interest in logically integrating distributed heterogeneous databases (see, for example, [Rade91], [SiStUl91]) has given new topicality to such an effort.

Research on a formal system of information management concepts (later called IMC) was initiated by the authors in 1972 when a rigorous description for the then much-discussed DBTG network data structures was desirable ([CODA73a], [DuRi72]). It turned out that the conceptual setup chosen was also helpful for the analysis of various other data models. The main goal of IMC was to provide a system of mathematically defined concepts for the formal description of structured information: information about physical and abstract objects is modelled in terms of so-called *constructs*, which in turn are *composed* of other constructs. "Information modelling by composition" was therefore preferred as being more to the point for the abbreviation IMC. Its basic ideas were presented to the public in the seventies ([DuRi74], [DuRi76]). In those days, there was much excitement about relational approaches, and emphasis on structural adequacy in response to semantic requirements was developing. In that context, attempts at more general conceptual frameworks for data and information structures ([Bosa62], [Zema68], [Chil68], [LuLaSt70], [Turs71], [Seve72]) received less attention than they deserved.

The more the three established data models came into practice, the more it became evident that substantial extensions were called for to satisfy actual information modelling needs. Two streams of development gradually became influential, andthus gave new impetus to dealing with general information structure concepts: data abstraction and enhancements within the compositional paradigm.

Data abstraction started from the programming language field and penetrated all other fields, in particular that of databases—though reluctantly in the latter case. Practical tools for information structure specification in the context of formal software specification, as, for example, the Vienna Development Method (VDM, [BjJo78]) and Z [Dill90], emanated from this strain and enjoyed wide recognition. In recent years, data abstraction has been put into the context of object-orientation: object-oriented database systems ([Banc88], [LeRi89], [Kim90], [Ditt90], [Otis91]) became a research field attempting to merge features of object-oriented programming with information modelling capabilities constituting an "object-oriented data model". From this point of view, the hierarchical and the network model class can today be regarded as the basis of "the ancient systems with object identity" [Ullm87], while the relational model class is seen as probably the first so-called "value-oriented" data model of practical relevance.

Enhancement of *compositional information models* was pursued in two ways: semantic constraints and increased compositional expressiveness. With the goal of capturing more meaning, non-compositional *semantic constraints* were added to existing compositional structures. Some of them served to compensate for compositional restrictions in a particular data model, while others were designed to express inherently non-compositional properties of information structures. *Compositional expressiveness* was augmented basically by relaxing structural restrictions. Unnormalized relations began to play a role when it was recognized that normalized relations had difficulties in coping with heterogeneous, richly structured information. In particular, NF^2 (*non-first-normal-form*) and other forms of nested relations were widely investigated ([ScSc84], [GyPaGu89], see also [PiTr86] and [ScSc89] for bibliographies).

Within this environment, IMC maintained its own application-oriented line of emphasis: to be general enough for conveniently describing all data structures usually occurring in programming languages and databases, but to be specific enough to provide easy access to basic structures, to incorporate generally held views on data structure, and to support visualization by composition diagrams. IMC is general in that it adequately covers all commonly discussed data models, including NF^2 and other nonconventional models with large or complex information objects and extensible type structures [HuKi87]. IMC is specific in that it is deliberately narrower than operational approaches (abstract data types). As a *value-oriented* model, IMC could be used for information modelling in value-oriented systems. For future applications of knowledge-base management and nonconventional database management these systems may be preferable to object-oriented systems "because they offer the user arbitrary access to data, with access expressed declaratively" [Ullm87] (see also [Comm91] and [SiStUl91]).

Much attention has been paid to finding languages that appropriately support IMC concepts. From the very beginning, two graphical languages have been developed along with the conceptual foundations, aiming at a conspicuous, yet formally defined representation of the compositional properties of complex information structures. In the eighties, a first-order IMC language, IMCL, was elaborated. Starting from built-in standard operators and predicates, application specific language elements can be defined, which allow one to specify arbitrarily nested information structures along with sophisticated integrity constraints across their components.

The merits of IMC/IMCL lie in the selection of an easily surveyed, still comprehensive functional basis for data structure description, its elaboration to considerable detail, and a systematic treatment of the spot concept, together with practical auxiliary concepts, operators, relations and pertinent language representations. The spot concept, which we found to be present in other work implicitly only, if at all, is a novel idea and a prominent feature of IMC. In a sense, it captures the common idea behind various concepts of access paths. Referring to spots in order to address information objects in their context turned out to be instrumental both in component manipulation on all levels of aggregation and in the definition of complex consistency constraints as they are required, for example, in CAD or CIM systems, office systems, spatial databases in geographic or environmental information systems, or in document management systems.

The characteristics of a design language are substantially determined by the way it handles abstractions. Although the compositional paradigm by itself does not convey the idea of abstraction, it does not impede it either. All abstraction capabilities a first-order language can offer are available in IMCL. One may defer decisions on compositional features until the appropriate design stages by introducing (abstract) operators and predicates. Thus, specification hierarchies and relationships between abstraction levels can be established.

IMCL can be used to specify information structures and transformations of a system if combined with a suitable model for systems and processes (e.g., a conventional programming language for sequential systems, or Petri nets for concurrent systems). Applications of experimental versions of IMCL—then called IML—for systems modelling can be found in [Rich81b], [RiDu82], and [HeRi86]. It is, however, not designed as a stand-alone system-modelling language since it does not include dynamic aspects.

As part of a system-modelling language, IMCL also conforms to the currently much-discussed paradigm of object-orientation. It meets two requirements for the definition of what elsewhere has been called *structurally object-oriented data models* [Ditt90]: recursive composition and user-definable types. Unrestricted recursiveness of construct composition is the basic structural principle of IMC. Composite constructs are always composed of other constructs that are objects in their own right and may be composite themselves. Admission of user-definable types, meaning that really new types can be introduced to the system by its users and afterwards dealt with in the same way as with predefined ones, is one of the strengths of IMCL. It permits arbitrary consistency constraints or "rules" to be established for user-defined types, and new operators tailored to such types and used like built-in ones to access and modify object structures on all levels of composition. In particular this feature has recently been applied to formally specify an international standard on office document architecture ([ApCaTe90], [Rugg90], [ISO91]).

In summary, IMC/IMCL comprises three major items: (i) a formal system of concepts for compositional information modelling, (ii) a set of graphical symbols and syntactic rules for the exact representation of compositional properties of information structures, and (iii) a first-order language for specifying arbitrarily nested information structures both on the specific and on the generic level. Experience and observation show that the compositional view of information structure is still a favorite way of thinking for many users. Data designers on all levels tend to think in terms of composition when they model information about the application world. They want this view to be supported at the interface of their application system. To the extent to which this is true, IMC/IMCL is claimed to be an appropriate choice.

How to read this manual

The sections of the manual serve different purposes and are of different importance. The following list provides a guide to the roles of the sections:

	1	Introduction	supplementary
→	**2.1**	**Constructs**	**basic concepts**
	2.2	Some well-known constructs	illustrative
→	**2.3**	**Spots**	**basic concepts**
→	**3.1**	**Language considerations**	**basic concepts**
→	**3.2**	**Language description**	**basic concepts**
	3.3	Examples	illustrative
	4	The development of IMC/IMCL in perspective	supplementary
	App. A	Constructs and spots in systems	supplementary
	App. B	Algebraic specification of IMC	supplementary

The arrows mark the essential sections. In principle, these are sufficient for understanding IMC and IMCL. For an informal understanding sufficient for the use of IMCL, the heart of the matter is covered in Sections 2.1.2, 2.3.2 and 3.2.

The sections on basic concepts are organized for sequential reading, although there are occasionally forward references in the earlier parts, in particular to the language IMCL introduced in Chap. 3.

Chapter 1

Introduction

Compositional versus operational view on data structure

Information structure description is a ubiquitous issue of information processing. Therefore it is highly desirable to make available a general conceptual frame appropriate for most, if not all, descriptional needs with respect to information structure.

In practice, there are basically two ways to look at information structure. One, the "inter-object" way, establishes relations between objects, where the objects themselves are considered elementary entities. Axiomatic set theory, for example, formally does not care about how a set is internally structured. Rather, it envisages elementary objects (classes), which are related by the abstract inter-object $\in$-relation. Thus, the number "2" is related to "natural numbers" by the is-element relation $\in$. It is not "part" of a composite object "natural numbers" (Fig. 1.1).

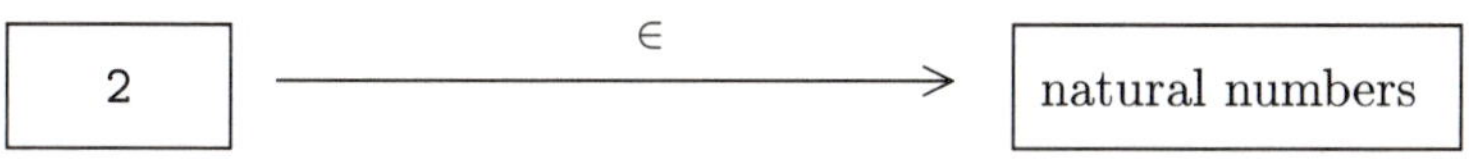

Figure 1.1 : The inter-object view: object related to another object

As another "operational" example, think of complex numbers characterized by their behavior under certain operations, for example, addition, multiplication and conjugation. Under this view, the imaginary part of a number, for example, is not a "component", but simply the result of certain combined operations.

The inter-object view is preferred in mathematical theories and in the formal semantics of predicate logic. It is most prevalent in algebra. "Inner" properties of objects are entirely dismissed. Only those properties are considered that an object displays under application of an operator. We call the inter-object view the *operational approach to information structure modelling*. ("Operational" is here understood as also including relations by way of "characteristic functions", that is, mappings of relation tuples to binary values.)

The other way to look at information structure is the "intra-object" one. Here, objects are considered as being composed of other objects. For this reason we call this view also the *compositional approach to information structure modelling*. Under this view, we call the objects **constructs**. Constructs have inner properties, seemingly independent from any operations that are or may be defined on them. For example, in the usual intuitive perception, a set is thought of as being composed from its elements. Thus the object "natural numbers" is seen as *containing* the number "2" (Fig. 1.2).

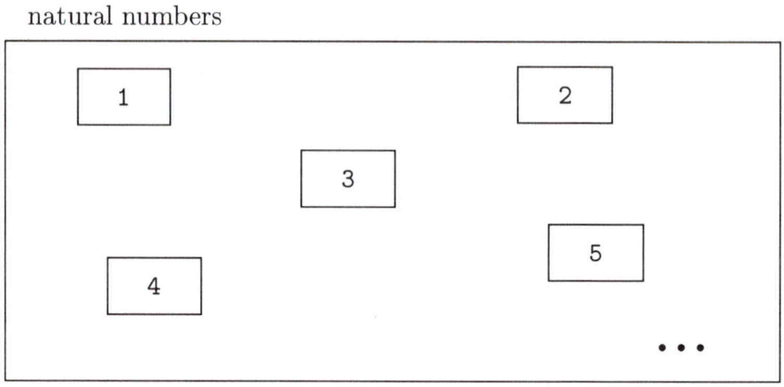

Figure 1.2 : The intra-object view: object composed of other objects

Its identity and qualities are considered independent of how many and which relations or operators are defined for it.

Similarly, under a compositional view, a complex number would be regarded as a construct made up of two components, the real and the imaginary part. Extraction of these parts would be performed by general decomposition operators supplied by the overall compositional framework. Conjugation, if required, could then be described by decomposition, negation and re-composition.

The compositional view is preferred in traditional programming languages and in database management systems. In particular, database people are accustomed to diagrams that show the composition of data objects up to any necessary degree of complexity.

Either way of viewing information structure has its own merits. The compositional way is more conspicuous and provides a stable reference for the introduction of new operators and relations. The operational way is more general and avoids questions about the distinction between compositional and non-compositional properties. (The latter arise for example when atomic compositional objects are to be defined: should a complex number be an atom or should it be considered a compound of a real and an imaginary part?)

Both views are closely related though they are not equivalent. Whereas compositional structures can always be described operationally as inter-object relations, the converse is not true. Compositional structure is based on some sort of component concept. This can always be "externalized", i.e., converted into an inter-object relation. For example, a set seen as being constituted of its elements becomes an elementary object for which an $\in$-relation connecting it to its elements is established. In contrast, there are a number of operational structures which cannot, or at least not naturally, be interpreted in a compositional way. In data structure considerations, one will hardly want to see the number "2" being treated as a component of the number "7" (as is done in the classical von Neumann definition of natural numbers in set theory).

An explicit elaboration of how compositional structure modelling can be translated into an operational one is given in Appendix B. This is rather straightforward.

As noted above, the compositional approach is more restricted than the operational one. However, restriction is not necessarily a disadvantage. In contrast, if done in the right way, it may more directly lead to the points of interest. Under this aspect, the relation between compositional and operational structure modelling acquires yet another appearance: Call *compositional algebra* an operational specification if it employs operators which satisfy axioms of an intuitively compositional nature. Compositional algebras have the advantage that part of the structure they provide can be made evident by compositional diagrams. There are obviously very many compositional algebras for a given compositional structure. In this sense, compositional structures can be considered as an abstraction of a class of algebras. Note that we have not provided a hard definition of what is a "compositional algebra". Although the task of finding such a definition would be interesting enough, it is not pursued here.

Another important aspect of information structure must be mentioned in this context: *pointers*. For a compositional approach, pointers are foreign. Nevertheless, they are a powerful means for expressing binary relations and handling them locally. They also allow for cyclic data structures. There was considerable temptation to put pointers on top of the compositional structure, but the authors resisted it, backed by the observation of others that pointers may be harmful to information structure in the same way as go-to's may be harmful to control structure ([Dijk68], [Hoar75]). Thus, pointers are not supported by IMC, although in IMCL, an IMC language proposed in this manual (Chap. 3), names can be abused for this, something we do not recommend (see also the discussion on names in Sec. 2.1.2.4).

The work presented here is dedicated to the elaboration of a fairly general framework for compositional information structure modelling. It is meant to support information handling in a uniform way as far as the compositional view is applicable. In particular, many classical as well as more recent "nonconventional" data models can adequately be described within this framework.

An important genuine compositional notion

In dealing with compositional structure, a very important and extremely useful concept has evolved. This concept is an abstract counterpart for the intuitive idea associated with pointing into an information structure diagram and saying "here", as in phrases like "this component here must be deleted" or "this component is to be replaced by another object". The salient point is, that in general the "here" is not identified uniquely by the component as such (a word may have several occurrences of the same letter), but rather by the context in which it appears. To deal conceptually with the idea of "here" requires a way of identifying contexts. This is done in IMC with the concept of **spot**. For example, the letter "i" occurs at two different spots in the word "information".

Languages for compositional information modelling

Beyond the *concepts* for dealing with compositional structure, *languages* for expressing objects in a compositional fashion are also provided. There are two pictorial languages (box notation and tree notation) which directly show the composition, and a textual language, IMCL (IMC language), which allows description of objects by reference to other objects and application of operators. The explicit use of operators in IMCL of course provides another link to the algebraic view. The language expressions are *precise* and to a desired degree *complete* descriptions of constructs. This is worth mentioning particularly for the pictorial languages, because very often pictures and diagrams are presented with no clearly defined semantics. They often obscure rather than clarify an issue.

Not only has IMCL to deal with constructs, but also with spots. Spots are actually the primary objects of manipulation and therefore are normally more prominent than constructs themselves in actual applications of IMCL. Spots are selected by selection criteria, which are not necessarily unique. Thus, the objects most naturally dealt with are not even spots, but rather sets of spots. Expressions for sets of spots are therefore the most important language features of IMCL. Because sets of spots are so important and so frequently mentioned, we term them **spotsets** for convenience.

Some elementary language expressions of IMCL are introduced in Chap. 2 as the concepts turn up. In Chap. 3, they are given a second time in a systematic and comprehensive fashion. To show how to customize IMCL to meet application-dependent descriptional needs, examples for the definition of language elements are given in Sec. 3.3.

In practical applications, information objects are dealt with in the context of information systems, that is, in the context of transformation, management and exchange of information. Because of the inherent dynamics of the environment in which they are considered, aspects beyond merely static structure turn up. They are all centred around the question of stability in the face of change (invariants). Important notions in that respect are *types* and *identity concepts*. For these, some key ideas are discussed in Appendix A.

Chapter 2

IMC: information modelling by composition

Remarks on notation

Usual mathematical and logical notation is presupposed in the description of IMC and IMCL, employing a few additional conventions as given below. This notation is for the purpose of the present manual only. The "Manual Language" must be distinguished from the language IMCL defined in Chap. 3.

The mathematical concepts used are mainly the elementary ones of set theory . In particular, we will need the concepts of set, function and sequence. We assume that functions and sequences are somehow defined, without being interested in the details of the definitions. However, for the usage envisaged in IMC, it is more appropriate to think of such concepts as being mutually exclusive, that is, that functions are not sequences and that neither functions nor sequences are sets. Further, we do not deal with transfinite constructions or infinite sequences. The following definitions provide concepts in response to these requirements. For any sets x and n, we define:

$\mathrm{S}(x) := \{\text{s-encode}(s) \mid s \subseteq x,\ s \text{ finite or countable}\}$,

$\mathrm{F}(n,x) := \{\text{f-encode}(f) \mid f\colon\ n \rightarrow x,\ f \text{ finite or countable function}\}$,

$\mathrm{Q}(x) := \{\text{q-encode}(q) \mid q \text{ finite sequence of elements from } x\}$.

In these, s-encode, f-encode and q-encode are arbitrary encoding functions the only requirements for which are that they are injective and have mutually exclusive ranges. (For instance, one could choose s-encode(s)=(1,s), f-encode(f)=(2,f), q-encode(q)=(3,q).) Thus, S(x), F(n,x) and Q(x) are mutually exclusive and there is a common inversion function "decode", for which decode(s-encode(s))=s, decode(f-encode(f))=f, decode(q-encode(q))=q. We will make use of these functions in the present section only.

We say, for a given set x:

"**subset** (of x)"	when we formally mean an element of S(x)
"**function** (from n to x)"	when we formally mean an element of F(n,x),
"**sequence** (over x)"	when we formally mean an element of Q(x),

and we use the usual set-theoretic symbols for encoded sets as well. For example, $a \cap b$ is meant to be s-encode(decode(a)$\cap$decode(b)), where the latter occurrence of "$\cap$" is meant as intersection in the ordinary set-theoretic sense. Similarly, in the following all other set-theoretic concepts are understood as applying to encoded objects in this sense.

Apart from the usual set-theoretical symbols, we also need symbolism for function application, function modification, explicit sequences and sequence concatenation. If f is a function and b is an object from its domain, then we write as usual $f(b)$ for the value of f on b in Chap. 2. (IMCL will employ a different notation, see Chap. 3.) Function modification is written in the form $f(x{\mapsto}y)$, which means the function identical to f, except for the argument x, for which the value y is assigned, regardless of f being defined for x or not. An explicit description of a (finite) sequence is denoted by a pair of parentheses enclosing a listing of the members. A sequence with only one member x is denoted (x). The sequence containing no members is denoted "()". Concatenation of finite sequences is denoted by the symbol "$\frown$". Thus

$$(a,b,c)\frown(b)\frown() = (a,b,c,b).$$

Predicate logic is used together with natural language. Where natural language is sufficiently precise and where it appears to give better guidance, it is preferred to predicate language. Also, within predicate logic expressions, concession is occasionally made to natural language habits. For example, "$x \in M \wedge y \in M$" is expressed by "$x,\ y \in M$".

2.1 Constructs

In this section, the ideas that lead to the notion of construct are outlined and the notion is formally defined. Subsection 2.1.1 discusses overall considerations. Subsection 2.1.2 gives an informal introduction to and motivations behind the various kinds of constructs adopted for IMC. Subsection 2.1.3 presents concise, formal definitions of the concepts considered so far. The formally-minded reader may find it more appropriate to skip Subsection 2.1.2 and go directly to Subsection 2.1.3 for looking at the structure on which IMC starts out. Subsection 2.1.4 outlines some ideas on extending IMC within the compositional paradigm.

2.1.1 Rationale of the approach

Constructs are the formal objects which are intended for interpretation as compositional models of structured information. There are two generic types of constructs, **atoms**, which are not composed of other constructs, and **compounds**, which are composed of other constructs. Only very few (i.e., three) composition principles are used to form compounds. But these may be applied repeatedly an arbitrary, but finite, number of times. Thus, provision is made for modelling information with any finite depth of nesting.

The admission of arbitrary nesting in compositional structures has been termed "recursive data structure" in [Hoar75], because their definitions (and, hence, their type structures) are recursive. The objects, however, are not recursive by themselves, since any particular object cannot be part of itself.

The constructs of which a compound is composed on the highest level are called **immediate components** of the compound. **Components** of a construct are those constructs which can be obtained by repeated selection of immediate components. Of course, immediate components are also considered components of the compound. (Later on (Sec. 2.3), the meaning of the word "component" will be extended.)

There are also compounds which do not have components. They are called **empty constructs**. Note that empty constructs are not considered atoms. This is for clarity of the aggregational complexity of the construct, and for convenience reasons. Operators can be defined more naturally if they can treat empty constructs as being composite.

IMC employs three composition principles (collections, nominations and catenations) to obtain information description of any desired compositional complexity. One will rightly ask, why exactly these three principles? The question has two aspects: (1) Why not the set-theoretic "$\in$" only, which is known to be sufficient for describing compositional structure? (2) Why not other, or more, composition principles?

Aspect (1) emphasizes formal properties. Whereas it is true that the "$\in$"-relation suffices, we are not interested in a minimal set of concepts, but rather in one that gives us direct access to views most often encountered in information structure considerations. Formally speaking, the composition principles are indeed defined on the basis of the $\in$-relation.

Aspect (2) addresses the practical value of the choice of the three principles. As a matter of experience in information modelling, we have found the selected composition principles on the one hand to be ubiquitous, on the other hand to be sufficient for most information structure description tasks, in particular in the area of databases. This does of course not preclude the desirability of other, fancier structures in particular applications. IMC is to be considered an attempt to make explicit a common smallest base on which information description can reasonably be handled. We have quite often encountered an urge to extend the repertoire of prefabricated compositional operators, because further structures appeared to be of high general interest. However, we deliberately refrained from extensions of this kind, because any step beyond would increase a bias towards specific fields of application. Some ideas on this issue can be found in Sec. 2.1.4.

2.1.2 Informal introduction to constructs

2.1.2.1 Box and tree notation

Compositional information structure shows its virtues particularly in its ability to support conspicuous pictorial representations. In addition to the linear notation of IMCL, boxes and trees are introduced as language elements for graphically representing constructs. The present section surveys principles of these languages. Individual language elements are introduced as they turn up.

In **box notation**, a construct is represented as a rectangular box (Fig. 2.1).

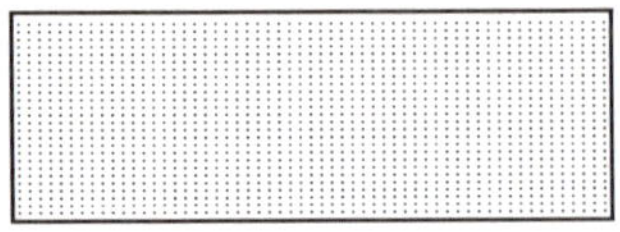

Figure 2.1 : Box notation for constructs: a framed construct description

The shaded interior of the box stands for an optional further description of the construct. There are two ways for such a description: (i) using an arbitrary language (which could be a natural language, but also a formal language such as IMC tree, linear, or again box notation), (ii) using a characteristic syntax which explicitly specifies the construct's immediate composition (see Fig. 2.2).

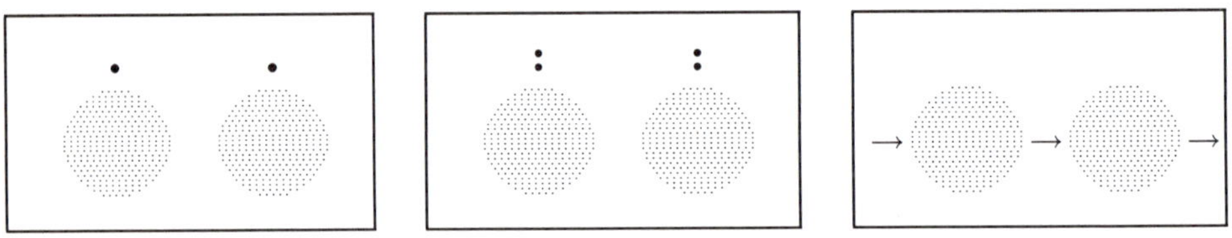

Figure 2.2 : Immediate composition in box notation

The characteristic symbols **•**, **:** and $\rightarrow$ indicate compositional structure which is explained later. The shaded regions stand for immediate component descriptions not specified here. These may, of course, themselves be in box notation.
An example may be useful to illustrate the conventions (Fig. 2.3).

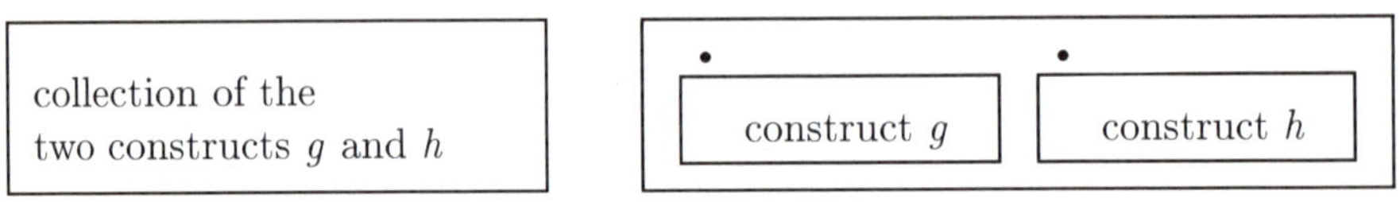

Figure 2.3 : Two ways of providing further description

The characteristic symbols indicate that explicit immediate composition syntax is used and are thus sufficient for distinguishing both kinds of description. At times, however, one may be concerned about possible confusion. Thus, if g is an arbitrary description of a construct (say, a variable the value of which is that construct), a box containing just g represents that construct, whereas when additionally tagged with a component symbol it represents a construct with g as its only component (Fig. 2.4).

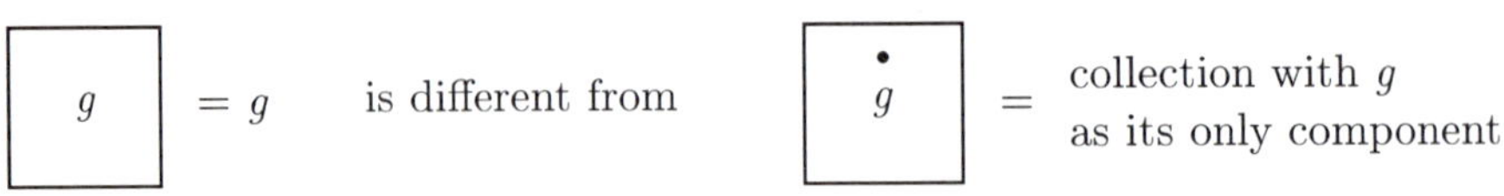

Figure 2.4 : A component symbol introduces a further level of nesting

Absence of characteristic component symbols may be emphasized by a horizontal bar on the bottom of the box, indicating that the object of the description is the entire construct rather than a single component (see Fig. 2.5).

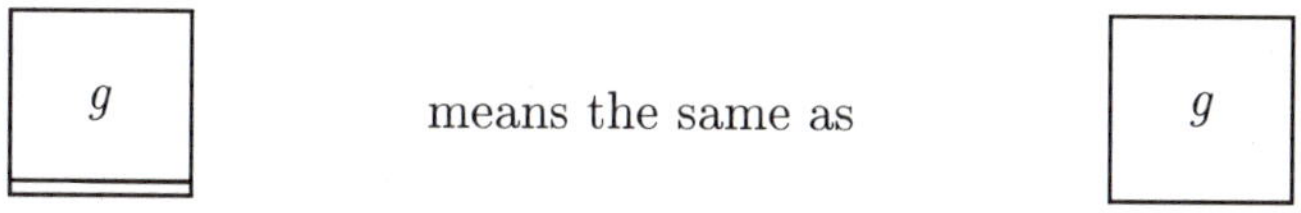

Figure 2.5 : Emphasizing the absence of characteristic composition symbols

A construct having no components cannot be represented in explicit immediate composition syntax. Special symbols for atomic and empty constructs are introduced below.

If one wants to represent an arbitrary construct without saying which one, an empty box is used (Fig. 2.6).

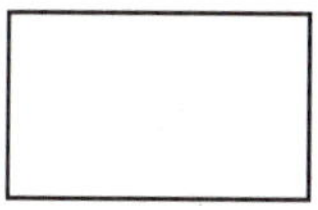

Figure 2.6 : Box notation for "any construct"

The **tree notation** for constructs is an alternative way of explicitly describing composition. The root of a tree corresponds to the comprising box while the next level nodes indicate the kind of immediate composition (Fig. 2.7). Also in this case, the shaded regions stand for construct descriptions which in turn may be in any notation, in particular again in tree notation.

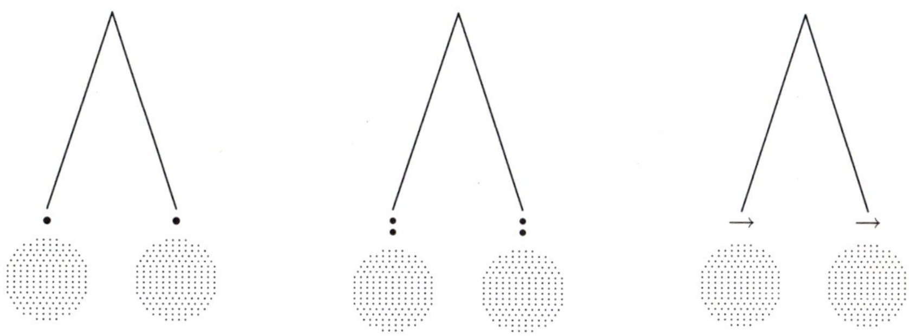

Figure 2.7 : Immediate composition in tree notation

2.1.2.2 Atoms

Each application determines which objects are to be considered atoms. There may be finitely or infinitely many atoms. The application also defines which operators are applicable to atoms. However, if such operators introduce structure which is compositional by nature, the atoms have probably been chosen inadequately. Resuming the complex number example of Chap. 1, think of an application with an emphasis on just pairing real numbers, but not on using complex arithmetic. In such a case, it would be more appropriate to see a complex number as a compound having real number components, rather than postulating complex number atoms. Operators REAL(z), IM(z) (extract real and imaginary part, respectively) and CMPL(x,y) (build complex number) would then appear as tools for composing and decomposing constructs rather than as abstract mappings between real and complex numbers.

Thus, one can assume that in an appropriate use of IMC for information modelling, all operators on atoms are non-compositional by nature and hence beyond the scope of IMC proper. They introduce structure not recognizable in the IMC conceptual frame. However, the language for describing constructs, IMCL (in its "nonstandard semantic specifications", see Sec. 3.1.2.1), also accomodates such foreign operators. It is particularly important for retrieval to have means for analysing properties of atoms. Arithmetic and Boolean operators as usually understood in programming languages are examples of standard non-compositional operators. An example of an application-dependent, non-compositional operator is one that transforms a calendar date atom into the number of the day in the year.

As an example of the necessity of application-dependent atom definition and handling, consider postal addresses. If addresses are used only as inscriptions for letters to be mailed, they can appropriately be treated as atoms. If for postal delivery the mail should be sorted according to ZIP code, a comparison operator on addresses could be introduced. Alternatively, one could decide to make the address a compound, where the ZIP code is a component. In this case, the standard arithmetic comparison operator "<" could be used to *induce* a (partial) ordering on addresses.

The question of what are atoms and what operators should be defined on them is very much the same as that of which structure one wants to see in a compositional way. Although there are many cases where a natural answer is quite obvious, there may also be difficult ones. For example, in a usual book-keeping environment nobody would suggest considering natural numbers as compounds with their prime factors as components. In a number theory application, however, this may be exactly what one wants to see. An example case where the decision may be difficult is the handling of text strings. Whether a word will be considered an atom or a compound built from syllables or characters much depends on the intended use and it is not unlikely that an initial decision will be revised later.

In box notation, an atom is designated by a rectangle with an inscription identifying the atom, for example, as in Fig. 2.8.

Figure 2.8: Box notation for "specific atom" (a) and for "any atom" (b)

If one wants to express that a construct is an atom without saying which one, a wiggle is used for the inscription (Fig. 2.8).

In tree notation, an atom has no particular symbol. For an atom as a node in a tree, box notation or linear notation could be used.

In the linear notation of IMCL, some commonly used atoms can be designated by a number in usual decimal notation, by `YES` or by `NO`. These language expressions are called *standard constants*. In addition, for introducing application-dependent *special* atoms, so-called *nonstandard constants* may be used. (Note, however, that the value of a nonstandard constant is not necessarily an atom.) A nonstandard constant is an arbitrary string enclosed in apostrophes, but not containing unpaired apostrophes ('). Examples for constants are:

`7     'ABC'     '7'`

Note that `7` is a standard constant designating a number atom, while `'7'` is a nonstandard constant.

2.1.2.3 Collections

A collection is a set of constructs. The set elements of a collection are its **immediate components**. Note that immediate components of a collection are constructs. Thus, not every set is a collection.

It is important to observe that, according to the axiom of extensionality, a collection is completely identified by the immediate components it has. That is, if collection a and collection b have the same immediate components, then $a{=}b$, no matter in what context they occur or with what intention they are used. Further, infinite collections are not excluded. It can be very convenient for modelling to have infinity concepts available as an abstraction of the notion of "larger than can sensibly be handled by enumerative methods".

Collections (sets), although commonplace in mathematics, have received relatively little attention in data processing. This is probably due to the sequential organization of physical stores and the sequential mode of operation of classical data processing machines. This has on the one hand caused a rather deep-seated sequential way of thinking in people concerned with structuring data, on the other hand, it has proved to be an obstacle to dealing elegantly with sets. Even the relational information model approach, which is genuinely based on the set concept, is biased toward sequentialization as soon as processing is involved (see, for example, the notion of "duplicate").

Nonetheless, set structures are natural in several cases and have, in fact, been advocated by some researchers. They have been proposed particularly in SETL and have also more recently been investigated from various points of view ([Kupe87], [Banc88], [HuSu89], [HaRi89]). If sequentialization is forced by the descriptional tool employed, overspecification ensues, which usually has detrimental effects on modularity (particularly for design changes), clarity of structural requirements and efficiency (when a processor is forced to adhere to a specific sequence although it could use a more efficient one, or even parallel processing).

In box notation, a collection is depicted as a rectangle containing representations for its immediate components, each marked by a bullet (Fig. 2.9).

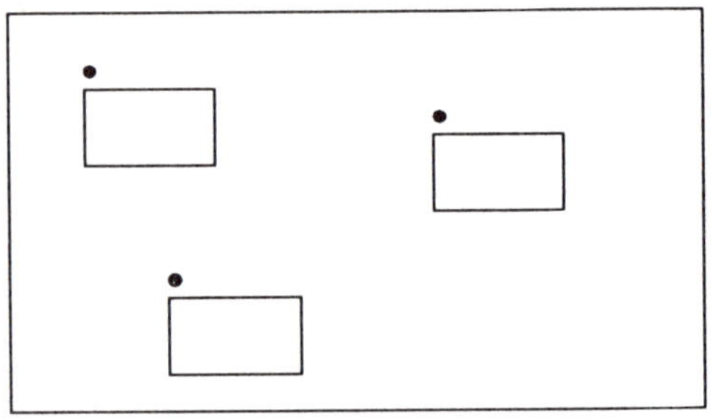

Figure 2.9 : Box notation for collection

Fig. 2.10 is an example of a (nested) collection. In this figure, as well as in subsequent representation examples, (strings of) lowercase letters are used as descriptional variables which stand for arbitrary constructs.

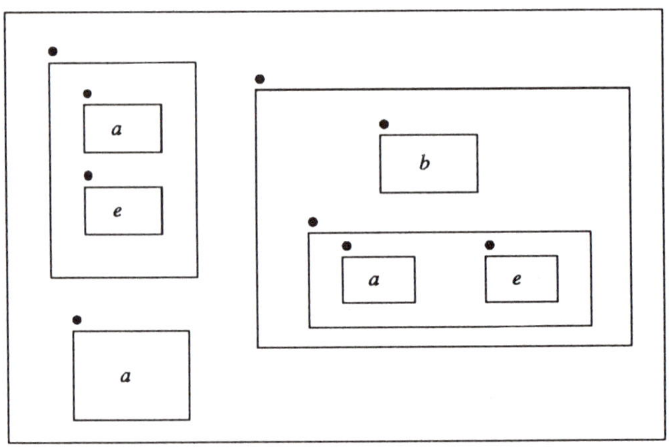

Figure 2.10 : Nested collection in box notation

The positioning, size and shape of the component boxes is irrelevant, so that the collection in Fig. 2.10 is the same as the one in Fig. 2.11.

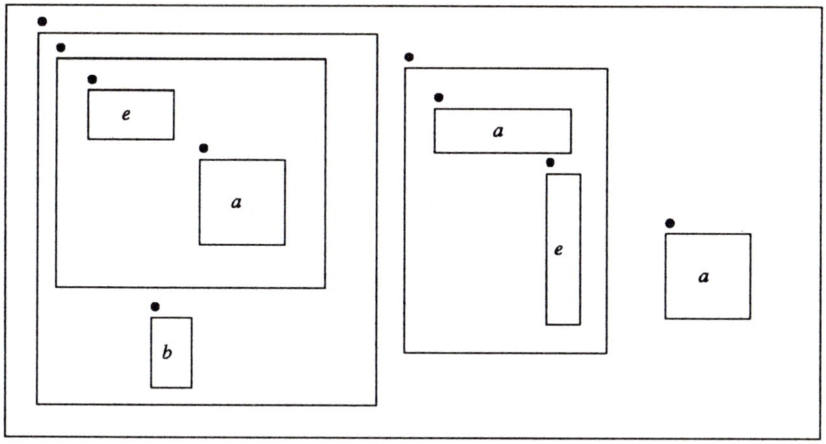

Figure 2.11 : The same collection as in Fig. 2.10

The empty collection is indicated by a diagonal bar with a bullet inserted (Fig. 2.12).

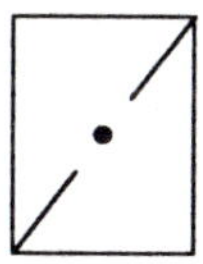

Figure 2.12 : Box notation for the empty collection

In tree notation, a collection is depicted by as many forking lines (branches) as the collection has immediate components, with bullets and representations of the immediate components appended, for example, as in Fig. 2.13.

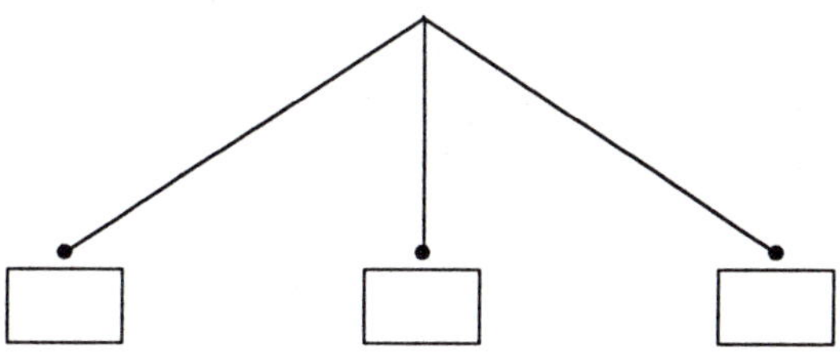

Figure 2.13 : Tree notation for collection

The nodes may be detailed further by representations of the immediate components, which may, in particular, in turn be trees. The order of the branches of a collection is immaterial. In a complete expansion, the above example could be rendered as in Fig. 2.14.

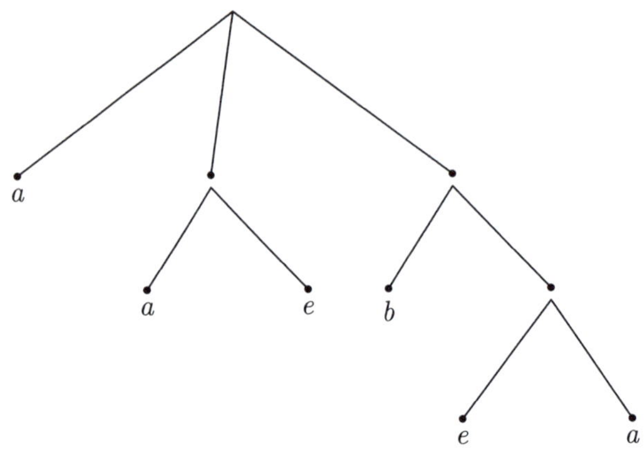

Figure 2.14: The collection of Fig. 2.10 in tree notation

In the linear notation of IMCL, a collection is designated by a list of constructs, where semicolons are taken as separation symbols and brackets as delimiting symbols. The order in the list is immaterial. The above example could be written

[a;[a;e];[b;[a;e]]]

or [[[a;e];b];a;[a;e]]

or any other sequence of the list or its sublists.

The empty collection is written [].

2.1.2.4 Nominations

A nomination is a function which maps names onto constructs. The names on which a nomination is defined constitute the **name set** of the nomination. For a nomination g, its name set is written NAMESET(g). The constructs which are function values of the nomination are its **immediate components**. Note that neither the names nor the (name,component)-pairs are immediate components. The prominent feature of nominations is that their names are *locally unique*. "Locally" means that uniqueness is required for the nomination itself only. This is not a restriction on name usage elsewhere, neither within the nomination's immediate components nor in a context in which the nomination occurs.

As opposed to collections, a nomination may have the same construct "several times" as immediate component, i.e., different names may be mapped to the same construct (the function is not necessarily injective). As with collections, nominations are understood in the strict extensional set-theoretic sense: a nomination is completely given by the set of (name,construct)-pairs. Neither context nor intention affect nomination identity. Also, nominations may be infinite.

Nominations have the structure most commonly used in classical data structure considerations. Examples are records in programming languages and databases as well as objects in the Vienna Definition Language [LuLaSt70].

In box notation, a nomination is depicted as a rectangle, containing representations for its immediate components, each marked by a name and a colon (Fig. 2.15). In this figure, as well as in subsequent representation examples, (strings of) uppercase letters are used as descriptional variables which stand for names.

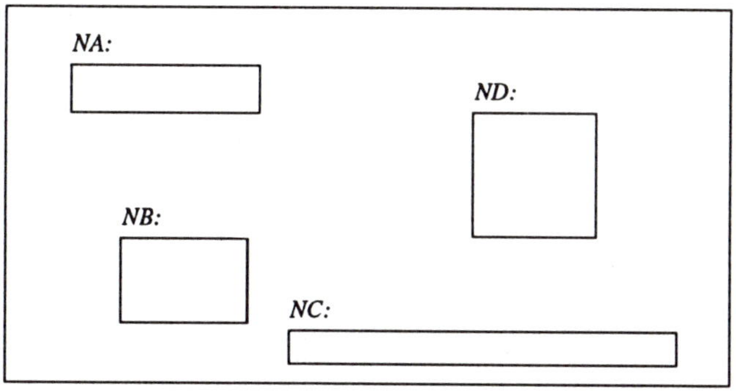

Figure 2.15 : Box notation for nomination

Fig. 2.16 is an example of a nomination obtained by adding names to the collection example of Fig. 2.10. It represents a function which maps names to constructs as shown in Fig. 2.17.

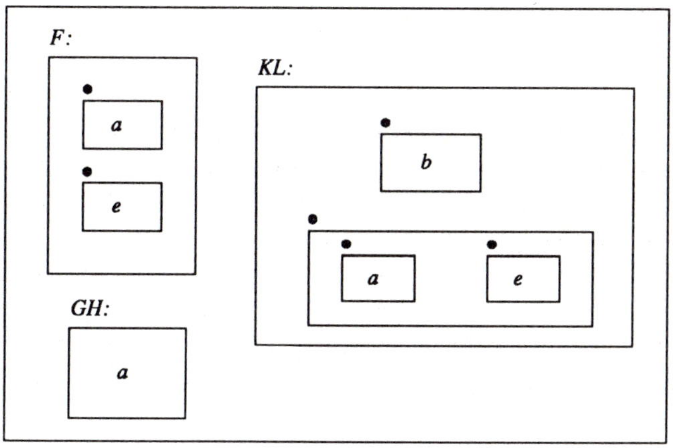

Figure 2.16 : A nomination obtained from the collection in Fig. 2.10 by adding names

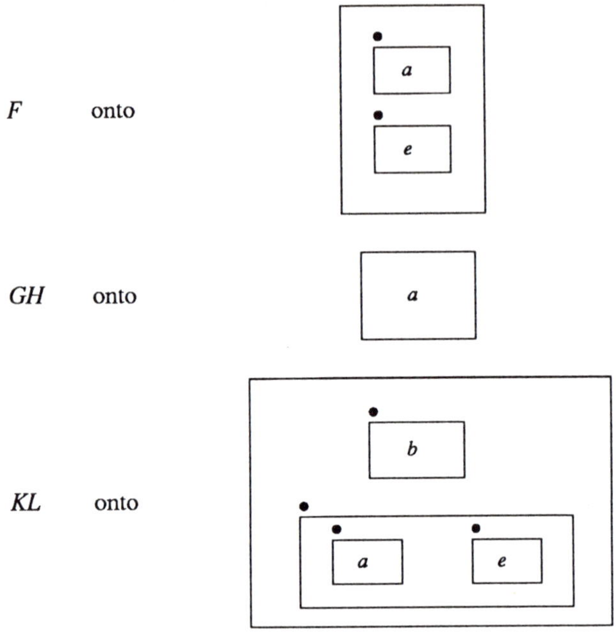

Figure 2.17 : The nomination of Fig. 2.16 seen as function

The empty nomination is indicated by a diagonal bar with a colon inserted (Fig. 2.18).

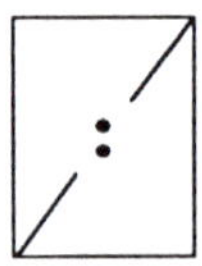

Figure 2.18 : Box notation for the empty nomination

In tree notation, a nomination is depicted by as many forking lines (branches) as it has names in its name set, with the names and representations of the immediate components appended, each name followed by a colon, for example, as shown in Fig. 2.19.

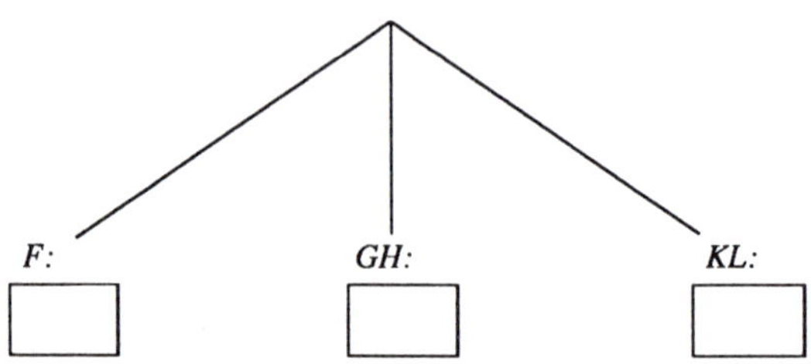

Figure 2.19 : Tree notation for nomination

The nodes may be detailed further by representations of the immediate components, which may, in particular, in turn be trees. The order of the branches of a nomination is immaterial. The example of Fig. 2.16 would render a tree as in Fig. 2.20.

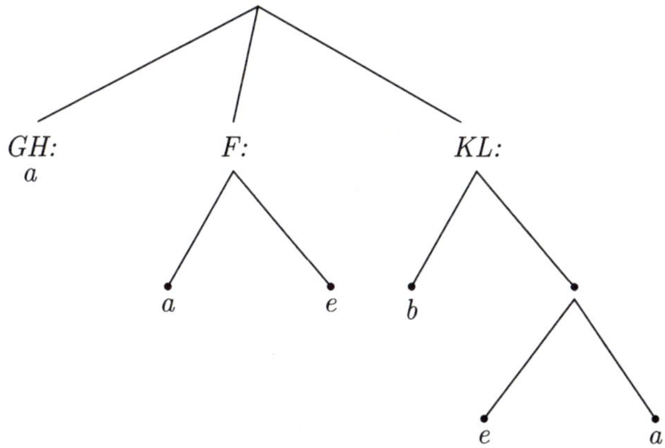

Figure 2.20 : The nomination of Fig. 2.16 in tree notation

If one is not interested in the particular names of the nomination, they may be omitted in the representation, so that the colons only remain.

In the linear notation of IMCL, a nomination is written as a list of (name,construct)-pairs, with semicolons as separation symbols and brackets as delimiting symbols. A name is separated from the construct by a colon. Note that the order in the list is irrelevant. The above example would be written in IMCL notation:

[*GH*: *a*; *F*: [*a*;*e*]; *KL*: [*b*; [*a*;*e*]]]

or [*GH*: *a*; *KL*: [*b*; [*a*;*e*]]; *F*: [*a*;*e*]]

or any other sequence of the list and its sublists.

The empty nomination is written [:].

"Name" is an undefined concept. Thus arbitrary things can be chosen for names. In particular, it is not prohibited to use again constructs for names. This may be very convenient at times. However, there is also a danger of obfuscating the structure in two respects: *name structure* and *references*. Without a restricting discipline for the use of constructs as names, names of arbitrary compositional complexity may be created. This is somehow counter to the original intention of considering names in nominations as abstract selectors of immediate components. If one finds it necessary to structure names, this can be taken as an indication that the names are in effect intended for compositional analysis and thus acquire properties typically applicable to components. In this case, one should convert names to components, for example, by using a relation in which the entries of a key column act as selectors (for more on relations see Sec. 2.2.2). The second aspect, referencing, concerns "external" name structure, that is, relations *between* names. It introduces non-compositional structure by way of an "implementation" (in IMC). If in one large construct a component construct is used as a name, the component can be interpreted as a reference to that part (or those parts) of the construct identified by the name. This makes it possible to impose arbitrarily complex network structure on a (compositional) IMC construct. Although this might be desirable at times, descriptionally it doesn't seem to be clean. At this point, one should remember that IMC is designed for compositional structure only. If network structure is needed, the proper solution would be to introduce additional "networking" operators. Alternatively, a standard escape for describing non-compositional structure is again the use of relations.

On the other hand, there is also a good reason to use constructs as names. This arises from a desire for language simplification rather than language expressiveness: if all names are constructs, no special language elements for handling names are required. The IMC language IMCL in fact takes advantage of this.

2.1.2.5 Catenations

A catenation is a finite sequence of constructs, which then are called the catenation's **immediate components**, also called **members** of the catenation. One may consider "sequence" to be defined in any way convenient for one's own thinking. However, one should avoid a view that uses natural numbers, as in Fig. 2.21. In a way, this is unnatural and can make catenation handling awkward. For the stringing together of catenations, for example, funny unsymmetric index translations would ensue. This is the reason why catenations are not simply considered nominations with special name sets. In mathematical terms, catenations can be considered elements of the free semigroup over the set of constructs.

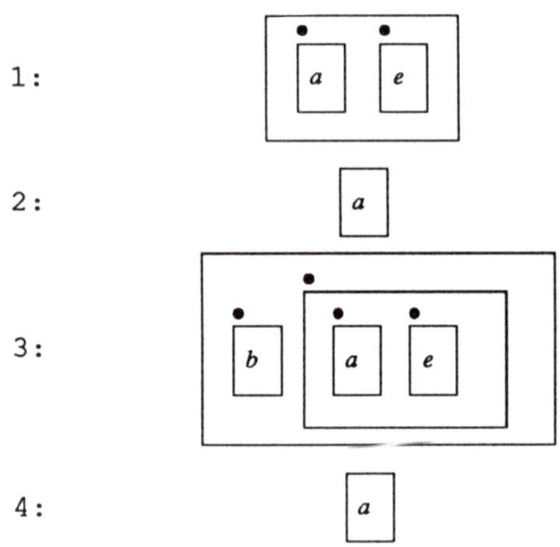

Figure 2.21: A catenation seen as a nomination with numbers

Catenations also occur very often in conventional data structures. They are most notorious in LISP-like languages and in any kinds of list or string handling facilities. But they are also commonplace for files, where collections of records would often conceptually suffice.

In box notation, a catenation is depicted as a rectangle containing representations for its immediate components, strung together by arrows (Fig. 2.22).

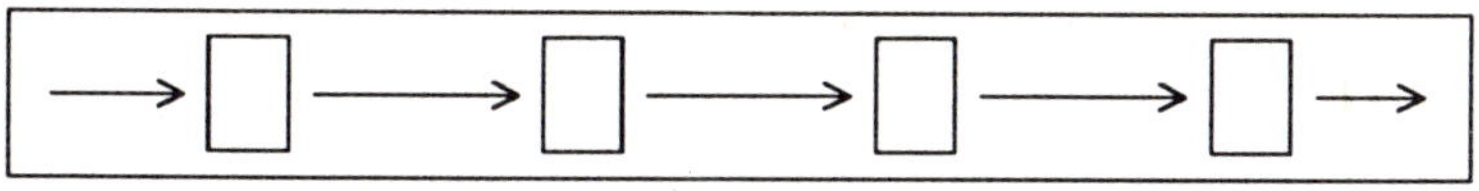

Figure 2.22 : Box notation for catenation

Fig. 2.23 is an example of a catenation having the same components as the example collection and the example nomination in the two previous subsections (see Fig. 2.10 and Fig. 2.16).

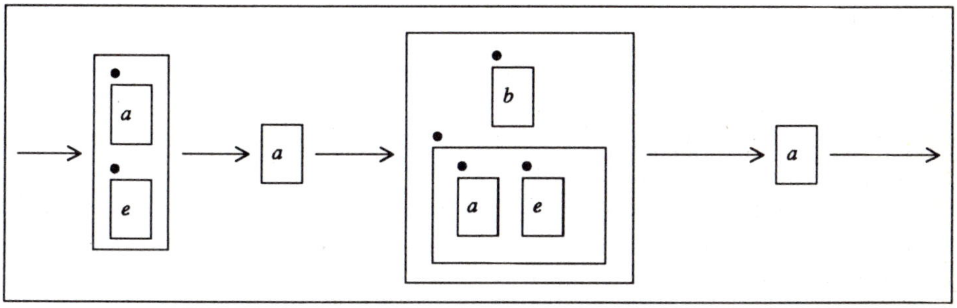

Figure 2.23 : A catenation in box notation

The empty catenation is indicated by a diagonal bar with an arrow inserted (Fig. 2.24).

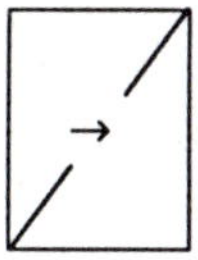

Figure 2.24 : Box notation for the empty catenation

In tree notation, a catenation is depicted by as many forking lines (branches) as it has members, with arrows and representations of the immediate components appended, for example, as in Fig. 2.25. This time, the order of the branches is essential.

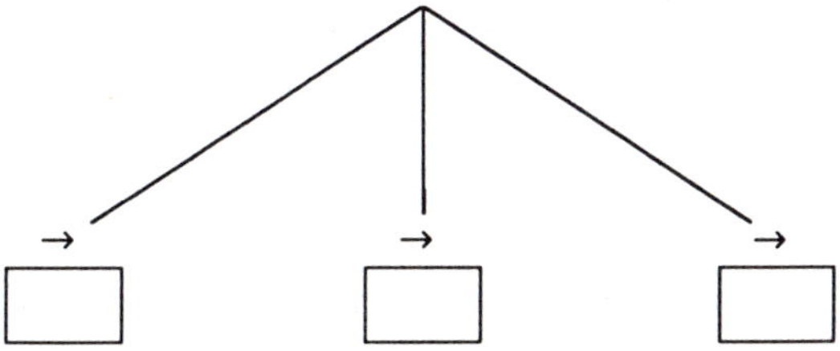

Figure 2.25 : Tree notation for catenation

The example of Fig. 2.23 would render a tree as shown in Fig. 2.26.

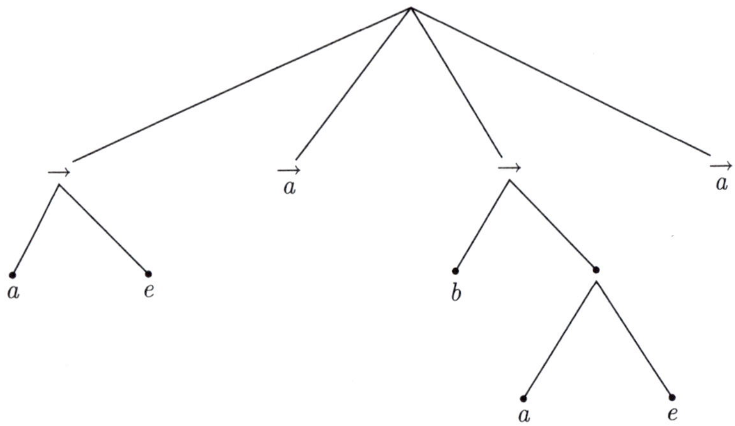

Figure 2.26 : The catenation of Fig. 2.23 in tree notation

In the linear notation of IMCL, a catenation is written as a list of constructs, with arrows as separation symbols and brackets as delimiting symbols. Again, the order in the list is essential. The arrows are meant to suggest exactly this idea. The above example would be written

$$[\rightarrow[a;e]\rightarrow a\rightarrow[b;[a;e]]\rightarrow a\rightarrow]$$

The empty catenation is written $[\rightarrow]$.

2.1.3 Formal definition of constructs

We start with two basic kinds of entities, **atoms** and **names**, from which all higher objects are derived (by means of set-theoretic constructions). Atoms are considered elementary constructs. Names are used for a certain kind of composition (nominations).

In this section, we call A the set of atoms and N the set of names. The set C of constructs is now defined:

Definition 1

$C_0 := A$

$C_{i+1} := C_i \cup S(C_i) \cup F(N,C_i) \cup Q(C_i)$

$C := \bigcup\{C_i \mid i \geq 0\}$

(Here, "$\cup$" and "$\bigcup$" are used in the ordinary set-theoretic sense.)

For $c \in C$ we say c is a **construct:**

Definition 2

c construct $:\Longleftrightarrow c \in C$

C is obtained by simultaneous recursion on forming subsets, functions and sequences. As a consequence, all the resulting types of constructs are lumped together in C. We now want to sort these out. This can be done by applying again operators S, F and Q on C. However, for S or F, the result contains objects not in C. (If, for example, s is a set having an element from each $C_i \backslash C_{i-1}$ (i>0), there is no n such that $s \in C_n$.) We have to restrict the result on C to obtain the desired classes of constructs, that is, the classes of **collections**, **nominations** and **catenations**:

Definition 3

c collection $:\Longleftrightarrow$ $c \in S(C) \cap C$
c nomination $:\Longleftrightarrow$ $c \in F(N,C) \cap C$
c catenation $:\Longleftrightarrow$ $c \in Q(C) \cap C$

(Because catenations are finite, $Q(C) \subseteq C$. Therefore, the restriction on C could as well be omitted for Q(C).)

We now define the concepts of **immediate component** and **component** already used earlier in an intuitive way:

Definition 4

c_1 immediate component of c_2 $:\Longleftrightarrow$

$$((c_2 \text{ collection} \wedge c_1 \in c_2) \vee (c_2 \text{ nomination} \wedge \exists n(c_1 = c_2(n))) \vee (c_2 \text{ catenation} \wedge \exists f,r(c_2 = f^\frown(c_1)^\frown r)))$$

Definition 5

c_1 component of c_2 $:\Longleftrightarrow$

$$c_1 \text{ immediate component of } c_2 \vee \exists c_3(c_1 \text{ component of } c_3 \wedge c_3 \text{ immediate component of } c_2)$$

If c_1 is component of c_2, c_2 is said to **comprise** c_1.

For easy reference, we introduce **compound** as a generic term for all three kinds of non-atom constructs:

Definition 6

c compound $:\Longleftrightarrow$ c collection $\vee$
c nomination $\vee$
c catenation

Catenations are finite in length. Other compounds, however, can have infinitely many (countably many) immediate components.

The **name set** of a nomination is its domain, that is, the set of names to which constructs are actually associated by the nomination:

Definition 7

$$\text{NAMESET}(c) := \begin{cases} \{n \mid c(n) \in C\} & \text{if } c \text{ is a nomination} \\ \text{undefined} & \text{otherwise} \end{cases}$$

Note that NAMESET(c) is a construct only if names are chosen to be constructs.

An **empty construct** is a compound which "has no parts" in the sense of the following definition:

Definition 8

c empty collection	$:\Longleftrightarrow$	c collection $\wedge \neg\exists x\ (x{\in}c)$
c empty nomination	$:\Longleftrightarrow$	c nomination $\wedge \neg\exists n\ (n{\in}\text{NAMESET}(c))$
c empty catenation	$:\Longleftrightarrow$	c catenation $\wedge \neg\exists x{,}s\ (c{=}(x)^\frown s)$

By definition, the empty constructs are compounds. In contrast, according to the above definition of *compound*, atoms are not compounds.

2.1.4 Further compositional structure

At times, it may be adequate to go beyond IMC when non-compositional structure must be considered. Aspects of non-compositional structure are discussed in the introduction (Chap. 1) and in connection with nominations (Sec. 2.1.2.4) and relations (Sec. 2.2.2). In the present section, we consider structure not leading out of the compositional paradigm, but dealing with other concepts of composedness.

The ways in which compounds are formed from component constructs could roughly be classified according to the structuring means employed to aggregate the components. Whereas collections are formed without any additional information objects, nominations are constructed with unordered index sets called their name sets. One could explore the idea of *index sets* in two directions:

- Concealment
  One could think of nominations with a "hidden" index set, i.e., with components which have unknown names. The presence of an abstract index set would still admit multiple occurrence of constructs within such an "anonymation" (nominations with unknown names). Constructs of this kind could, for instance, be used to model multi-sets or "bags".
- Order
  One could think of nominations with a linear order established on the index set (for example, using natural numbers as names). Such an order would induce a serialization of the components: first, second, ... component of a nomination. Unlike components of catenations, components of such "catenominations" could not only be addressed by their positions but also by their names. This is frequently to be found in record structures. Also, lists with named items could be modelled with this kind of construct.

Combining both ways into a single one leads to a view of catenations as nominations with a hidden ordered index set. Because in this view the index set is concealed, operations on catenations (insertion and deletion of members, concatenation) do not require explicit index translation (see also Sec. 2.1.2.5).

The diagram in Fig. 2.27 summarizes the ideas of how to add structure to IMC through the various uses of index sets.

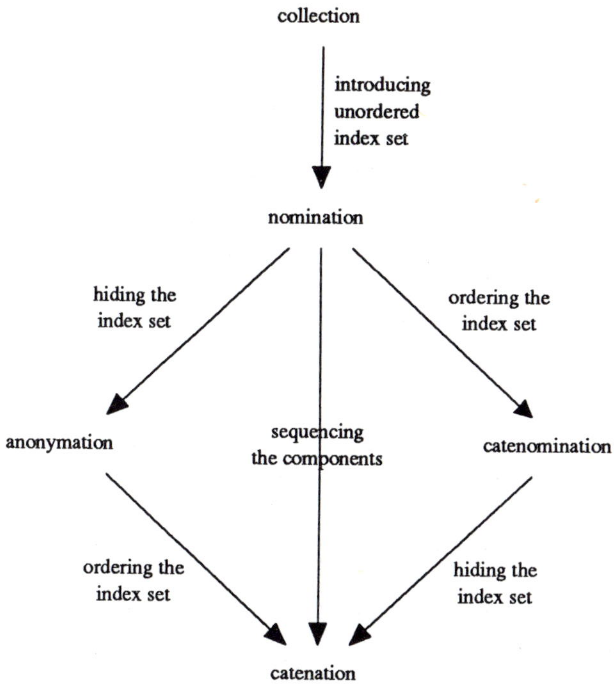

Figure 2.27 : Index sets in compositional structures

Cyclic lists are another information structure which could be modelled in a compositional way. A corresponding construct could be thought of as a catenation whose ends are "bent" together such that the last member becomes the immediate predecessor of the first member. The notions of first and last member would, of course, no longer be applicable.

It would probably not make sense to develop a compositional model for cyclic lists only, without investigating the whole world of directed and undirected graphs. Graphs are information structures with a widespread field of application. A compositional model for graphs would depend on the intended use of the graphs. Frequent access to nodes would call for a "node oriented" model, where a graph is composed of arcs and an arc is composed of a parent (from) and a child (to) node. A "substructure oriented" model would be more adequate if the nodes primarily served to address subgraphs (as is possible for trees): a graph is composed of nodes and "their" subgraphs. The concepts of IMC (with the definition tools of IMCL) allow one to define both kinds of models. Whatever model is chosen, operations and predicates tailored to the intended use of the graphs can be defined, such that a natural way of working with those graphs can be maintained.

2.2 Some well-known constructs

2.2.1 Records

A record is normally thought of as a grouping of named fields and thus closely corresponds to a nomination. Fields may be nested, and so may nominations. Thus, part of a record the type of which is specified by a COBOL data description

```
 .
 .
 .
03     B PIC ...
03     C
   04  E PIC ...
   04  F PIC ...
   04  G PIC ...
03     H PIC ...
 .
 .
 .
```

could be seen as in Fig. 2.28.

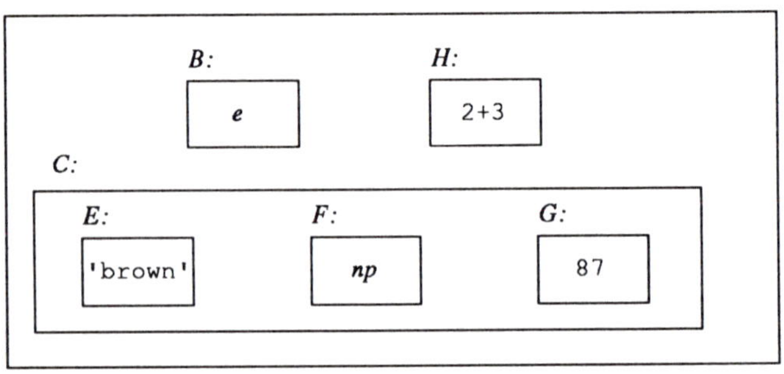

Figure 2.28 : A record modelled as a nomination, leaving out sequence information

One will note that the nomination lacks sequence information implied by the COBOL data description. To represent it, one could use catenations. But then the identifiers could no longer be used as IMC names, but must rather reappear as components (and hence necessarily be constructs). This would yield a construct as in Fig. 2.29.

Alternatively, one could extend the name set by natural numbers and give each component two names, the original identifier and a number (Fig. 2.30).

This solution would entail the necessity of special consistency conditions, to guarantee that the component constructs under alias names are equal. If IMC were extended to allow for "catenominations" (see Sec. 2.1.4), this would provide a third alternative.

There are more alternatives conceivable. One might argue that such solutions are unduely complicated or implausible. However, one should take into account that the double structuring of a COBOL record (by name and by sequence) is indeed relatively complex, a fact that is sometimes overlooked and that has been laid open by the IMC representation. Also, the question must be raised whether the double-structure is itself reasonable. The sequence of fields comes into effect mainly when a RENAMES clause is specified or a MOVE to a differently structured record is used. Both features are suspected to support dirty programming and it would probably be an improvement to COBOL or related data languages to eliminate the field sequence in records.

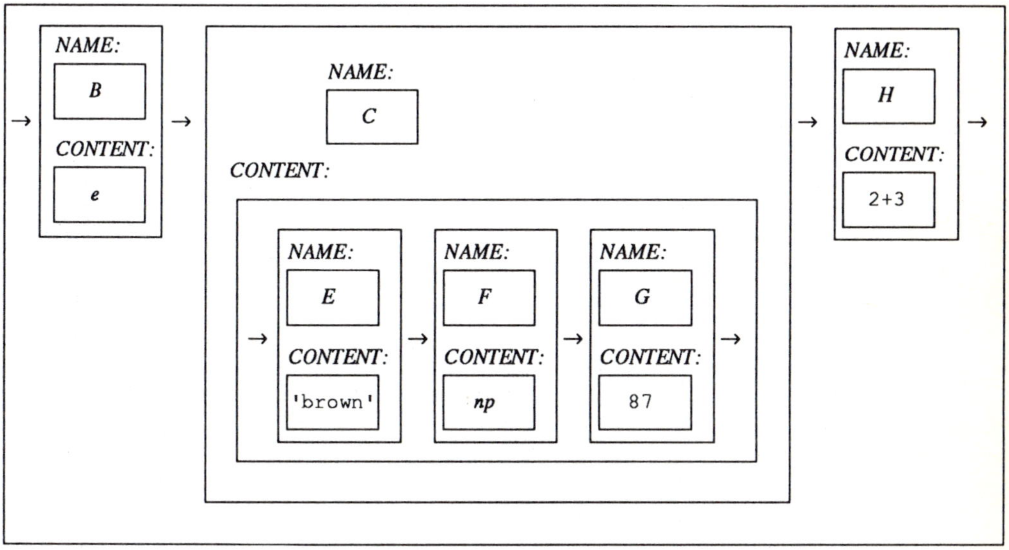

Figure 2.29 : A record modelled as a catenation

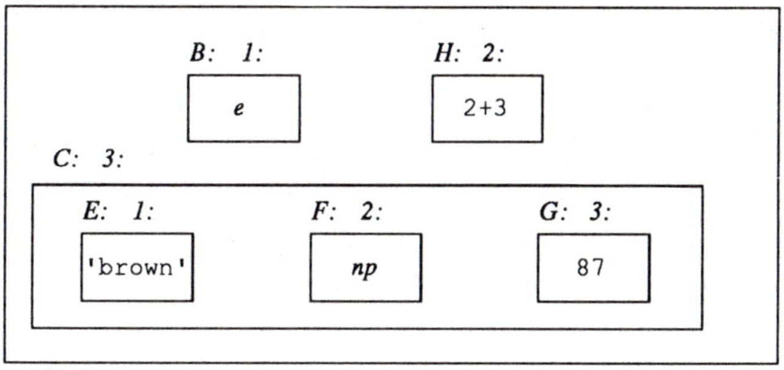

Figure 2.30 : A record modelled as a nomination, maintaining sequence information

2.2.2 Unordered tables

Unordered tables are the dominant idea of all relational approaches. In these, sets of homogeneously structured constructs, often called *rows*, are considered. The standard way in mathematics to conceive a relation is to see it as a set of n-tuples. An n-tuple is usually defined as the result of nested pairings or as a mapping from natural numbers 1,...,n to the tuple elements. Both ways have the effect of inducing a sequence on the tuple elements. In information processing, this is normally not desirable because it introduces conceptually irrelevant structure and thus forces overspecification. "Generalized" relations, also a notion of long standing, admit any arbitrary index set instead of natural numbers ([Bour68]). Under this view, a tuple is a mapping from an index set onto the tuple elements, and an unordered table (called *relation*) is a collection of tuples with the same index set. The mappings that make up a relation are then termed its **rows**, and the indices of the common index set its **attributes**. A similar view is also taken in [BaKh86].

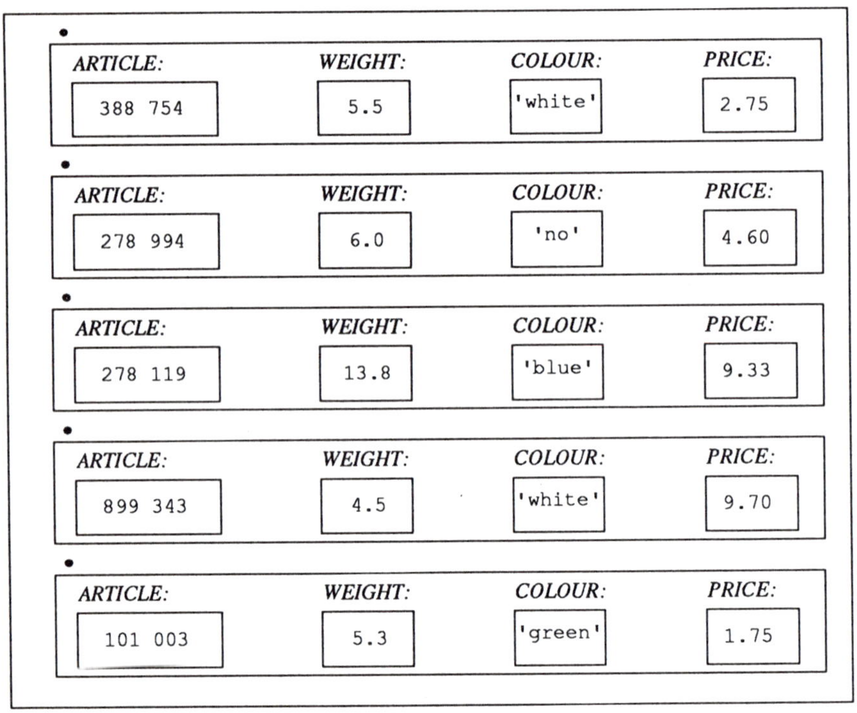

Figure 2.31 : An unordered table in box notation

The IMC representation of an unordered table understood in this way is straightforward. The rows are nominations with identical name sets (i.e., the relation attributes). The **unordered table** is the collection of rows. An example of an IMC representation of an unordered table is shown in Fig. 2.31. A representation of the same unordered table in a condensed form, called **table notation**, is shown in Fig. 2.32. The notation capitalizes on the homogeneous structure of tables by "factoring out" the names.

ARTICLE	*WEIGHT*	*COLOUR*	*PRICE*
388 754	5.5	'white'	2.75
278 994	6.0	'no'	4.60
278 119	13.8	'blue'	9.33
899 343	4.5	'white'	9.70
101 003	5.3	'green'	1.75

Figure 2.32 : The table of Fig. 2.31 in table notation

Such a collection of rows would be quite adequate for dealing mathematically with unordered tables. However, for the purpose of information handling there is still something unsatisfactory about it. One wants to modify unordered tables, in particular, insert or delete rows. The attribute set does not change under these operations, except in the extreme case when the last row is removed. What then remains is the empty collection, the attribute set is lost. Also, there is only one empty unordered table. This

TEMPLATE:

ARTICLE:	*WEIGHT:*	*COLOUR:*	*PRICE:*
'value'	'value'	'value'	'value'

ROWS:

ARTICLE	*WEIGHT*	*COLOUR*	*PRICE*
388 754	5.5	'white'	2.75
278 994	6.0	'no'	4.60
278 119	13.8	'blue'	9.33
899 343	4.5	'white'	9.70
101 003	5.3	'green'	1.75

Figure 2.33 : The unordered table of Fig. 2.31 with a row template

is counter-intuitive. It seems more appropriate to attach the attributes to the unordered table, independent of the presence or absence of rows. This can be done by forming a higher construct that, in addition to the collection of rows, contains a separate listing of attributes (cf. [DuSi83], [Date90], [GyPaGu89]). An example is given in Fig. 2.33. Here, the names *TEMPLATE* and *ROWS* and the component construct `'value'` are arbitrarily chosen for use in all unordered tables. `'value'` serves as a dummy for table entries. With these provisions, the attribute set is preserved if all rows of a table are deleted. Also, there are several empty unordered tables, one for each attribute set.

Unordered tables with such an extension occur fairly often, so that it is reasonable to introduce a more compact notation for them. Fig. 2.34 displays a convention taken from [DuSi83].

ARTICLE	*WEIGHT*	*COLOUR*	*PRICE*
388 754	5.5	'white'	2.75
278 994	6.0	'no'	4.60
278 119	13.8	'blue'	9.33
899 343	4.5	'white'	9.70
101 003	5.3	'green'	1.75

Figure 2.34: The table of Fig. 2.33 in extended table notation

The table notation, in its plain form as well as in its extended form, is also readily expanded to accomodate hierarchical attribute structure. This is not detailed here. (For an elaboration see [DuSi83].) If, in addition to attribute hierarchies, structured table entries are considered, it is necessary to distinguish names within such entries from those used as attributes. The explicit mention of attributes in the *TEMPLATE*-component also resolves this issue.

With an adequate representation of relations in IMC, an access to a wide variety of mathematical structures is provided. In particular, order structures can readily be modelled with binary relations. However, one should be careful not to carry IMC too far beyond its proper domain, which is the compositional paradigm of information modelling.

2.2.3 Ordered tables

In addition to unordered tables, (linearly) ordered tables are also frequently considered, even in the context of relations for information processing, in particular where procedural and implementational aspects come in. An ordered table is an unordered table with

ARTICLE	*WEIGHT*	*COLOUR*	*PRICE*
388 754	5.5	'white'	2.75
278 994	6.0	'no'	4.60
278 119	13.8	'blue'	9.33
899 343	4.5	'white'	9.70
101 003	5.3	'green'	1.75

Figure 2.35 : An ordered table in table notation

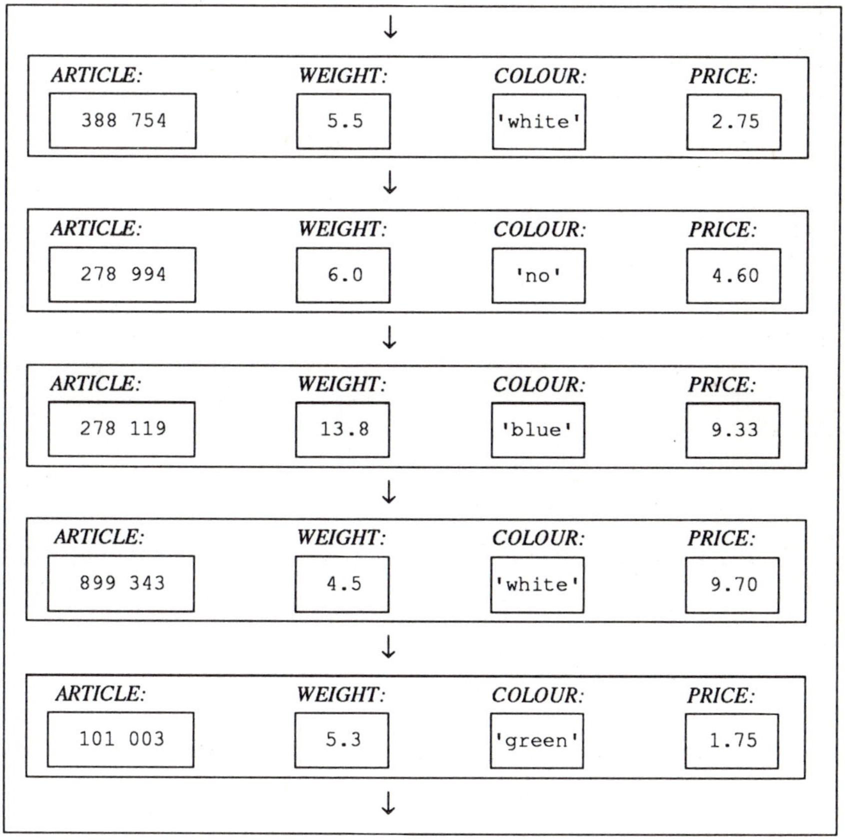

Figure 2.36 : The table of Fig. 2.35 in box notation

additional information on the sequence of the rows. Ordering entails the possibility of duplicates, which is in sharp contrast to unordered tables. In IMC, sequential ordering is most naturally expressed by a catenation. Thus, an **ordered table** is defined to be a catenation of nominations ("rows") with equal name sets.

The conventions for a compact graphical notation of unordered tables can be adapted to the needs of a compact representation of ordered tables. The appearance is nearly the same as with unordered tables, the only difference being that the left-hand side of the overall box is extended upwards and downwards and ends with an arrow head thus indicating catenation.

Let the unordered table of articles in the preceding subsection (Fig. 2.32) be ordered according to the scheduled order of shipments. While for unordered tables the order of rows in the diagrammatic representation is immaterial, it is essential for ordered tables, because it displays their sequence. In Fig. 2.35, the sequence of rows may for instance be seen as reflecting an order of shipments. Fig. 2.36, which gives the same table in box notation, reveals its character as a catenation.

2.2.4 Lists

Lists are finite linearly ordered arrangements of information objects. Each element or *entry* of a list has an ordinal position within the list. Depending on context, lists in this sense are commonly seen as (mathematical) n-tuples, strings (e.g., of characters), or, more abstractly, elements of a free semigroup.

A direct way of modelling lists in IMC is to represent them as catenations. As an example, an ordered table is defined in Sec. 2.2.3 to be a catenation of rows. Of course, other constructs can be designed, which model a list in a way tailored to a particular application field (for example, nested constructs for representing LISP-like structures).

2.3 Spots

2.3.1 A case for the spot concept

The spot concept as it is introduced in this chapter is an abstract counterpart of the intuitive idea of pointing into a data diagram, saying "here". Although such pointing is fairly commonplace, it is frequently impaired by an uncertainty as to whether the object itself is meant or the particular context in which it occurs. Consider the example

`information`
↑ (pointing at the second `i`)

together with the sentences

(1) The indicated letter is "`i`".
(2) The indicated letter is to be deleted.
(3) "`i`" is to be deleted.

Given (1), one should expect (2) and (3) to be equivalent. However, (2) would normally be interpreted to yield "`informaton`", whereas (3) results in "`nformaton`".

The confusion arises because (2) is interpreted in two different ways. If the noun part "The indicated letter" is understood as identifying the letter "`i`" as an object without regard to its context, both (2) and (3) yield "`nformaton`". If the noun part is meant to refer to the particular context in which the indicated letter occurs, then (2) does not talk about a construct, but a particular spot, and thus is different from (3).

Lack of distinction between an object and its occurrence in a comprising context can lead to unclear explanations of even simple composed objects. For example, in [HoUl79], the basic notion of *string* is explained as a "sequence of symbols", with the additional explanation "for example, a, b and c are symbols and $abcb$ is a string. The *length* of a string is the number of symbols composing the string. For example, $abcb$ has length 4". As, however, a, b and c are symbols, the number of symbols composing the string is 3 rather than 4: there is no fourth symbol in the string $abcb$. On the other hand, it is true that $abcb$ has length 4. In IMC the string would be modelled as a catenation with four (immediate) component spots. Thus, the length of a string is not the number of component constructs, but the number of component spots.

Normally, such ambiguity is not expected to cause trouble because it is clear from context what is meant. On the other hand, there are enough cases where the meaning is unclear. This easily occurs if a writer or speaker rapidly and repeatedly switches between both interpretations and, in particular, if he himself is not aware of the distinction. Once one is alerted to the problem, one will surprisingly often be able to track down difficulties of communication to exactly this point. Moreover, if we want to speak formally about data structure, the distinction must be made explicit.

As an alternative to distinguishing "object proper" from "object in context", or, as we shall say, "construct" from "spot", one could desist from using the spot concept at all. One could argue that a spot is identified for the purpose of "doing" something at this spot. If object selection and object manipulation were always tied together in one single operation, there would in principle be no need for an explicit spot concept. For instance, in a "delete record" operation, the selection criteria for the record to be deleted would be provided as parameters to the operation. Finding the spot at which the deletion takes place and execution of the deletion would then be one indivisible operation. This kind of thinking is particularly present in the operational approach to data structuring.

In contrast, it can be convenient to separate pointing from manipulation. For example, one might want to inspect a component at a spot before it is deleted at that spot. The operational approach would first require selecting the component in question for inspection and then re-evaluating the same selection criteria for deletion. This is not only inefficient, but can also be a descriptional nuisance and introduce errors. It can be avoided if the spots retrieved in the first step can be remembered (using spot variables) and subsequently used for various local operations.

Apart from component manipulation, there is an additional, even more important aspect of using spots: information structure description, as, for example, in type declarations, must be able to cope with complex local context properties in deeply nested constructs. If spots are not available, the usual way is to decompose the construct, somehow remembering its composition (externalized structure), deal with the thus extracted components with respect to their externalized structure, and possibly recombining them. As a typical example, think of the definition of list concatenation in LISP.

This awkwardness of dealing with complex properties involving components that are more or less distant in the reference construct is probably the reason for considering "constraints" as something special and on top of type declarations, as is usual in the database world. It also accounts for the many varied approaches to "constraints" for specialized data models created in response to several attempts to provide a richer structure for capturing real life semantic requirements. With spots, a uniform way of penetrating a complex construct and relating selected parts of it is provided, which comes close to reducing the expressional complexity to that unavoidable degree inherent in the descriptional task.

Most programming and database languages use some concept for pointing. A classical example is the Network Database Language NDL [ISO87a], where FIND can strictly be separated from record manipulation (although there are also "automatic" insertion and deletion mechanisms which bypass prior spot selection). On the other hand, relational database languages like SQL [ISO87b] emphasize the pointerless approach, at least in their pure forms. For practical reasons, compromises are accepted, for example, retrieval result lists, tuple identifiers or cursors for tuple-at-a-time operations.

2.3.2 Informal introduction to the spot concept

We want to capture formally the intuitive idea of a "spot" in a construct. The formal definition is given in the next section. In the present section, the guiding considerations and motivations are outlined.

Very often, a spot can be identified by the component occurring at that spot, as in the example in Fig. 2.37. In this and in the following figures, upright triangles ("$\triangle$") are used to refer to spots informally. The triangles themselves do not belong to the construct description. The spot $\triangle_1$ is identified by the component 27, the spot $\triangle_2$ is identified by the component 29.

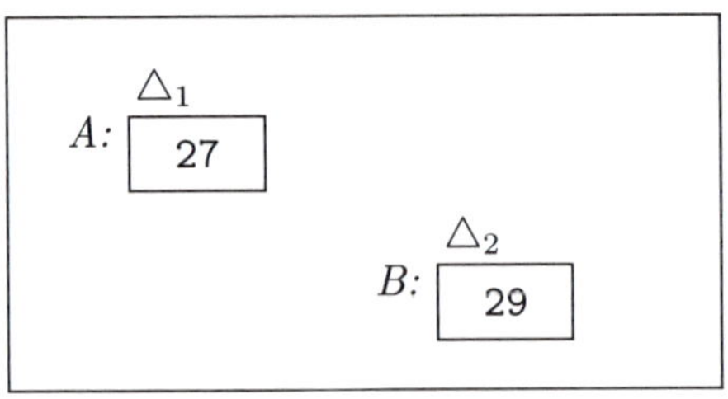

Figure 2.37: Spots identifiable by component constructs

That spots can be identified by components is, however, a favourable exception rather than the rule. In general, the same construct may be a component at different spots. This may appear trivial, but for approaching the concept of spot it is at the heart of the matter. Fig. 2.38 illustrates a case where the component does not identify a spot. Here, $\triangle_1$ is certainly understood to mean a different spot than $\triangle_2$.

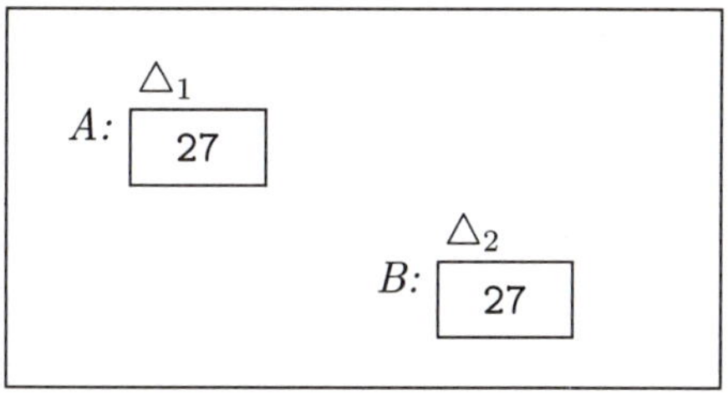

Figure 2.38 : Spots not identifiable by component constructs

Thus, the component construct alone is not suitable for identifying a spot (just as in the introductory example in Sec. 2.3.1, "`i`" did not identify a spot in "`information`"). In this particular case, one may be led to use the attached name instead. This works for nominations, but names are not available in collections and catenations. However, the idea of using the name, if suitably generalized, leads in the right direction of looking at the *context* of the considered component.

Several well-known languages deal with spots by using pointing devices, sometimes called references, cursors or currency indicators. However, these are normally treated as variables for which the nature of their values is not explicitly specified. They are defined by their effects on operator outcome, which may be satisfactory in each particular case. This does not suffice for a more general compositional approach like ours, which is intended to cover an entire class of operationally specifiable structures, as explained in the introduction. Some languages explicitly provide values for pointer variables, such as addresses or database keys. These are, however, spot-identifying components of constructs, specifically introduced for that purpose. Because it is our aim to conceptually identify *any* spot in a construct, not just a few selected ones equipped with special spot identifiers, we cannot make use of this kind of solution. Rather, we have to extract the essence of the spot idea and define it as a concept in its own right.

There are two approaches to the spot concept, the "full context" approach and the "route class" approach. They are closely related and lead to similar results.

In the "full context" approach, the idea is to see a spot as a component construct together with the complete context in which the component occurs. The component construct is, of course, described as constructs usually are, but how can a complete context be described? This is, in fact, quite easy for an immediate component. It is the construct in which the immediate component is considered, together with an indication of the way in which the immediate component is embedded in this construct. This is most easily achieved by taking the comprising construct itself, except that exactly one occurrence of the component in question is substituted by a **placeholder**. The placeholder is a special entity which is not a construct. Consequently, the "context" is not a construct either. We call it an **immediate context shell**. In the previous example the immediate context indicated by $\triangle_2$ would be represented by the immediate context shell given in Fig. 2.39. The spot is then this immediate context shell together with the construct 27.

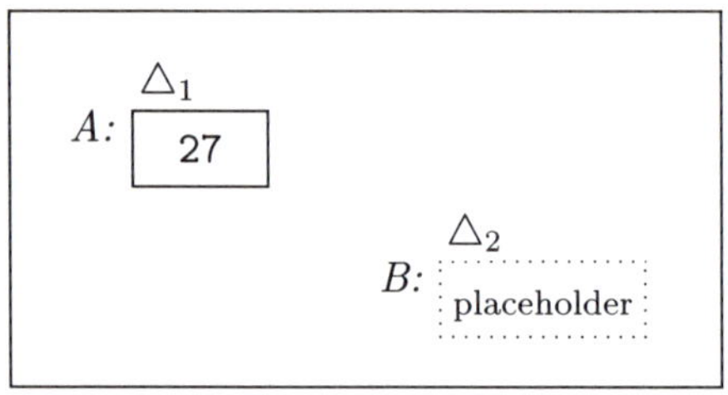

Figure 2.39 : An immediate context shell

We can now actually take this as the basic idea for a spot concept for immediate component occurrences. The next step is to extend it to any arbitrary depth of nesting. This can be achieved by recursively tracing the composition of the construct. Once we have a spot at some given level, it can be extended by appending a description to it of how a component occurrence on the next inner level is to be considered an immediate component of the component at the given spot. Thus, a spot is basically a sequence of immediate contexts closing in on the component in question, and it is in fact *the* complete context. How this is technically carried out in detail is described in Sec. 2.3.3.

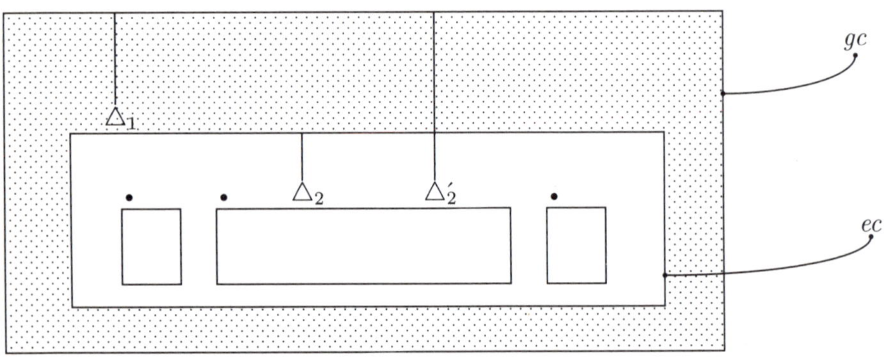

Figure 2.40 : Spots in nested constructs

Fig. 2.40 illustrates the recursive definition of the spot concept. The shaded area is meant to contain other (unspecified) structure. $\triangle_1$ marks the spot supposed to be already given. *ec* is the construct at this spot. It is drawn as a collection, but could as well be a nomination or catenation. $\triangle_2$ marks the spot in question, but *relative to ec* only. As such, it is defined in the manner described above for immediate component occurrences. $\triangle_2'$ denotes the spot in question relative to the outermost construct *gc*. The spot $\triangle_2'$ is obtained essentially by "appending" $\triangle_2$ to $\triangle_1$.

We now turn to the other approach, dubbed "route class" approach. In this, the starting point is to consider a spot to be identified by an arbitrary route description. Depending on the selection criteria used, there can be very many routes leading to the intuitively "same" spot. Thus, any one of them *describes* the spot, but, for the present, there is no reason to distinguish any of them as *being* the spot. Rather, the class of all routes leading to the intuitively "same" spot should be defined to be the spot. Route equivalence is also mentioned in [Ullm87], where the question is asked whether "two methods [for data access] commute".

To elaborate this approach formally, two preconditions must be met: (i) there must be a fixed language for route descriptions (for otherwise it would depend on the language which routes are in the class; the class would therefore formally be language-dependent); (ii) it must be clear by what criterion two route descriptions lead to the "same" spot. The preconditions are not independent. In particular, whenever the language required by (i) is extended, it is necessary to invoke the intuitive idea of spot sameness to redefine the equivalence relation postulated by (ii). This comes out most blatantly in an algebraic specification as given in Appendix B.

Once one has such a spot defining equivalence relation, one can deal with spots by using representatives of the equivalence classes. It would be nice to have a unique, distinguished representative for each class. This would, for example, facilitate tests on spot equality. Irrespective of the particular route description language, one should expect the following properties to hold for the distinguished representative:

- it is uniquely determined by the route class,
- it depends on the most general properties of constructs only,
- it goes strictly inwards into the construct (i.e., it does not change directions).

Now the complete context description of the "full context" approach can be considered a special route description that in fact meets the above requirements. Thus, it reconciles both approaches. It has the particular advantage of being interpretable as the distinguished representative of a route equivalence class for any route description language in which it is expressible.

To summarize this section, the spot concept is adequately captured by a component construct and a sequence of immediate context shells, starting with the construct relative to which the spot is considered. Such a sequence can be considered a full context description or a distinguished representative of a route description class.

Based on these considerations, the next section introduces a formal definition of the spot concept.

2.3.3 Formal definition of the spot concept

As explained in the previous section, the notion of spot is built on two ideas: that of the context of an immediate component and that of stringing such contexts together to obtain spots on arbitrary levels of nesting. The next two subsections provide formal definitions of these notions.

Before we start out, a terminological convention is introduced to facilitate talking about spots. So far, the term "component" has been used to mean a construct as a part of a comprising construct. Now, as we direct our attention to the fact that the same construct may occur several times as a building block in another construct, we have a need for a discriminating terminology. The common language word "component" has both connotations, that of a construct and that of a spot. In compositional information modelling, the distinction between both is crucial. Therefore, we say **component construct** when we really mean a construct, and **component spot**, when a spot in a comprising construct is under consideration. Thus the same component construct may be at different component spots.

For convenience, although with some danger of confusion, the term **component** will still be used. It is intended to mean both "component construct" and "component spot", whatever is sensible in a given context. Often, even both interpretations make sense and are then in fact intended.

2.3.3.1 Immediate context shells

The formal definition of an **immediate context shell** (**ics**) will be different for each of the three generic kinds of constructs, that is, collections, nominations and catenations. However, all three definitions obey a common principle, which is to describe the context of an immediate component occurrence by reproducing all of its comprising construct *except the component occurrence in question*, which is replaced by the non-construct "placeholder", as mentioned already in Sec. 2.3.2. Thus, the immediate context of △ in Fig. 2.41 will be described by a diagram as in Fig. 2.42.

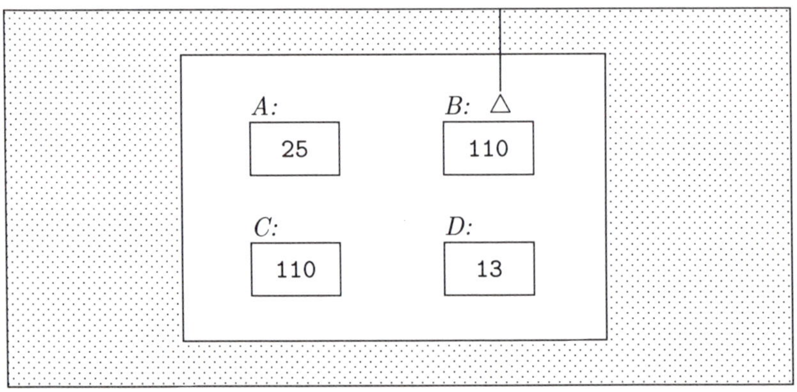

Figure 2.41 : An informally defined spot

Let the non-construct placeholder be denoted by "@". Since the components of a compound must be constructs, anything composed with @ is not a construct. An ics will be something which looks almost like a construct, but has @ for exactly one of its immediate component occurrences:

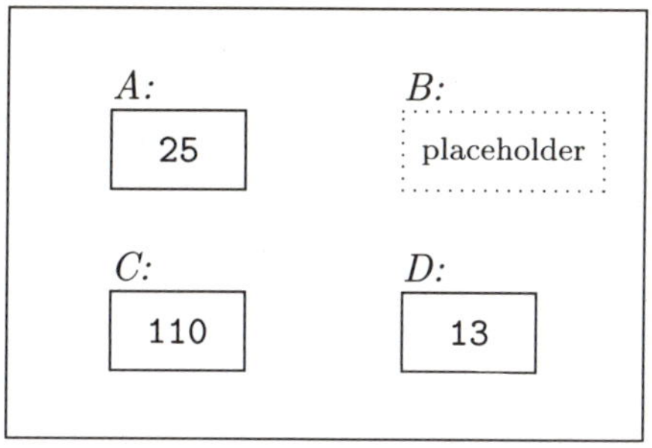

Figure 2.42 : The immediate context of the spot in Fig. 2.41

Definition 9

$$
\begin{aligned}
x \text{ ics} :\Longleftrightarrow\ & \exists g \quad (g \text{ collection} \wedge x{=}g{\cup}\{@\}) \vee \\
& \exists g{,}n\ (g \text{ nomination} \wedge n \text{ name} \wedge x{=}g(n{\mapsto}@)\ ) \vee \\
& \exists g{,}h\ (g,\ h \text{ catenations} \wedge x{=}g^\frown(@)^\frown h\ )
\end{aligned}
$$

For discussing spots, it is useful to have an easy way of referring to the construct obtained from an ics x when @ is replaced by a construct h (h **plugged into** x).

Definition 10

$$
\text{PLUG}(x{,}h) := \begin{cases} g{\cup}\{h\} & \text{if } x{=}g{\cup}\{@\} \\ g(n{\mapsto}h) & \text{if } x{=}g(n{\mapsto}@) \\ f^\frown(h)^\frown g & \text{if } x{=}f^\frown(@)^\frown g \end{cases}
$$

If h occurs in a collection-like ics x, then, on plugging h into x, the h substituted for @ collapses with the one already present. Thus, PLUG($x{\cup}\{h\}$,h)=PLUG(x,h), so that we could have different immediate context shells ($x{\cup}\{h\}$ and x) for what we want to be the same spot. This is undesirable, because ultimately we want a unique formal representation for spots. Uniqueness is forced by postulating absence of the construct to be substituted for @. This is referred to as "receptiveness". An ics is defined to be **receptive of** h if it does not already have h as a set element. In the following definition, the concept of receptiveness is extended to sequences of ics's as well in order to exclude collapses also on higher composition levels.

Definition 11

$$
\begin{aligned}
x \text{ receptive of } h\ :\Longleftrightarrow\ & (x \text{ ics} \wedge (\ x\backslash\{@\} \text{ collection} \Longrightarrow h{\notin}x\ )\ ) \vee \\
& (x \text{ sequence of ics's} \wedge \\
& \ (x{=}() \vee \\
& \ \ \exists q{,}y\ (x{=}q^\frown(y) \wedge y \text{ receptive of } h \wedge \\
& \qquad\qquad q \text{ receptive of PLUG}(y{,}h))))
\end{aligned}
$$

2.3.3.2 Spots

Based on the informal considerations in Sec. 2.3.2 and having available immediate context shells, a **spot concept** is now easily obtained by stringing immediate context shells into sequences. Obviously, the reference construct must be derivable from a spot. Thus, one might be inclined to take as a spot a pair (r, q), where r is the "reference" construct in which the spot is considered and q is a sequence of ics's leading from outside inward to the intuitively intended "spot". However, the ics's in q would then have to be "compatible" with r, that is, each ics has to be almost a copy of the component construct of r to which it refers. The compatibility requirement amounts to a consistency condition on (r, q) which is somewhat awkward to formalize. A simpler way is to avoid such a consistency requirement by omitting the highly redundant reference construct in the definition. The reference construct can in fact be derived from q and the construct "at the spot" only. This way, an almost free combination of arbitrary ics's is admissible for composing spots. The only restriction comes from the difficulty already encountered in the previous section, which led us to introduce receptiveness.

Definition 12
s spot $:\Longleftrightarrow$ $\exists q,g$ $(s=(q,g) \wedge g$ construct $\wedge$ q receptive of $g)$
The sequence q may also be empty (cf. "ownspot", Sec. 2.3.4).

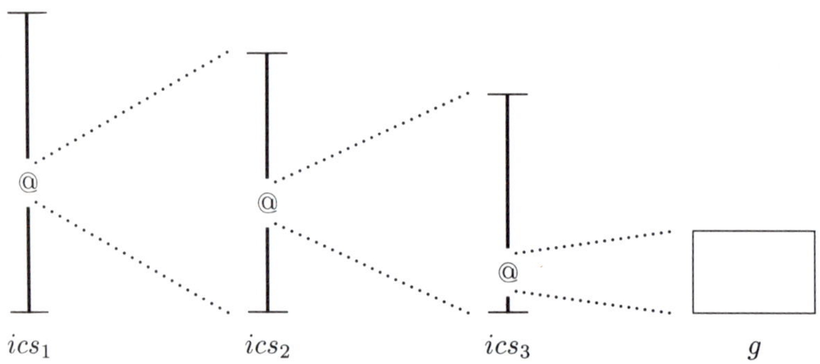

Figure 2.43 : Repeated substitutions yield a spot's reference construct

With this definition, the reference construct is obtained by repeated substitution of placeholders. A formal definition is given in the next section. Fig. 2.43 illustrates how the reference construct is obtained by successively plugging a construct into an immediate context shell (from right to left), that is, by

substituting @ in ics_3 by g,
substituting @ in ics_2 by the previous result and
substituting @ in ics_1 by the previous result.

2.3.4 Some derived notions

In this section, some derived notions of general interest are given.

As announced in the previous section, we first give a formal definition of the reference construct.

Definition 13
$\mathrm{REFCON}(((),g)) := g$
$\mathrm{REFCON}((q^\frown(x),g)) := \mathrm{REFCON}((q,\mathrm{PLUG}(x,g)))$
The **reference construct of** (q,g) is $\mathrm{REFCON}((q,g))$.

To facilitate talking about spots, we also say that a spot is a **spot in** its reference construct.

The "ownspot" of a construct is the "out-of-the-blue" spot at which the construct occurs when it is not considered as a component of some comprising construct.

Definition 14
For a construct g, $((),g)$ is the **ownspot of** g.
An **ownspot** is the ownspot of some construct.

Since $\mathrm{REFCON}(((),g))=g$, the reference construct of the ownspot of a construct is again this construct.

A spot is **immediately inward** of another spot if its sequence of ics's has exactly one more member appended, the second component of course being appropriately adjusted.

Definition 15

$$s \text{ immediately inward } t \quad :\Longleftrightarrow \quad s,\, t \text{ spots} \wedge \exists\, q,x,g\ (s=(q^\frown(x),g) \wedge t=(q,\mathrm{PLUG}(x,g))$$

$$t \text{ immediately outward } s \quad :\Longleftrightarrow \quad s \text{ immediately inward } t$$

The transitive and reflexive closure of "immediately inward" and "immediately outward", **inward** and **outward**, respectively, are also needed.

Definition 16

$$s \text{ inward } t \quad :\Longleftrightarrow s,\, t \text{ spots} \wedge (s=t \vee \exists x\ (s \text{ immediately inward } x \wedge x \text{ inward } t))$$

$$t \text{ outward } s \quad :\Longleftrightarrow s \text{ inward } t$$

Note that, according to this definition, any spot is inward and outward of itself. The reason for such an abuse of a natural language word is that, on the one hand, the non-reflexive closure (for which "inward" and "outward" would have been more appropriate) is of little interest, and that, on the other hand, a better word could not be found for the interesting case.

The relations immediately inward, immediately outward, inward and outward are also applied to sets of spots in the following way: a spotset s is said to be **inward of** a spotset t if for any $s_1 \in s$ and $t_1 \in t$ holds s_1 inward t_1. The other relations are analogously applied to spotsets. These generalizations to spotsets are arbitrary in a way. Other, still "natural", generalizations would be conceivable (for example, for any $s_1 \in s$ *there is* a $t_1 \in t$ such that s_1 inward t_1). However, we need the extension mainly for cases where at least one operand is a singleton spotset. For these, the differences vanish.

Sometimes one wants to refer to all spots immediately inward of a given spot. For a spot s, this set of spots could be described by $\{t \mid t$ immediately inward $s\}$. However, if s is already at the bottom of the composition hierarchy, a subtle distinction should be made. If the construct at s is empty, this is a special case of a compound, that is, one with zero components. Hence, the resulting set of spots should be empty. In contrast, if the construct at s is an atom, the search for a component is just not applicable. Consequently, the result should be undefined in this case. In the following definition this view is expressed and at the same time generalized for a *spotset* as argument instead of a single spot.

Definition 17

$$\text{IMINWARD}(s) := \begin{cases} \{t \mid \exists x (x \in s \wedge t \text{ immediately inward } x)\} & \\ & \text{if the constructs at all spots of } s \text{ are compounds} \\ \text{undefined} & \text{otherwise} \end{cases}$$

In particular, if s is the empty spotset, IMINWARD(s) is the empty spotset, too.

Similarly, IMOUTWARD(s) is defined to be the set of all spots immediately outward of the spots of s. This time, the case to be specifically regarded is when the spotset contains an ownspot, because there is no spot immediately outward of an ownspot.

Definition 18

$$\text{IMOUTWARD}(s) := \begin{cases} \{t \mid \exists x (x \in s \wedge t \text{ immediately outward } x)\} & \\ & \text{if } s \text{ does not contain an ownspot} \\ \text{undefined} & \text{otherwise} \end{cases}$$

Again, if s is the empty spotset, IMOUTWARD(s) is the empty spotset, too.

Without proof, we state for spots the tree properties with respect to "immediately inward/outward". In the set of all spots with the same reference construct holds:

(1) For each spot there is at most one other spot immediately outward of it.
(2) There is exactly one spot which is outward of any other one.
(3) For each spot there is exactly one path of spots starting with the outermost spot guaranteed by (2) and ending with the given spot, such that any two subsequent nodes of the path are in the immediately-inward/outward-relation.

We call the tree of all spots in one construct the **spot tree** of that construct. The spots of a spot tree can be considered to emanate from the common root of that tree. The following definition accounts for that view.

Definition 19
The **rootspot of** a spot s is the spot outward of s for which there is no other outward spot. A **rootspot** is the rootspot of some spot. A rootspot is also called an **outermost** spot.

Note that "rootspot" and "ownspot" (without *of* ...) are synonymous, although they differ in emphasis, since for "rootspot" the idea of a reference to a spot is invoked, whereas with "ownspot" the reference is to a construct.

The spots at the other end of the spot tree are called "leafspots".

Definition 20
A **leafspot of** a spot s is a spot inward of s for which there is no other inward spot. A **leafspot** is a leafspot of some spot. A leafspot is also called an **innermost** spot.

If (q, g) is a leafspot, g is either an atom or an empty construct.

For spots which are not inward or outward of each other, a "closest proximity" is sometimes interesting.

Definition 21
s_0 neighbor of s_1 $:\Longleftrightarrow$ $\exists s(s$ immediately outward $s_0 \wedge s$ immediately outward $s_1)$

If s_0 is neighbor of s_1, s_0 and s_1 are said to be **neighbors**. Neighboring is an equivalence relation the classes of which are called **neighborhoods**. Thus, a spot always belongs to its own neighborhood.

It is sometimes useful to display a spot tree as a diagram. A spot tree diagram is somewhat similar to a construct tree diagram. It is all the more important to note the difference. Fig. 2.44 shows a construct tree diagram and a spot tree diagram of the example catenation $[\rightarrow[a;e]\rightarrow a \rightarrow[b;[a;e]]\rightarrow a \rightarrow]$ given in Sec. 2.1.2.5. The spots are marked by $\triangle$-symbols to make the diagrams comparable. In the construct tree diagram (left), the $\triangle$-symbols are for reference purposes only; they do not belong to the construct.

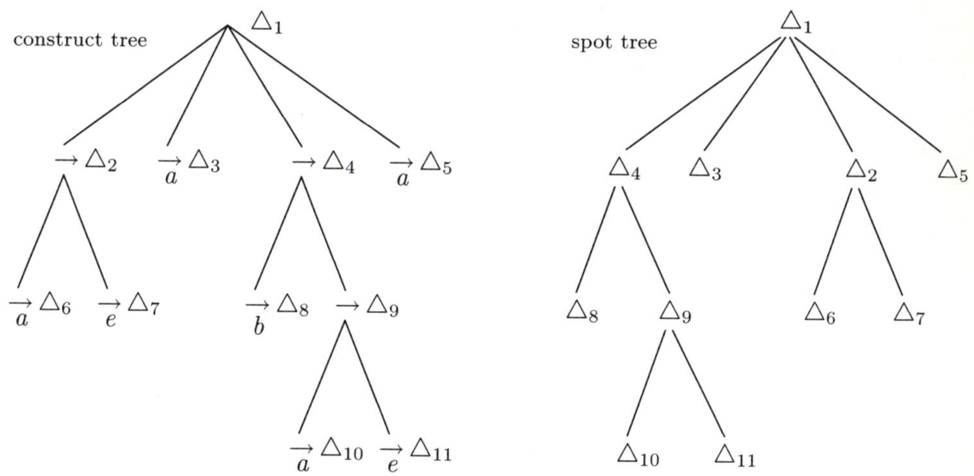

Figure 2.44: Contrasting a spot tree with a construct tree

In a spot tree, the order of branches is always immaterial, because each node represents a complete spot. This is in contrast to a construct tree representation of a catenation. The nodes of the spot tree diagram in Fig. 2.44 are deliberately rearranged to illustrate independence of a particular sequence. Notice also that the topmost node of a spot tree diagram represents the rootspot of all inward spots. Hence, there is always a $\triangle$-symbol at its top.

Mostly, one considers spots from only one spot tree (i.e., spots which all have the same reference construct). Sometimes, however, one needs to relate a spot to a "shorter" spot leading to the same component, but relative to some component in between. For this, we introduce spot embedding as visualized by the diagram in Fig. 2.45.

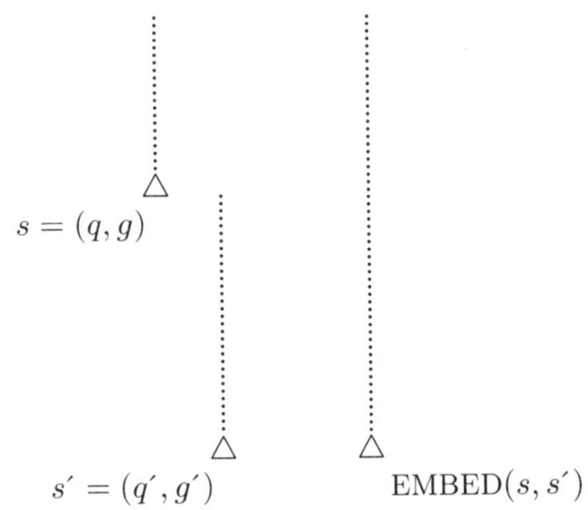

Figure 2.45: Spot s' embedded at spot s

Definition 22

$$\text{EMBED}((q,g),(q',g')) := \begin{cases} (q \frown q', g') & \text{if } g = \text{REFCON}((q', g')) \\ \text{undefined} & \text{otherwise} \end{cases}$$

By definition, all spots of a spot tree have a common reference construct. Thus, a spot tree does not account for the fact that each component construct is also at all spots relative to some intermediate component. In Fig. 2.46, these embeddings (inclusive of ownspots) are depicted for *all* spots of the construct shown in Fig. 2.44.

We now turn to a few other useful derived notions concerning single spots.

For a given spot, there are two distinguished constructs: its reference construct "at the outer end" of the spot, and, at the opposite end, the "construct at the spot". The following definition introduces terminology for the latter.

Definition 23

The construct g is the **construct at** the spot (q, g).
If (q, g) is not an ownspot, g is also said to be the **component construct at** (q, g).
Also, the spot (q, g) is said to **lead to** the (component) construct g.

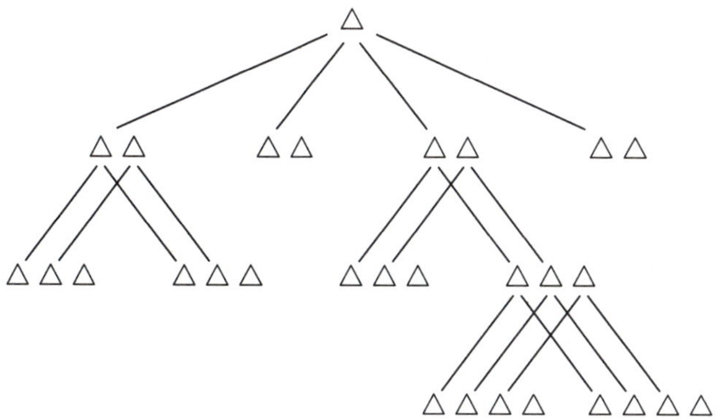

Figure 2.46 : Spots with nested reference constructs

Definition 24
The name n is the **name at** the spot $(q\frown(g(n\mapsto @)), h)$.

In the latter case, g is of course a nomination. Thus, the name at a spot is defined if and only if the construct at the spot immediately outward of the given spot is a nomination.

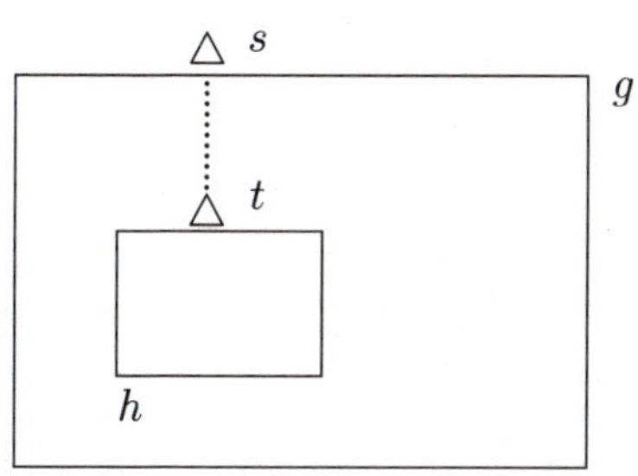

	t	g	h
s	$\underline{s}$ rootspot of t	$\underline{s}$ ownspot of $\underline{g}$	
t		t spot in $\underline{g}$	t leads to $\underline{h}$
g	$\underline{g}$ reference construct of t		
h	$\underline{h}$ construct at t		

Figure 2.47 : Terminology for spots in a construct

For ease of expression a generic way of referring to particular kinds of spots is useful: if g is a construct of some kind ... (in particular, collection, nomination or catenation), then a spot (q, g) is said to be **a ... spot** (for example, "a nomination spot").

Fig. 2.47 provides an overview of the terminology used for the relations between a construct g, the ownspot s of that construct, a spot t in the construct, and the construct h at that spot. s and t may be equal, in which case, of course, g is also equal to h. An underlined parameter is uniquely defined by the other parameter.

As an example of an application of the spot concept, the definition of two typical string operations is given. A spot immediately inward of a catenation spot can be used to define partial catenations in the same manner as a character occurrence in a word cuts the word into a front part and a rear part. The diagrams in Fig. 2.48 and Fig. 2.49 may help to visualize the situation and to understand the definition below. They also show that the rootspot of the spot that defines the position (s) is immaterial for cutting the catenation into two parts: it can be any outward spot, in particular the ownspot of the catenation.

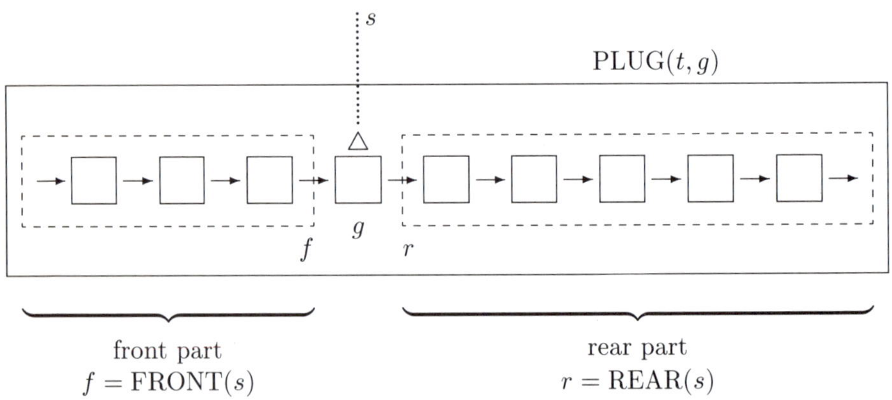

Figure 2.48 : Front and rear part with respect to spot s

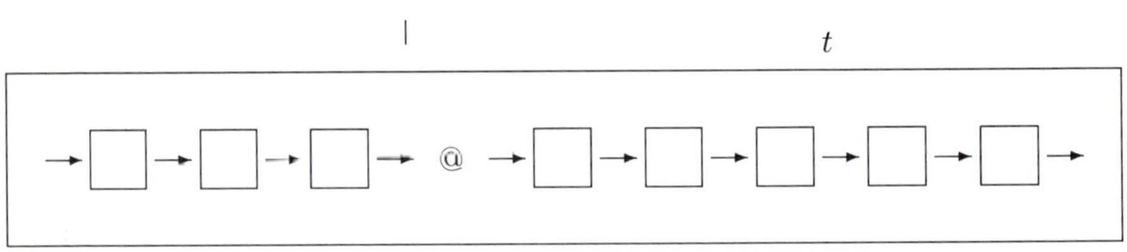

Figure 2.49 : Immediate context shell t of component g in Fig. 2.48

Definition 25

$$\text{FRONT}(s) := \begin{cases} f & \text{if } \exists\, q,t,g,r(s=(q^\frown(t),g) \wedge t=f^\frown(@)^\frown r) \\ \text{undefined} & \text{otherwise} \end{cases}$$

$$\text{REAR}(s) := \begin{cases} r & \text{if } \exists\, q,t,g,f(s=(q^\frown(t),g) \wedge t=f^\frown(@)^\frown r) \\ \text{undefined} & \text{otherwise} \end{cases}$$

Note that in this definition the concatenation operator "$^\frown$" is used in two quite different "directions": in $q^\frown(t)$ it appends an ics to a sequence of ics's (a "vertical" or "inward" step in the spot hierarchy), in $f^\frown(@)^\frown r$ it fits @ into a catenation to produce an ics (a "horizontal" operation on catenations).

Catenations are the IMC way to represent sequences. A spot immediately inward of a catenation spot represents what is commonly termed a "member" of the sequence. Therefore, we say **member spot** for a spot immediately inward of a catenation spot. We say "member" for the member spot as well as for the construct at that spot in the same ambiguous way as we use the word "component" (see introduction of Sec. 2.3.3).

Chapter 3

IMCL: an IMC language

3.1 Language considerations

3.1.1 Principles of language design

This section explains the guiding principles for IMCL design decisions and trade-offs between conflicting goals, and gives some related considerations.

Richness

A language should be as small as possible, but not smaller than reasonable. What is reasonable depends on several parameters and cannot be decided upon for all application situations. In particular, there are the conflicting requirements of ease of learning (small) and ease of use (elaborate). For IMCL, a compromise is sought on the ground of two principles: anticipated general need and language extensibility. First, a number of language elements beyond the bare functional minimum are included that are expected to make life significantly easier in a majority of specification tasks. IMCL with only the predefined language elements (inclusive of predicate and operator symbols defined in Sections 3.2.2 and 3.2.3) will be referred to as **plain IMCL**. Second, the language is made easily extensible by use of well-known mechanisms. Plain IMCL enriched by consistent definitions of new predicate and operator symbols will be called an **IMCL extension**.

The trade-off between conciseness and elaboration is difficult: on the one hand, the decisions for the basic language are bound to reflect a particular view and will not satisfy everybody. On the other hand, extensibility—though often applauded—puts part of the burden of language design onto the user and, moreover, threatens communication between users.

Expression orientation

IMCL is primarily intended as a specification language. Hence, any procedural connotation has been banned. This applies in particular to conditional terms and to operators which suggest set enumeration.

Usage

IMCL is designed for human communication as well as for machine processing. For machine processing, the admission of mixed notation (pre-, post-, in- and distfix) may be a source of parsing problems for user-defined extensions. In case of such difficulties, language users can employ parentheses to locally fix them. In a trade-off between flexibility of syntax and ease of parsing it was decided to impose minimal restrictions on the syntax.

Undefinedness

IMCL does not have undefined expressions since formally all functions are total and formulae always do have a truth value. A special entity "undefined" is provided for representing pathological cases. For this value, a "contamination principle" is adopted for all operators of plain IMCL: a single subterm that has the value "undefined" causes the entire term to have the value "undefined". The only exception is the conditional-term, the value of which is that of the selected branch, no matter whether the unselected branch evaluates to a defined value or not. (For a classical discussion of several ways to deal with undefined values see [Supp57], which does not, however, introduce a contamination principle.)

Precedence rules

Precedence rules are kept small. However, to comply with general usage and for convenience in some frequent and important cases, a few rules beyond the bare minimum are introduced (cf. Sec. 3.2.1, EXPRESSION).

Overloading

In principle, predicates and operators are specialized on types of entities. In particular, spotsets are carefully distinguished from constructs in general. However, there are a few exceptions for convenience and to comply with traditional usage: equality and inequality ($=$, $\neq$) apply to all entities. Set predicates ($\subset$, $\subseteq$, $\supset$, $\supseteq$), set operators ($\cap$, $\cup$, $\setminus$, CARD) and the total-operator-term (TOTAL ...) are applicable to collections as well as to spotsets.

Character set

IMCL expressions should be producible with generally available character sets. Thus, fancy symbols have been avoided. The spotset-related symbols "$\langle ... \rangle$", "$\hat{}$" and "$\hat{\in}$" may be considered exceptions. However, as it seemed rather important to distinguish spotsets typographically, the decision has been taken to use these symbols, even at the expense of possible representation problems on hopefully rare occasions. In case the symbols are not available, they must be substituted by others (see also *Symbol substitution* in Sec. 3.1.5).

3.1.2 Principles of language semantics

3.1.2.1 IMCL semantic mappings

An IMCL semantics is given by specifying the meaning of each expression of the language. Technically, this is broken down into

1) Specifying a **Universe of Entities** (**UoE** for short). This is a set the elements of which are called **entities**.
2) Assigning an entity to each constant.
3) Assigning a predicate on entities to each predicate symbol.
4) Assigning an operator on entities to each operator symbol.
5) Specifying how the meaning of an expression is derived from specifications 1) through 4).

In this, we have made reference to IMCL language elements *constant*, *predicate symbol*, *operator symbol*, and *expression*. These are explained in detail in Sec. 3.2. At present, it is only important to know that

- the language elements are syntactically recognizable,
- predicate symbols and operator symbols have "arities", that is, for each of them a fixed number of parameter positions is defined,
- constants are special expressions.

Further, on the "semantic side" and independent of the IMCL syntax, the notions of *predicate on entities* and *operator on entities* are used. It is sufficient to envisage a predicate as something which has an arity, too, and for which a *truth value* "true" or "false" is defined if applied to a tuple of entities the length of which matches the arity of the predicate. Similarly, an operator is something which has an arity and for which an *entity* is defined if applied to a tuple of entities the length of which matches the arity of the operator. Most commonly, an n-ary predicate is seen as an n-ary mathematical relation over the UoE, i.e., a subset of the n-fold Cartesian product of the UoE. Similarly, an n-ary operator is seen as an $(n+1)$-ary relation with a functional dependency.

There are several semantics possible for IMCL, depending on how specifications 1) through 5) are carried out. Any application may choose its own semantics according to the concepts relevant to its problem area. However, we want to introduce a body of common semantic rules, referred to as the **standard semantic specifications**, independent of the particular application and valid for all applications. Semantics that is beyond the standard semantic specification is called the **nonstandard semantic specification**. The present section is concerned with identifying the standard/nonstandard borderline and describing general aspects of the standard semantic specifications. Specific aspects of the standard semantic specifications are deferred until Sec. 3.2.

Standard semantic specifications

1) Entities

   The UoE contains at least
   - an entity "undefined",
   - entities called **common atoms**, which are the binary atoms "yes-atom" and "no-atom", and the rational numbers.

   The UoE is closed with respect to
   - forming compounds of constructs in the UoE,
   - forming sets of component spots of constructs in the UoE.

2) Constant semantics

   There is a fixed assignment of entities to standard-constants (see Sec. 3.2.1).

3 Predicate symbol semantics

   There is a fixed assignment of predicates to distinguished predicate symbols (see Sec. 3.2.2).

4) Operator symbol semantics

   There is a fixed assignment of operators to distinguished operator symbols (see Sec. 3.2.3).

5) Expression semantics

   There is an assignment of facts about the UoE to formulae and an assignment of entities to terms (see Sec. 3.2.1). These are defined on assignments for subformulae and subterms, and are ultimately based on assignments provided by standard and nonstandard specifications according to items 2), 3) and 4).

A particular application is free to provide additionally

Nonstandard semantic specifications

1) Entities supplement

   New atomic entities called **special atoms**.

2) Constant semantics supplement

   An assignment of entities to nonstandard-constants.

3) Predicate symbol semantics supplement

   An assignment of predicates to predicate symbols, except for those for which a standard interpretation is provided.

4) Operator symbol semantics supplement

   An assignment of operators to operator symbols, except for those for which a standard interpretation is provided.

5) No expression semantics supplement

   Nothing can be specified about the derived meaning for formulae and terms.

Standard-constants are used for denoting common atoms and a few non-atoms (see Fig. 3.2 below). Nonstandard-constants may denote any entity. In particular, they are used to make special atoms syntactically available.

The semantics of nonstandard-constants, predicate symbols and operator symbols is not necessarily given by an assignment according to items 2) through 4). It can also be left open or specified by providing appropriate definitional formulae ("axioms").

A *fact* in item 5) of the standard semantic specifications is understood to be a *conceivable fact*. A fact may hold or may not hold. Thus, a truth value "true" or "false" is associated with each fact that holds or does not hold, respectively. We assume the existence of abstract facts **valid** and **invalid**, that is, the facts of truth and falsity with truth values "true" and "false", respectively. Since a fact is assigned to each formula and a truth value is assigned to each fact, a truth value is indirectly also assigned to each formula. Thus, there is a three-tier staging for the semantics of IMCL formulae:
- the language,
- the facts,
- the truth values.

The following three figures illustrate the IMCL semantics. First, a breakdown of the UoE into mutually exclusive classes is given.

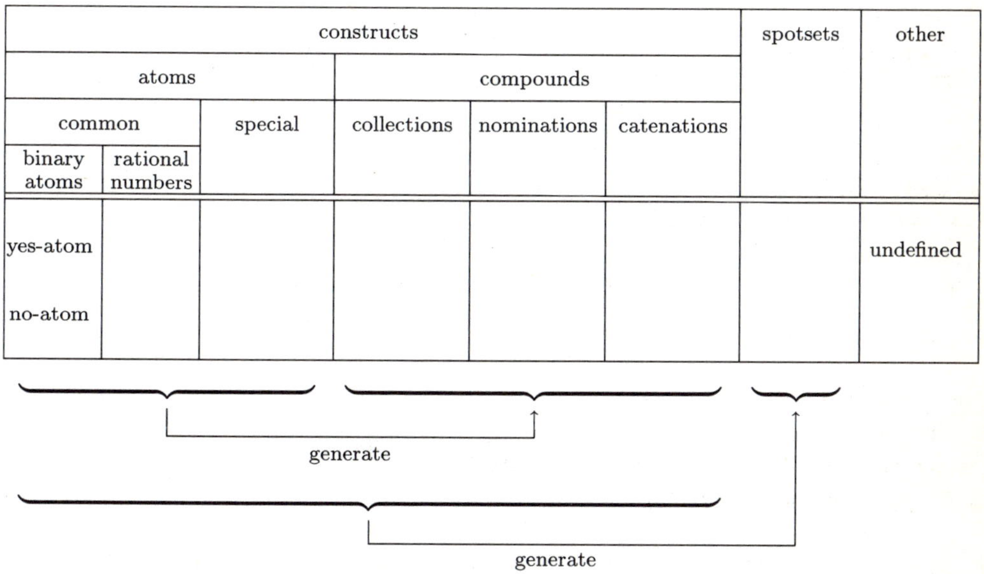

Figure 3.1 : The UoE of IMCL

The next two figures show the breakdown of the IMCL semantics into the various standard and nonstandard assignments. Fig. 3.2 illustrates semantic assignments for terms and formulae as given by items 1), 2) and 5) of the above semantic specification lists. It shows examples for each kind of assignment. Fig. 3.3 deals with operators and predicates according to the remaining items 3) and 4). Again, examples are given for each kind of assignment.

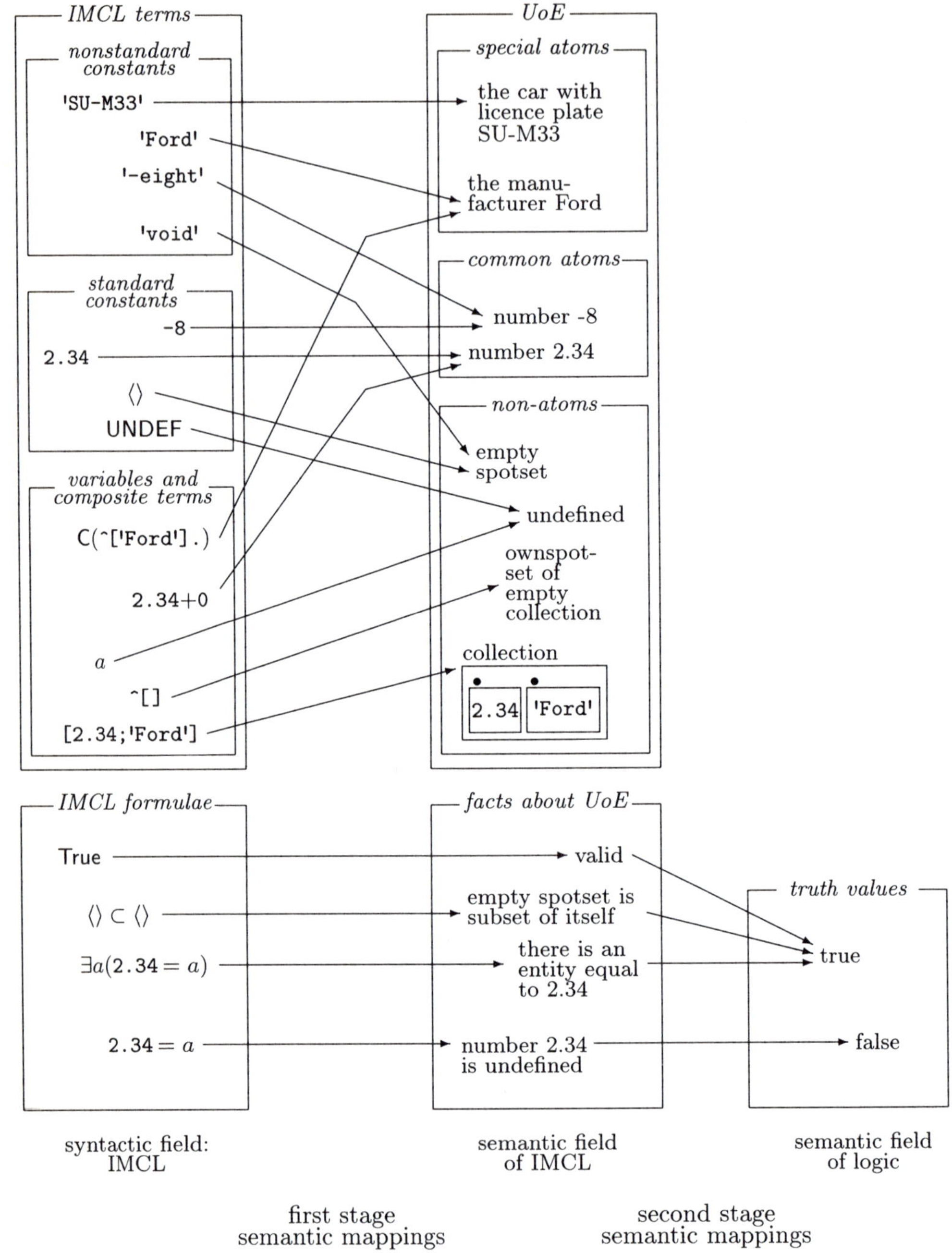

Figure 3.2: Semantic mappings of IMCL

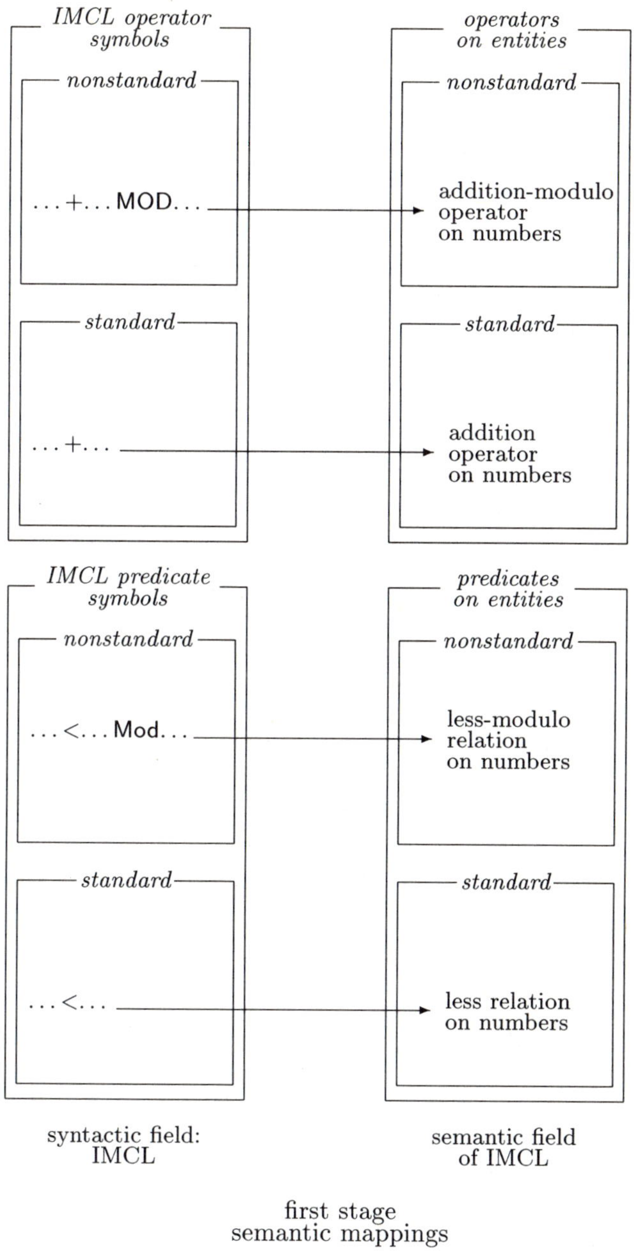

Figure 3.3: Assigning operators and predicates to IMCL symbols

There are three features which deserve special mention:

- Though nonstandard-constants are provided in the language primarily to make special atoms syntactically available, their use is not restricted. They may denote any entity. (Example: `'eight'` denoting the number 8. For a more complex example see `'translation table'` in Sec. 3.3.1.)

- Most standard-constants denote atoms (common atoms, never special ones). However, a few of them denote non-atoms of very general interest. (These are `UNDEF`, ⟨⟩, `[]`, `[:]` and `[→]`, denoting "undefined" and the empty entities, respectively.)
- Except for a few particularly simple ones, compounds and spotsets are primarily representable by composite terms and variables. However, by explicit assignment, compounds and spotsets may also be values of nonstandard-constants. (Example: `'void'` being specified to denote the empty spotset.) In turn, variables and composite terms may denote any kind of entity. (Example for a composite term: `C(^['Ford'].)`, denoting the manufacturer Ford as special atom.)

Whereas general mathematical language is used for defining IMC concepts (Chapters 1 and 2), IMCL is a restricted, precisely circumscribed language. Not all concepts employed for IMC are explicitly used in IMCL, and vice versa. The following table contrasts IMC and IMCL usage. A horizontal bar in the examples indicates that the concept is not considered in the respective context.

concept	considered in	
	IMC (example)	IMCL (example)
atom	7	7
name (other than construct)	*NA*	———
compound	{7,a}	[7;'a']
placeholder	@	———
immediate context shell (ics)	{7,@}	———
spot	(({7,@},{b,@}),a)	———
spotset	$\{s \mid s$ spot $\wedge\ s \hat{\in} t\}$	$\langle u \mid u \hat{\in} t \rangle$
set (other than collection or spotset)	$\bigcup\{C_i \mid i \geq 0\}$	———
sequence, pair (other than catenation)	(q,g)	———
"undefined"	———	UNDEF

Figure 3.4 : IMC concepts vs. IMCL concepts

3.1.2.2 Truth values and binary atoms

Paired values, usually called *binary values*, *truth values*, or *Boolean values*, depending on context, are also used in IMCL. They appear in different roles which have to be clearly kept apart. The difficulty of distinction lies in their structural similarity. It is therefore important to use some notational discipline so as not to confuse the levels of consideration.

In IMCL, there are two standard nullary predicate symbols, True and False. These are mapped onto "valid" and "invalid", respectively. Thus, the three-tier staging of the semantics of IMCL-formulae described in the previous section yields for the roles of paired values:

True	and	False	on the level of the IMCL syntactic field,
"valid"	and	"invalid"	on the level of the IMCL semantic field,
"true"	and	"false"	on the level of general logic

Note that "valid", "invalid", "true" and "false" are not IMCL language expressions (as opposed to True and False).

To maintain these distinctions is not difficult, but it requires some attention. To make things worse, paired values also appear in a completely separate context, i.e., that of terms and entities. In the same way as there are numbers in any IMCL-UoE, there are also the two common binary entities "yes-atom" and "no-atom". They just happen to have the same kind of algebra as truth values. In IMCL they are denoted by YES and NO. The operators of the algebra are not given in plain IMCL, but can be defined within IMCL, if needed (see Sec. 3.3.2.2). Note again that YES and NO are IMCL terms, but "yes-atom" and "no-atom" are meta-language expressions. Fig. 3.5 illustrates how the resulting five kinds of paired values are related. It uses the frame of Fig. 3.3, but shows the paired values only.

3.1.2.3 Constructs used as names

IMC does not specify what are names (see Sec. 2.1.2.4). In particular, names can also be constructs. If a user decides to take constructs for names, he must be expected to have reasons for distinguishing components in names and/or for having names as components in other constructs. Consequently, he will also have the corresponding descriptional needs. The language should be responsive to such requirements. One way is to treat names as constructs from the outset. This attitude is adopted for IMCL. From a language point of view, this has the additional advantage of uniformity of expression and syntactical economy. On the other hand, a penalty is paid in terms of lack of type separation and, hence, fewer possibilities of syntactic (static) term validation.

3.1.2.4 Spotsets rather than spots

As mentioned in the introduction (Chap. 1), the semantic field of IMCL contains spotsets, but it contains no single spots. Though spots are conceptually prerequisite to spotsets, they are rarely of direct concern in an environment of IMCL usage. Most operations deal naturally with spotsets. To keep the IMCL syntax and semantics straight,

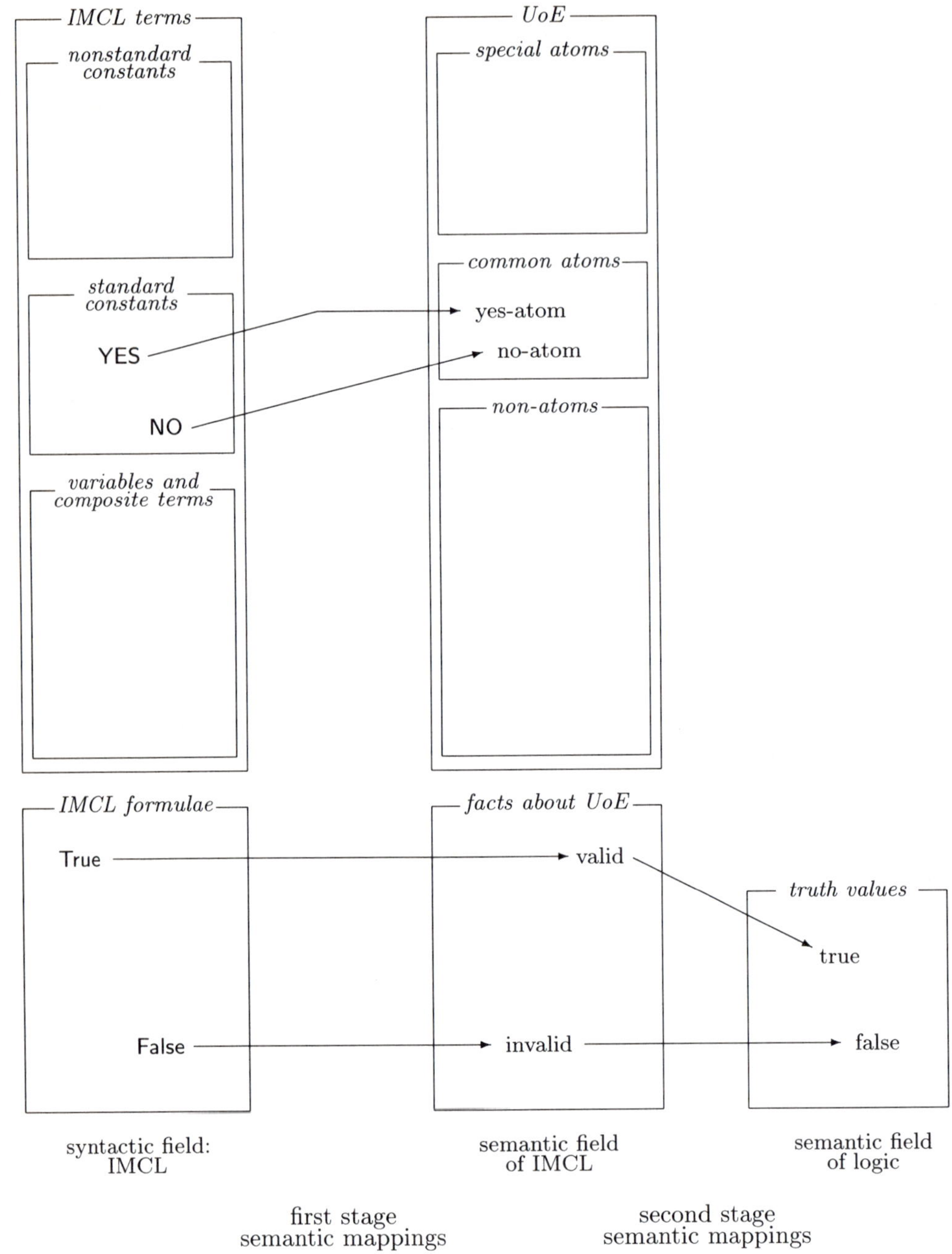

Figure 3.5 : Binary atoms vs. truth values

the few cases where it is important to refer to single spots are handled by using singleton spotsets. Thus, from the point of view of IMCL, spots do not exist as entities, but are auxiliary concepts for defining spotsets as entities of concern.

3.1.3 Remarks on the IMCL description

The exposition of IMCL in Sec. 3.2 proceeds along the formal syntax given in a top-down arrangement of BNF rules. The formal syntax, however, does not cover all syntactic properties. This is partly due to the necessity of expressing context-sensitive properties, partly to the fact that, without loss of precision, some syntactic properties are more easily expressed in natural language than in BNF. Complementary syntactic specification as well as explanations are given in the text following a BNF production rule. Also, the semantics is specified in this text. Throughout, the text is structured into portions marked *Syntax* or *Semantics* for better guidance.

Generally, the text following a production rule applies to this rule only. Details about nonterminal syntactic categories on the right-hand side of the production rule are postponed until the discussion of their own production rule.

For some language elements (spot-selection-clause, conditional-term, particularization-term, extensional-collection-term, extensional-spotset-term) it is necessary to talk about an arbitrary formula. This is referred to by a bold-face f (**f**). Thus, a displayed expression containing **f** is not an IMCL expression, but rather a schema of IMCL expressions. Although **f** is meant to denote any formula, in most cases an interesting situation only occurs if **f** contains the variable under discussion as a free variable.

The description contains short illustrative examples. These make use of syntactic liberties explained in Sec. 3.1.5 and of language features introduced in still later parts of this manual. Thus, they may sometimes be fully understandable only after having read these parts. Small examples are scattered throughout the text, those needing a few phrases are in separate paragraphs marked *Example* .

To understand discussions of IMCL language elements and examples, it is normally helpful and sometimes almost indispensable to use diagrams like those introduced in Chap. 2. In some cases, such diagrams are provided in the text. Where they are missing the reader is urged to visualize the considered situation by himself. The authors have extensively used diagrams for the development of this manual, many more than have finally been included.

3.1.4 Notation for the IMCL syntax

The IMCL syntax given in Sec. 3.2 employs a few usual conventions for describing formal languages. The following characters are used as meta-language symbols:

::=	as production symbol,
|	for separating alternative portions of text,
...	for repeating a portion of text one or more times,
$\equiv$	for indicating that no space is admissible at this place,
{ }	for delimiting a portion of text,
[ ]	for delimiting a portion of optional text,
-. .-	for delimiting a comment in the meta-language text.

One or more blanks are required between any two syntactical units, except where they are prohibited by "$\equiv$". (Later, this rule is somewhat relaxed, see next section.)

3.1.5 Syntactic liberties

For a particular application, one may want to shape IMCL to local needs. One way to do so is to introduce new predicates and operators by definitional equations within the IMCL language. In addition, one may want to derive IMCL variants not expressible in this way, for example, taking into account the character set available. Of course, any dialect can be invented. However, to facilitate reshaping of the language and to prevent unnecessary variations, some suggestions are made for representational variants. These liberties are also employed in examples of this manual.

Blanks
Blanks may be omitted if no ambiguities arise.

Parentheses
Parentheses may be omitted if no ambiguities arise. In addition, instead of using parentheses, a nesting structure may informally be expressed by a layout pattern, particularly by indentation.
A means of supporting perspicuity of the parenthesis nesting structure is to use variations of parentheses, for example, by attaching "attributes" like indices. An example of attributed parentheses is $({}_3 \cdots {}_3)$. This same facility is usable for other paired symbols, that is, [...] and $\langle ... \rangle$.

Variables
Strict IMCL syntax composes variables from letters, digits, and the underscore ("_"). To name variables systematically, one often wants to append or even insert other discriminatory characters. In particular, indices are a generally applied means to distinguish variants in a class of closely related variables, for example x_1, x_2, x_3 for the three coordinates of a point in space. Also, apostrophes (primes) are a common means of distinguishing variants. However, the use of apostrophes for this purpose is not recommended for IMCL, since here apostrophes occur in the strict syntax (for nonstandard-constants), so that confusion, if not ambiguity, may arise.

Decimal fractions
Some countries prefer a decimal comma to a decimal point. This can also be done in IMCL if some care is given to possible ambiguities in parameter lists.

Symbol substitution
The character set on the available printing device may lack some characters used in strict IMCL. Composite symbols could be used instead, such as "| |" for "||", "^∈" for "$\hat{\in}$", or "UNION" for "∪". On the other hand, when the character set is rich enough, one may find it convenient to introduce one-character symbols for frequently used word symbols. As an example, "$\prec$" may appropriately be used in place of "Prec".

Restricted quantification
Logical formulae are sometimes more readable when range restrictions on quantified variables are syntactically made conspicuous. Thus

$\forall x(x\in\mathbf{m} \Longrightarrow \mathbf{formula})$	is written	$\forall x\in\mathbf{m}(\mathbf{formula})$,
$\exists x(x\in\mathbf{m} \wedge \mathbf{formula})$	is written	$\exists x\in\mathbf{m}(\mathbf{formula})$,
$\forall x(x\hat{\in}\mathbf{m} \Longrightarrow \mathbf{formula})$	is written	$\forall x\hat{\in}\mathbf{m}(\mathbf{formula})$,
$\exists x(x\hat{\in}\mathbf{m} \wedge \mathbf{formula})$	is written	$\exists x\hat{\in}\mathbf{m}(\mathbf{formula})$,

where **m** stands for a term.

3.2 Language description

3.2.1 Formulae and terms

EXPRESSION ::=
FORMULA | TERM

Syntax An expression may be **closed** or **open** (see explanations of VARIABLE below).

Semantics An expression is a language element which is semantically complete in the sense that it denotes an entity or states a fact about the IMCL Universe of Entities (IMCL-UoE). This applies to closed expressions in the first place, but it is also true for open expressions for a given assignment of entities to all of its free variables. If in the following open expressions are treated as having a meaning, this is understood as referring to an assumed assignment of entities to its free variables.

Syntax The general precedence rule is left-to-right reduction. It can be overruled by parentheses. The following exceptions are made to the general rule:
- operators have precedence over predicates,
- predicates have precedence over logical connectives,
- logical connectives have precedence $\neg$, $\wedge$, $\vee$, $\Longrightarrow$, $\Longleftrightarrow$, $\not\Longleftrightarrow$, ordered by decreasing strength,

with precedence among operators as follows:
- "^" (ownspot) has highest operator precedence,
- postfix operators have precedence over prefix operators other than "^" (name-specifications following a shift-operator-symbol and spot-selection-clauses are treated as postfix operators in this regard),
- prefix operators have precedence over infix operators,

– "**" has precedence over "*" and "/",
– "*" and "/" have precedence over "+" and "−".

Example The effect of the precedence rules is illustrated by the following example:

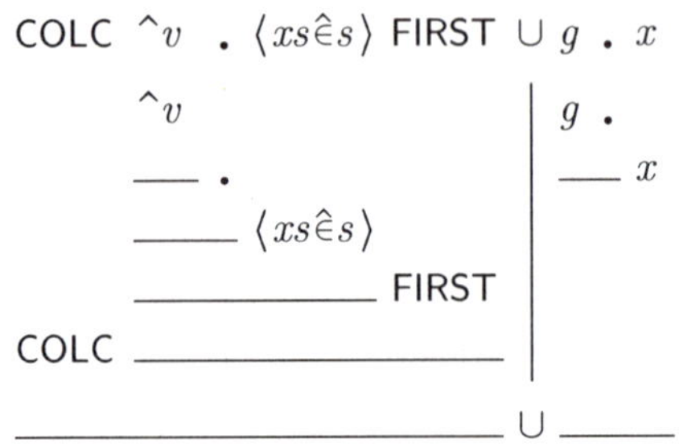

FORMULA ::=

PRIME-FORMULA |
¬ FORMULA | FORMULA { ∧ | ∨ | ⟹ | ⟺ | ⇎ } FORMULA |
∃ VARIABLE (FORMULA) | ∀ VARIABLE (FORMULA) |
(FORMULA)

Semantics A formula is an expression that states a fact about the IMCL-UoE. The fact (and thus indirectly the formula) has a truth value "true" or "false". Note that truth values are not entities *in* the IMCL-UoE. Rather, they are attributed to facts *about* the IMCL-UoE (see Sec. 3.1.2.2). A formula with the truth value "true" ("false") is said to *be* true (false).

Syntax Formulae may be composed in the usual way by using logical connectives and quantifiers. The precedence of connectives is in the order as given in the syntax definition, ordered by decreasing strength of binding, i.e., "∧" is the strongest, "⇎" is the weakest binary connective, "¬" is stronger than any binary connective. In a formula beginning with a quantifier (∀ or ∃), the VARIABLE is bound in the entire formula (for variable binding see explanation of VARIABLE).

Semantics The meaning of a composite formula is defined by the meaning of the constituent formulae and the connective or quantifier as usual in the semantics of predicate logic.

Syntax Any formula enclosed in parentheses yields another formula. Parentheses may be used to confirm or to overrule inherent precedence.

Semantics Parentheses around a formula don't change its meaning.

PRIME-FORMULA ::=

[PARAMETER-PART] PREDICATE-SYMBOL-PART ...
[PARAMETER-PART PREDICATE-SYMBOL-PART ...] ... [PARAMETER-PART]

Syntax A prime-formula is one which is not directly composed of other formulae. (A prime-formula may, however, indirectly contain another formula within a term.)

Syntax A prime-formula is a sequence of predicate-symbol-parts with interspersed parameter-parts, possibly beginning and/or ending with a parameter-part. A liberal syntax like this is elsewhere called "distfix" (see [Jone86]). It admits prefix, infix and postfix positions for predicate-symbol-parts to allow for more informative expressions, as opposed to the usage in formal logic, where prefix position is the rule. For PARAMETER-PART see description close to the end of this section.

Semantics The meaning of a prime-formula is given by the meaning of its pattern of predicate-symbol-parts (i.e., its *predicate symbol*, see below). It has the truth value "true" if the predicate denoted by the predicate symbol holds for the entities denoted by the parameter-parts, otherwise it is "false".

PREDICATE-SYMBOL-PART ::=
[PREDICATE-CHARACTER ≡] ... CHARACTERISTIC-PREDICATE-CHARACTER
[≡ PREDICATE-CHARACTER] ... |
UPPERCASE-LETTER [≡ LETTER | ≡ DIGIT | ≡ _] ... ≡ LOWERCASE-LETTER
[≡ LETTER | ≡ DIGIT | ≡ _] ...

Syntax A predicate-symbol-part is a string of predicate-characters that contains at least one characteristic-predicate-character, or a string of letters and possibly digits and underscore characters that starts with an uppercase-letter and contains at least one lowercase-letter. The characteristic-predicate-character or a lowercase-letter, respectively, syntactically distinguishes a predicate-symbol-part from an operator-symbol-part (see below for OPERATOR-SYMBOL-PART). For the definitions of PREDICATE-CHARACTER and CHARACTERISTIC-PREDICATE-CHARACTER see descriptions close to the end of this section.

Syntax In the following, a pattern of predicate-symbol-parts (i.e., a sequence of predicate-symbol-parts with parameter positions) is called a **predicate symbol**. A predicate symbol is identified by its sequence of predicate-symbol-parts. Thus, the predicate symbols of the following prime-formulae are different from each other (the t_i stand for parameter-parts):

t_1 Knows t_2
t_1 Knows t_2 To Manage
t_1 Knows $t_2 < t_3$

For the related notions of **parameter position**, **parameter term** and **parameter**, see explanation of PARAMETER-PART close to the end of this section.

For a given predicate symbol, the parameter positions are fixed. That is, the same predicate symbol may not be used with a different number or distribution of parameter positions. Thus, "t_1 Knows To Manage t_2", or "t_1 Knows (t_2,t_3) To Manage" could not coexist with the above "t_1 Knows t_2 To Manage".

Syntax The general IMCL syntax does not care about syntactic ambiguity of predicate symbols. Each application that introduces its own predicate symbols is responsible for their uniqueness.

Semantics A predicate symbol is interpreted as an n-ary predicate, where n is the number of parameter positions (its *arity*). Different predicate symbols, even when they have common symbol parts, are semantically completely unrelated (unless connections are explicitly established). The meaning of a predicate symbol is either given in a standard or nonstandard semantic specification (see Sec. 3.1.2.1), or it may be left open or specified by the user. If a predicate symbol has a standard semantics, this cannot be overruled. Standard semantics for predicate symbols is given in Sec. 3.2.2.

Semantics The meaning of a predicate symbol for which no standard semantics is given can be freely defined. Thus, "IsNatOrZero t" could be given any arbitrary meaning, though the choice of the predicate symbol rather suggests

$$\forall x(\mathsf{IsNatOrZero}\ x \iff \mathsf{IsNat}\ x \lor x{=}0)$$

as a reasonable definition.

Semantics The meaning of a predicate symbol can be specified in various ways. A precise way is to relate the predicate symbol through a definitional formula to other concepts for which a semantics is already established, as in the above example. As another example, one could define "$t_1 = t_2$ Modulo t_3" by postulating

$$\forall x,y,m(x = y\ \mathsf{Modulo}\ m \iff \exists n(x = n * m + y)).$$

Both examples have the form

$$\forall x(\mathsf{NewPred}\ x \iff ...x...x...\ ),$$

which a definitional formula for a predicate symbol should preferably take in general.

TERM ::=
VARIABLE |
CONSTANT |
OPERATOR-TERM |
SPOT-SELECTION-TERM |
ELLIPTIC-COMPONENT-SELECTION-TERM |
SUBSTITUTION-TERM |
AUGMENTATION-TERM |
DELETION-TERM |
TOTAL-OPERATOR-TERM |
CONDITIONAL-TERM |
PARTICULARIZATION-TERM |
EXTENSIONAL-COLLECTION-TERM |
EXTENSIONAL-SPOTSET-TERM |
EXPLICIT-COMPOSITION-TERM |
VALUATION-TERM |
(TERM)

Semantics A term is an expression that denotes an entity of the IMCL-UoE, that is, a construct, a spotset, or the entity "undefined". At this point it seems appropriate to recall that spots by themselves are not in the IMCL universe of entities and hence there are no terms to denote spots. In talking about the semantics of terms, we use several locutions: **associated** entity, **assigned** entity, **meaning** of a term, **semantics** of a term, term is **interpreted as**, term **has interpretation**, term **denotes** entity, or term **has value**. Often it is convenient to talk about a term as if it were the entity it denotes. Thus, for example, if g and h are construct terms, we might say "g **is** a component of h" when we mean "the construct denoted by g is a component of the construct denoted by h". Moreover, for a term which denotes the entity "undefined", we also say the term *is* undefined. Note, however, that "undefined" is an entity in the IMCL-UoE, and that, without exception, every term has a value. To further facilitate talking about the "undefined" entity, we adopt the convention that if something is said to be **required** for a term, this means that the term is undefined if the requirement is not met. For example, "in $x+y$, the values for x and y must be numbers" means that $x+y$ has the value "undefined" if x or y is not a number. For, say, x undefined, the term $x+y$ is still meaningful. It has the definite value "undefined". Also, $x+y=$UNDEF is then true rather than indefinite.

Syntax Any term enclosed in parentheses yields another term. Parentheses may be used to confirm or to overrule inherent precedence.

Semantics Parentheses around a term don't change its meaning.

VARIABLE ::=

LOWERCASE-LETTER [≡ LETTER | ≡ DIGIT | ≡ _] ...

Syntax Syntactically, a variable can be recognized by the initial lowercase letter. An occurrence of a variable in an expression may be **free** or **bound**. If it is bound, it has a well-defined **scope** to which it is said to be bound. If two different scopes overlap, one of them is completely contained in the other one. In an expression, a variable may have free and bound occurrences at the same time. An expression is called **closed** if all of its variable occurrences are bound, otherwise it is called **open**.

Syntax In IMCL, variable bindings occur in the following expressions:

quantification	$\forall x(...)$, $\exists x(...)$	
spot-selection-term	**term**$\langle x \| ... \rangle$	scope is $\langle x \| ... \rangle$
substitution-term	SUBST ... FOR ALL x OF ...	
augmentation-term	AUG ... FOR ALL x OF ...	
total-operator-term	TOTAL ... FOR ALL x OF ...	
particularization-term	THAT x (...)	
extensional-collection-term	$[x\|...]$	
extensional-spotset-term	$\langle x\|...\rangle$	
valuation-term	$(x=)(...)$, $(...)(=x)$	wider scope

The scopes are the entire expressions, except for the spot-selection-term, for which the scope is the spot-selection-clause $\langle x \| ... \rangle$ only (see SPOT-SELECTION-CLAUSE), and the valuation-term, which has a wider scope (see VALUATION-TERM).

Semantics A variable is a language device used for context bindings. Variables do not have genuine meanings by themselves. However, for the technicalities of defining the semantics of expressions it is convenient if all terms have a meaning, without any exception. We force this by assigning the value "undefined" to variables. This is, however, a default assignment which is altered locally for bound variables in the definitional mechanism that specifies the semantics of an expression. A variable in an expression will retain the default assignment of "undefined" in free occurrences only. Intuitively, this matches quite well with the idea that an expression with free variables does not really have any immediate sense when considered out of context. Expressions with free variables are auxiliary language elements the semantics of which, although technically important and well-defined, should not be overemphasized. This applies in particular to variables themselves, since they are special terms.

Semantics Variables with different scopes are treated as semantically different, even if they are homonymous. In particular, a variable is inaccessible within the scope of a homonymous variable if the scope of the latter is contained within the scope of the former. The effect is that for nested scopes of homonymous variables the outer scope is exempted within the inner scope. Homonymous variables must not have identical scopes.

CONSTANT ::=
STANDARD-CONSTANT |
NONSTANDARD-CONSTANT

Semantics A constant has a fixed interpretation, i.e., the assignment of entities to constants is permanently established for a given environment of IMCL usage. Although there are other terms with fixed interpretation, *constants* are the only such terms not comprising other expressions. As an example, 21 is a constant which has the natural number twenty-one as its meaning. In contrast, 21+0 is a term denoting the same number, but it is not a constant.

Semantics The meaning of a standard-constant is defined for all application environments of IMCL. The meaning of a nonstandard-constant is application-dependent.

STANDARD-CONSTANT ::=
UNDEF | YES | NO |
EMPTY-CONSTANT |
NUMBER-ATOM-CONSTANT

Semantics A standard-constant has an obvious standard semantics. UNDEF denotes the entity "undefined", YES denotes the binary atom "yes-atom", and NO denotes the binary atom "no-atom".

EMPTY-CONSTANT ::=
[ ] | [:] | [→] | ⟨ ⟩

Semantics [ ] denotes the empty collection, [:] denotes the empty nomination, [→] denotes the empty catenation, ⟨ ⟩ denotes the empty spotset.

NUMBER-ATOM-CONSTANT ::=
  [+ ≡ | − ≡] DIGIT [≡ DIGIT] ... [≡ . ≡ DIGIT [≡ DIGIT] ...]

Syntax Number-atom-constants have the usual syntax of decimal number representation. A rather small segment of possible number representations is selected for IMCL since calculation is not a focal point of this language.

Semantics A number-atom-constant means a rational number in the usual way. Not all rational numbers are expressible as number-atom-constants.

NONSTANDARD-CONSTANT ::=
  ' ≡ CHARACTER [≡ CHARACTER] ... ≡ '   -. apostrophes must be paired .-

Syntax A nonstandard-constant is any nonempty string of IMCL characters enclosed in apostrophes, but containing apostrophes in pairs only. Thus `'A''B'` is a nonstandard-constant, but `'A'B'` is not.

Semantics The semantics of a nonstandard-constant is defined by and specific to an application environment (see Sec. 3.1.2.1). Any entity may be assigned to a nonstandard-constant. Nonstandard-constants must not be confused with catenation-words.

OPERATOR-TERM ::=
  [PARAMETER-PART] OPERATOR-SYMBOL-PART ...
  [PARAMETER-PART OPERATOR-SYMBOL-PART ...] ... [PARAMETER-PART]

Syntax An operator-term is a sequence of operator-symbol-parts with interspersed parameter-parts, possibly beginning and/or ending with a parameter-part. The syntax admits prefix, infix and postfix positions for parameter-parts (see also "distfix" in the explanations for PRIME-FORMULA.) For PARAMETER-PART see description close to the end of this section.

Semantics The meaning of an operator-term is given by the meaning of its pattern of operator-symbol-parts (i.e., its *operator symbol*, see below). It is the result of applying the operator denoted by the operator symbol to the entities denoted by the parameter-parts.

OPERATOR-SYMBOL-PART ::=
  [OPERATOR-CHARACTER ≡] ... CHARACTERISTIC-OPERATOR-CHARACTER
  [≡ OPERATOR-CHARACTER] ... |
  UPPERCASE-LETTER [≡ UPPERCASE-LETTER | ≡ DIGIT | ≡ _] ...

Syntax An operator-symbol-part is a string of operator-characters that contains at least one characteristic-operator-character, or a string of uppercase-letters and possibly digits and underscore characters. The characteristic-operator-character or the absence of lowercase-letters, respectively, syntactically distinguishes an operator-symbol-part from a predicate-symbol-part (see above for PREDICATE-SYMBOL-PART). For the definitions of OPERATOR-CHARACTER and CHARACTERISTIC-OPERATOR-CHARACTER see descriptions close to the end of this section.

Syntax Analogously to predicate symbols, we call a pattern of operator-symbol-parts an **operator symbol**. An operator symbol is identified by its sequence of operator-symbol-parts. Thus, the operator symbols of the following operator-terms are different from each other (the t_i stand for parameter-parts):

$$t_1 + t_2$$
$$t_1 + t_2 \ \mathsf{MOD}\ t_3$$
$$t_1 + t_2 \ \mathsf{MOD}\ t_3 \ \mathsf{INV}$$

For the related notions of **parameter position**, **parameter term**, **parameter** and **operand**, see explanation of PARAMETER-PART close to the end of this section.

For a given operator symbol, the parameter positions are fixed. Consequently, the same operator symbol may not be used with a different number or distribution of parameter positions. Thus "$(t_1,t_2) + \mathsf{MOD}\ t_3$" or "$t_1 + t_2\ \mathsf{MOD}\,(t_3,t_4)$" could not coexist with the above "$t_1{+}t_2\ \mathsf{MOD}\ t_3$".

Syntax The general IMCL syntax does not care about syntactic ambiguity of operator symbols. Each application that introduces its own operator symbols is responsible for their uniqueness.

Semantics An operator symbol is interpreted as an n-ary operator, where n is the number of parameter positions (its *arity*). Different operator symbols, even when they have common symbol parts, are semantically completely unrelated (unless connections are explicitly established). The meaning of an operator symbol is either given in a standard or nonstandard semantic specification (see Sec. 3.1.2.1), or it may be left open or specified by the user. If an operator symbol has a standard semantics, this cannot be overruled. Standard semantics for operator symbols is given in Sec. 3.2.3.

Semantics The meaning of an operator symbol for which no standard semantics is given can be freely defined. Thus, "GREATEST FACTOR OF t" could be given any arbitrary meaning, though the choice of the operator symbol rather suggests

$$\begin{aligned}&\forall x\ \ (\mathsf{GREATEST\ FACTOR\ OF}\ x = \\ &\quad \mathsf{THAT}\ z\ (\quad \mathsf{IsNat}\ z \wedge \exists y\ (\mathsf{IsInt}\ y \wedge y{\neq}1 \wedge x{=}z{*}y) \wedge \\ &\qquad\qquad \forall k (\mathsf{IsNat}\ k \wedge \exists y\ (\mathsf{IsInt}\ y \wedge y{\neq}1 \wedge x{=}k{*}y) \Longrightarrow k{\leq}z\ )\ )\ )\end{aligned}$$

as a reasonable definition.

Semantics The meaning of an operator symbol can be specified in various ways. A precise way is to relate the operator symbol through a definitional formula to other concepts for which a semantics is already established, like in the above example. This has the form

$$\forall x,y(x\ \mathsf{NEWOP}\ y = \mathsf{THAT}\ z(\ \ldots\ x\ \ldots\ y\ \ldots\ z\ \ldots\ )),$$

which a definitional formula for an operator symbol should preferably take in general. It guarantees the uniqueness property of functions, whereas

$$\forall x,y,z(x\ \mathsf{NEWOP}\ y = z \iff \ldots\ x\ \ldots\ y\ \ldots\ z\ \ldots\ )$$

would require careful checking that ... x ... y ... z ... specifies a unique z for any given x and y.

Semantics Operator symbols with no parameters are also admitted. They are interpreted as nullary operators. Nullary operator symbols provide an alternative way for terms with constant entity assignment, in addition to standard-constants and nonstandard-constants introduced earlier. Semantically, they are equivalent, since nullary operators and entities are interchangeable concepts.

SPOT-SELECTION-TERM ::=
TERM SPOT-SELECTION-CLAUSE |
ELLIPTIC-SPOT-SELECTION-TERM

Semantics The term is required to denote a spotset. In the case of a spot-selection-clause, the value of the spot-selection-term is the subset of this spotset as specified by the spot-selection-clause. The elliptic-spot-selection-term is a special syntactic variant of the first case.

SPOT-SELECTION-CLAUSE ::=
⟨ VARIABLE || FORMULA ⟩ |
⟨ FORMULA ⟩ |
⟨ NAME-SPECIFICATION [, NAME-SPECIFICATION] ... ⟩

Syntax The merit of the spot-selection-clause is that repeated selection, interspersed with other spotset operations, can be written in natural sequence, rather than requiring nesting. The last two alternatives are abbreviated syntactic variants of the first one for simple but frequently occurring cases.

Syntax In the first alternative, the VARIABLE is bound in the entire spot-selection-clause. In the second alternative, the standard variable xs is bound in the entire spot-selection-clause.

Semantics The spot-selection-clause specifies a subset of the spotset given by the term to which it refers. If s denotes a spotset and **f** stands for a formula, then $s\,\langle x \| \mathbf{f}\,\rangle$ denotes the set of those spots of s, the singleton spotsets of which satisfy **f** if assigned to x. Formally:

$$s\,\langle x \| \;\mathbf{f}\;\rangle = \langle s_0 |\; s_0 \hat{\in} s \wedge \exists x (x{=}s_0 \wedge \mathbf{f})\;\rangle$$

Semantics If **f** is a formula, $\langle \mathbf{f}\,\rangle$ means the same as $\langle xs \| \mathbf{f}\,\rangle$, that is, if the standard variable xs is taken for the bound variable, it need not be explicitly specified after the opening angle bracket ("xs" stands for "x-spot").

Semantics The normal rules for scope nesting of variables apply to the standard variable xs. That is, in

$$s\,\langle \mathsf{N}\,(xs){=}\texttt{'A'} \wedge \mathsf{CARD}\,(xs\,\texttt{.}\langle \mathsf{C}\,(xs){=}\texttt{[]}\rangle){>}0\rangle$$

the xs in the inner angle brackets is semantically different from the xs outside. However, to avoid confusion, nesting of the same variable (standard or not) is not recommended.

Semantics The third alternative provides a particularly simple way for selection in nominations. If s denotes a spotset and n_1, ..., n_k are name-specifications, then

$$s\langle n_1,...,n_k\rangle = s\langle \mathsf{N}\,(xs){=}n_1 \vee \;...\; \vee \mathsf{N}\,(xs){=}n_k\rangle$$

NAME-SPECIFICATION ::=
NONSTANDARD-CONSTANT | VARIABLE

Semantics The construct denoted by a name-specification is used as a name for spot selection in a nomination.

ELLIPTIC-SPOT-SELECTION-TERM ::=
TERM SHIFT-OPERATOR-SYMBOL NAME-SPECIFICATION

SHIFT-OPERATOR-SYMBOL ::=
. | · | (.) | (·) | ↓ | ↑

Syntax In the special syntactic case that a spotset term ends with a shift-operator-symbol, a particularly convenient way for further simple subset selection is provided.

Semantics For the semantics of the shift-operators see Sec. 3.2.3.

Semantics If $\otimes$ stands for a shift-operator-symbol and n is a name-specification, $s \otimes n$ is equivalent to $s \otimes \langle n \rangle$. The term `s.'ABC'` is an example. In programming languages, this kind of syntax is well-known as "name qualification". Since the term syntax allows for repeatedly appending "$\otimes$ NAME-SPECIFICATION" (an elliptic-spot-selection-term is a term), "nested" qualifications can be expressed in the usual way, e.g., `s.'ABC'.'x3'.'T'`, as far as the construct at s consists of nested nominations. Note that for IMCL this is a special case. The general IMCL spot selection syntax also permits penetration in cases where the encountered constructs are not nominations.

Example The following examples illustrate the various forms of spot-selection-terms. Let the variable p denote an unordered table with attributes `'salary'` and `'empname'`. The term

$$\hat{}p.\langle emp|| \,(\mathsf{C}\ emp.\langle \mathsf{N}\ xs = \texttt{'salary'}\rangle) < 1500\rangle.\langle\texttt{'empname'}\rangle$$

contains all three kinds of spot-selection-clauses, namely

- the full notation: $\langle emp||(...emp...) < 1500\rangle$
- the notation using the standard variable xs: $\langle \mathsf{N}\ xs = \texttt{'salary'}\rangle$
- the particularly simple notation: $\langle\texttt{'empname'}\rangle$

The entire term can be rewritten in a most compact form also employing elliptic-spot-selection-terms:

$$\hat{}p.\langle \mathrm{C}\ xs.\texttt{'salary'}<1500\rangle.\texttt{'empname'}$$

It denotes the set of all those spots with name `'empname'`, which are inward of a row spot *emp* (or xs in the latter form), whose immediately inward component spot xs with name `'salary'` leads to a construct which is less than 1500.

ELLIPTIC-COMPONENT-SELECTION-TERM ::=
VARIABLE . NAME-SPECIFICATION [. NAME-SPECIFICATION] ...

Syntax The elliptic-component-selection-term provides a syntactic simplification for a special, but frequently occurring construct term. It should be noted that a very specific case is singled out by this language element.

Semantics For an elliptic-component-selection-term, the variable must denote a nomination. If it denotes any other construct, the term is undefined. If it denotes a spotset, it is defined, but is an elliptic-spot-selection-term rather than an elliptic-component-selection-term. For a variable v denoting a nomination and name specifications n_1, ... , n_i, the term $v\,.\,n_1\,.\;...\;.\,n_i$ is equivalent to $\mathsf{C}(\hat{}v\,.\,n_1\,.\;...\;.\,n_i)$. This allows for "name qualification" in the traditional way. It starts from a nomination and yields a construct (as opposed to the elliptic-spot-selection-term, which starts from a spotset and yields a spotset).

SUBSTITUTION-TERM
AUGMENTATION-TERM
DELETION-TERM
TOTAL-OPERATOR-TERM

In the following, four kinds of terms, substitution-terms, augmentation-terms, deletion-terms and total-operator-terms, are introduced, which have some common features that are explained first.

Syntax All these terms follow the general pattern

... WITH object term FOR ALL [VARIABLE] OF range term [IN subject term]

although with some individual variations. The three dots stand for either SUBSTC, SUBSTN, AUGCOL, AUGNOM, AUGCAT, AUGBEFORE, AUGAFTER, DELETE or TOTAL. In the pattern above, the terms in parameter positions have been given distinguishing names for easier reference. The variable is bound in the entire term. It makes sense only if it occurs freely in the object term. However, it must *not* occur freely in the range term nor in the subject term. This is a syntactic requirement to exclude semantically not resolvable (as opposed to "undefined") specifications.

Semantics The subject term must denote a construct, subsequently called the **subject construct**. The range term must denote a spotset, called the **range spotset**, the spots of which are in the subject construct, that is, the subject construct must be the common reference construct of the spots in the range spotset. The spots of the range spotset are called **range spots**. A singleton spotset formed from a range spot is called a **range value** of the variable. (Note that a variable can never assume single spots as values, since single spots are not IMCL entities.) The set of range values is called the **range** of the variable. The object term must denote a construct if the variable assumes any of its range values. This construct is called the **object construct** (for a given range value).

Semantics The subject construct is that on which the operation is performed. An object construct is the construct to be used in the operation at each range spot when the associated range value is assigned to the variable.

Semantics Operations that modify the subject construct at range spots must be considered as being executed in two steps:
– for each range spot the associated object construct is determined,
– at each range spot, the operation is performed with the associated object construct.

Execution of operations in the second step has to be regarded as one instantaneous transformation of the original construct, because sequential substitution would spoil the original spots.

Semantics The idea for substitution-, augmentation- and deletion-terms (not for total-operator-terms) is that the result of the operation is a variant of the subject construct. Some attention must be paid to the possibility of a **collection collapse**. This occurs if originally different immediate components of a collection "become the same". This is not regarded as an error. The collapse may also occur indirectly on any level outward of the range spots.

Semantics The optional omissions allow for more concise notation in special, but frequent, cases. If "IN subject term" is omitted, this is taken to be equivalent to "IN C((range term)↑)", that is, the common reference construct is taken for the subject construct. However, if the range spotset is empty, the subject construct cannot be calculated from the range term since no reference construct is available, and C((range term)↑) would thus yield UNDEF. To account for this, the subject term parameter is provided as a means of explicitly specifying the reference construct if from the context an empty range spotset cannot be excluded. In this case, "IN subject term" must be specified.

Semantics The variable may be omitted if the object construct does not depend on the range spot, that is, if the same object construct is used for all range spots.

Semantics If the range spotset is empty, the result is the unaltered subject construct. If in this case the subject construct is not specified, the result is undefined.

SUBSTITUTION-TERM ::=
SUBSTC WITH TERM FOR ALL [VARIABLE] OF TERM [IN TERM] |
SUBSTN WITH TERM FOR ALL [VARIABLE] OF TERM [IN TERM]

The features substitution-terms have in common with augmentation-terms, deletion-terms and total-operator-terms are described above.

Semantics The range spots of a substitution-term are called **substitution spots**. SUBSTC substitutes components, SUBSTN substitutes names. The substitution-term denotes the construct obtained from the subject construct by substituting the component constructs or names, respectively, at the substitution spots.

Semantics For SUBSTC, the object construct is the construct to be inserted at each substitution spot. Substitutions at spots more inward of other substitution spots are without any effect, because it is the construct related to the most outward substitution spot (see "first step" above) which will replace the original construct at that spot. So all substitutions at more inward spots are overruled by the most comprehensive substitution.

Example Let $g =$ `['number':[3;[4;5; 6]]]` be given (Fig. 3.6).

SUBSTC WITH CARD(t.) FOR ALL t OF ^g(.)⟨IsCol(C xs)⟩

is then the nomination `['number':2]`.

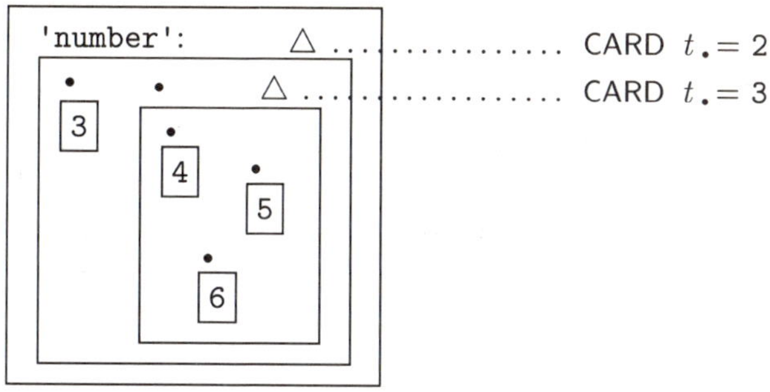

Figure 3.6 : Most comprehensive substitution overrules all others

Semantics For SUBSTN, the substitution spots must be immediately inward of nomination spots. The object constructs are the names by which the names at the substitution spots are to be substituted. Of course, the substitution may not result in a duplication of names for different component constructs of one nomination. Yet, a **nomination collapse** may occur if nomination components with the same construct, but originally different names, acquire the same name. This is not regarded as an error.

AUGMENTATION-TERM ::=

AUGCOL WITH TERM FOR ALL [VARIABLE] OF TERM [IN TERM] |
AUGNOM WITH TERM FOR ALL [VARIABLE] OF TERM [IN TERM] |
AUGCAT WITH TERM FOR ALL [VARIABLE] OF TERM [IN TERM]
[ACC TERM] |
AUGBEFORE WITH TERM FOR ALL [VARIABLE] OF TERM [IN TERM] |
AUGAFTER WITH TERM FOR ALL [VARIABLE] OF TERM [IN TERM]

The features augmentation-terms have in common with substitution-terms, deletion-terms and total-operator-terms are described above.

Semantics An augmentation-term beginning with AUGCOL, AUGNOM or AUGCAT denotes a construct which results from the subject construct by augmenting component constructs of a specified kind (referred to by the suffix -COL, -NOM or -CAT) at all range spots by an object construct of the same kind. The subject construct itself may also be among those to be augmented. AUGBEFORE and AUGAFTER refer to catenations, as does AUGCAT, but they have their range spots immediately inward of the catenation spots. Fig. 3.7 schematically outlines the situations.

Semantics Augmenting means to fuse the component construct at a range spot (or, in the case of AUGBEFORE or AUGAFTER, immediately outward thereof) with the object construct in a way which depends on the kind of these constructs. The range spots of an augmentation-term are called **augmentation spots**.

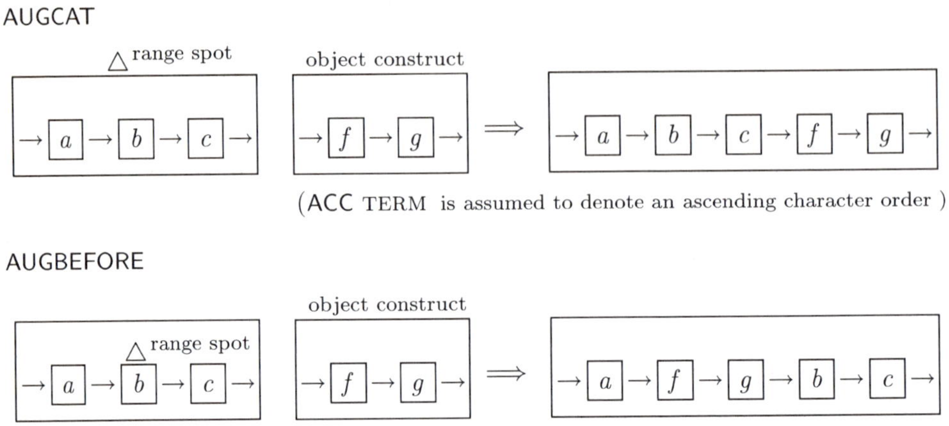

Figure 3.7: AUGCAT vs. AUGBEFORE

Semantics For "AUGCOL WITH object term FOR ALL VARIABLE OF range term IN subject term" to be defined, the constructs at the augmentation spots as well as the object constructs must be collections. The augmentation-term denotes the construct which results from the subject construct by substituting the component construct at each augmentation spot by the union of the collection at this spot with the associated object construct.

Semantics For "AUGNOM WITH object term FOR ALL VARIABLE OF range term IN subject term" to be defined, the constructs at the augmentation spots as well as the object constructs must be nominations. The augmentation-term denotes the construct which results from the subject construct by substituting the component construct at each augmentation spot by the *merge* of the nomination at this spot with the associated object construct. The merge $n_1{:}\cup n_2$ of two nominations n_1 and n_2 is given by the union of their (name,component)-pair sets, barring name conflicts (see Sec. 3.3.2.3).

Semantics For "AUGCAT WITH object term FOR ALL VARIABLE OF range term IN subject term ACC order pattern term" to be defined, the constructs at the augmentation spots as well as the object constructs must be catenations. AUGCAT has a special "order pattern term" parameter, which specifies how the catenation at an augmentation spot must be split for linking in the object catenation. The order pattern term must denote a collection of catenations (order pattern) if the variable is assigned any of its range values. There must be exactly one way to *link* the object catenation into the catenation at the augmentation spot such that the resulting catenation is in the order pattern. (More precisely, there must be catenations y and z such that $y /\!/ z$ is the catenation at the augmentation spot and $y /\!/$(object catenation)$/\!/ z$ is in the order pattern, and for any such choice of y and z the result is the same. Note that there may be several ways to decompose the original catenation and still achieve a unique result, as can be seen from the example of linking [→*a*→] into [→*a*→*a*→*a*→]. Hence only the result is required to be unique, not the partial catenations y and z. ("//" is the "concatenation operator" introduced in Sec. 3.2.3.) The augmentation-term denotes the construct which results from the subject construct by replacing the component construct at each augmentation spot with the catenation obtained by linking the associated object catenation into the catenation at the augmentation spot such that the result is in the order pattern. Thus, the order pattern may vary for different augmentation spots. If the order pattern is not specified, this is equivalent to specifying "ACC [object term]". It follows that, in the latter case, the augmentation term is defined only if the catenation at the augmentation spot is empty.

Example As an example, let g be a construct describing some public service agency. Let s be a singleton spotset of g such that the construct at s is the catenation of those days of the week in natural order on which the services are available, for example

g=[... [→'Mon'→'Tue'→'Fri'→] ...]
C(s)= [→'Mon'→'Tue'→'Fri'→]

Assume that the services are additionally made available on Wednesdays. The following term denotes the updated construct:

AUGCAT WITH [→ 'Wed' →] FOR ALL OF s IN g ACC *dayorder*

with the order pattern *dayorder* = [q | $\exists d$ (q=CATC(d) $\wedge$ $d\subseteq$^*daysequence*.)], where

daysequence = [→'Mon'→'Tue'→'Wed'→'Thu'→'Fri'→'Sat'→'Sun'→]

Semantics For "AUGBEFORE WITH object term FOR ALL VARIABLE OF range term IN subject term" to be defined, the object constructs must be catenations; the augmentation spots must be *immediately inward* of catenation spots. The augmentation-term denotes the construct which results from the subject construct by linking just before each augmentation spot the associated object catenation into the catenation immediately outward of this spot.

Semantics The semantics for AUGAFTER is analogous to that of AUGBEFORE.

DELETION-TERM ::=

DELETE FOR ALL OF TERM [IN TERM]

The features deletion-terms have in common with substitution-terms, augmentation-terms and total-operator-terms are described above.

Syntax The deletion-term does not have an object term parameter, nor a variable for range spots.

Semantics The range spots of a deletion-term are called **deletion spots**. The ownspot of the subject construct itself must not be among the deletion spots. The deletion-term denotes the construct obtained from the subject construct by removing the components at the deletion spots.

Semantics Removal of a component means just taking it away if it is an immediate component of a collection. If it is an immediate component of a nomination, the name is also deleted. If it is an immediate component of a catenation, the parts left and right of the deletion spot are concatenated to form a new catenation that is shorter by one member.

TOTAL-OPERATOR-TERM ::=

TOTAL (OPERATOR-SYMBOL-PART ...) WITH TERM FOR ALL OF TERM |
TOTAL (OPERATOR-SYMBOL-PART ...) WITH TERM
FOR ALL VARIABLE OF TERM [ALL VARIABLE OF TERM] ...

The features total-operator-terms have in common with substitution-terms, augmentation-terms and deletion-terms are described above.

Syntax The total-operator-term does not have a subject term parameter. On the other hand, it may have several variables, each with its own range term. If the clause "ALL VARIABLE OF TERM" is repeated, the variables must all be different from each other.

Semantics The range terms are required to denote nonempty finite sets, which can be spotsets, or—as a special feature of TOTAL—collections. If t_2 denotes a collection, TOTAL (**op**) WITH t_1 FOR ALL x OF t_2 is equivalent to TOTAL (**op**) WITH t_1' FOR ALL y OF $\hat{}t_2$., where t_1' is t_1 with all free occurrences of x substituted by C(y). For ease of description, and to conform with the common feature description, we assume in the following that all range terms denote spotsets. As another special feature of the total-operator-term, the object term can denote a construct *or a spotset* if the variable assumes any of its range values.

Semantics The sequence of operator-symbol-parts is required to constitute an operator symbol denoting a commutative, associative binary operator. The value of a total-operator-term with only one ALL-OF-clause is obtained in the following way: the range spots are successively selected in arbitrary sequence. The object construct associated with the first range spot is taken as an initial intermediate result. Subsequent intermediate results accrue from applying **op** to the most recent intermediate result and the object construct associated with the next range spot. The last intermediate result is the final value. Commutativity and associativity of **op** make the result independent of the particular sequence chosen for range spot selection. If the range spotset is empty, the result is undefined. (Since the total-operator-term does not have a subject term parameter, the general rule that an empty range spotset yields the subject construct does not apply.)

Semantics If more than one ALL-OF-clause is used, the value is analogously obtained, each variable ranging independently over its associated range spotset. That is, the object term is in effect evaluated on the Cartesian product of all of these sets. For each point of the Cartesian product, the operator **op** is applied to produce a new intermediate result.

Example For illustration consider the following applications of the total-operator-term:

TOTAL (+) WITH 1 FOR ALL OF t

  yields the cardinality of t

TOTAL (+) WITH C(x) FOR ALL x OF t

  yields the sum of all numbers at the spots of t

TOTAL (GCD) WITH C(x) FOR ALL x OF t

  yields the greatest common divisor for all numbers at the spots of t, if GCD(x,y) denotes the greatest common divisor of two numbers x and y

TOTAL (∪) WITH C(x) FOR ALL x OF t

  yields the union of all collections at the spots of t

TOTAL (:∪) WITH [C(x):C(x)] FOR ALL x OF ^c.

  yields the nomination obtained from a compound c by using each immediate component for its own name

TOTAL (∪) WITH [x:∪y] FOR ALL x OF *tab_a* ALL y OF *tab_b*

  yields the natural join of two tables with disjoint name sets

TOTAL (MAX) WITH x FOR ALL x OF *numset*

  yields the maximum number from a collection of numbers *numset*. MAX(a, b) is assumed to deliver the maximum of a and b

The last two examples have collections as ranges.

CONDITIONAL-TERM ::=

  IF FORMULA THEN TERM ELSE TERM

Syntax A conditional-term IF ... THEN ... ELSE ... is not regarded as an operator-term, since a formula is not a parameter-part.

Semantics For a formula **f** and terms t_1 and t_2, IF **f** THEN t_1 ELSE t_2 denotes the same as t_1 if **f** is true; it denotes the same as t_2 if **f** is false. Formally, IF **f** THEN t_1 ELSE t_2 is equivalent to THAT $z((\mathbf{f} \wedge z{=}t_1) \vee (\neg \mathbf{f} \wedge z{=}t_2))$.

PARTICULARIZATION-TERM ::=

  THAT VARIABLE (FORMULA)

Syntax The **particularizator** THAT makes a term from a formula. The variable is bound in the entire particularization-term.

Semantics For a formula **f**, the term THAT x (**f**) denotes that entity, which, if assigned to x, makes **f** true. In general, this makes sense only if **f** contains x as a free variable. If there is not exactly one (i.e., none or more than one) entity satisfying **f**, the term is undefined. Formally, particularization is characterized by

$$\forall y\ (y = \text{THAT}\ x\ (\mathbf{f}) \iff (\exists! x(\mathbf{f}) \wedge \mathbf{f}_y) \vee (\neg\exists! x(\mathbf{f}) \wedge y{=}\text{UNDEF}))$$

where $\mathbf{f}_y$ stands for $\exists x(\mathbf{f} \wedge x{=}y)$, $\exists! x(\mathbf{f})$ stands for $\exists y(\mathbf{f}_y \wedge \forall x(\mathbf{f} \Longrightarrow x{=}y))$, and **f** is assumed not to contain y as a free variable.

Semantics Unexpected things may occur if the formula is not carefully designed. For example, THAT x ($\forall z$ ($z \in x \iff$ IsConstruct z)) is not a collection, because the class of all constructs is not a construct. Here we are in the vicinity of the paradoxes of naive set theory. Since we have a well-established universe, the conclusion is simply that there is no such entity x satisfying the formula. Hence, the term is undefined.

EXTENSIONAL-COLLECTION-TERM ::=
[VARIABLE | FORMULA]

Syntax For the frequently occurring case of specifying a set by a formula, well-known in set theory in the form of $\{x|...x...\}$, extensional-collection-terms are introduced to make sets of constructs more easily recognizable. The variable is bound in the entire extensional-collection-term.

Semantics The meaning of an extensional-collection-term is a collection. Using predicate symbols introduced in Sec. 3.2.2, it is defined by the following equation:

$$[\ x \mid \mathbf{f}\ ] = \mathsf{THAT}\ z\ (\forall x\ (x \in z \iff \mathbf{f}\ )\ )$$

If $\mathbf{f}$ is satisfied by a non-construct x_0 (i.e., a spotset or "undefined"), $[x \mid \mathbf{f}\ ]$ is undefined, because there is no z such that $x_0 \in z$.

Example The extensional-collection-term

$$[n \mid \exists x,y\ (n = [x;y] \wedge \mathsf{IsNat}(x) \wedge \mathsf{IsNat}(y) \wedge x+y=4)\ ]$$

denotes the collection of collections [[1;3];[2;2]] . An example of an undefined extensional-collection-term is

$$[x \mid \mathsf{Box\_in\_Box}\ x\ ],$$

where Box_in_Box is recursively defined by

$$\forall x(\mathsf{Box\_in\_Box}\ x \iff x=[\,] \vee \exists y(x=[y] \wedge \mathsf{Box\_in\_Box}\ y)),$$

because constructs must have finite depth of nesting. Though any single x satisfying Box_in_Box(x) is finitely nested only, the set of all such constructs has unlimited depth of nesting.

EXTENSIONAL-SPOTSET-TERM ::=
⟨ VARIABLE | FORMULA ⟩

Syntax As for collections, special syntax is also introduced for spotset specification by extensional-spotset-terms. The variable is bound in the entire extensional-spotset-term.

Semantics The meaning of an extensional-spotset-term is a spotset. Using the predicate symbol $\hat{\in}$ introduced in Sec. 3.2.2, it is defined by the following equation:

$$\langle\ x \mid \mathbf{f}\ \rangle = \mathsf{THAT}\ z\ (\forall x\ (x \hat{\in} z \iff \mathbf{f}\ )\ )$$

If $\mathbf{f}$ is satisfied by something which is not a singleton spotset x_0 (i.e., by a construct, "undefined", or a spotset containing zero or more than one spots), $\langle\ x \mid \mathbf{f}\ \rangle$ is undefined, because there is no z such that $x_0 \hat{\in} z$.

Semantics The value of an extensional-spotset-term is on the same aggregational level as the (singleton) spotsets which contribute to the result. This is in contrast to the extensional-collection-term, where the constructs which contribute to the result are aggregated as immediate components of the resulting collection.

Example The extensional-spotset-term

$\langle\ s \mid s\ \hat{\in}$ (^"data"). $\wedge$ C(s)= 'a' $\rangle$

denotes the set consisting of the two component spots of the catenation "data" at which the 'a' appears. (The spot-selection-term ^"data".$\langle$C(xs)='a'$\rangle$ denotes the same spotset.)

EXPLICIT-COMPOSITION-TERM ::=

[TERM ⌊ ; TERM ⌋...]|
[TERM : TERM ⌊ ; TERM : TERM ⌋ ...]|
[→ TERM ⌊ → TERM ⌋ ... →]|
CATENATION-WORD

Semantics An explicit-composition-term lists terms for all immediate components of a construct. If not all of t_1, $t_2, \ldots, t_n$ denote constructs, the entire explicit-composition-term is undefined. If the explicit-composition-term is of the form [t_1 ; t_2 ; ... ; t_n], it denotes the collection the components of which are t_1, $t_2, \ldots, t_n$. If the explicit-composition-term is of the form [$n_1 : t_1$; $n_2 : t_2$; ... ; $n_n : t_n$], it denotes the nomination with name set [n_1 ; n_2 ; ... ; n_n], which maps n_i onto t_i. The term is undefined if the same n_i occurs more than once, but with different t_i. If the explicit-composition-term is of the form [→t_1→t_2→ ... →t_n→], it denotes the catenation of constructs t_1, $t_2, \ldots, t_n$ in the given sequence.

CATENATION-WORD ::=

" ≡ CHARACTER ⌊ ≡ CHARACTER ⌋ ... ≡ "   -. quotes must be paired .-

Syntax A catenation-word is any string of characters, enclosed in quotes, that contains quotes only in pairs, if any.

Semantics Catenation-words allow concise terms for catenations in special cases. If each member of a catenation is denoted by a nonstandard-constant consisting of one character only, the catenation can be represented by correspondingly lining up these characters in a catenation-word. Thus "abca" stands for the catenation [→'a'→'b'→'c'→'a'→]. Pairing of quotes allows one to deal with quotes in catenations. A pair of quotes stands for a single one. Thus "a""b" is the same as [→'a'→'"'→'b'→]. As a cautionary remark, note that "abca" is a catenation-word, whereas 'abca' is a nonstandard-constant.

Semantics It seems appropriate to draw attention to the fact that, from a language point of view, the catenation-word is a somewhat peculiar construction. Although IMCL semantics does not look into the particular composition of nonstandard-constants, the catenation-word distinguishes the syntactically shortest ones, i.e., those consisting of a single character. Thus, if one chooses in an application to denote train car types by 'hopper', 'tank', 'open', etc., the catenation

[→'hopper'→'hopper'→'tank'→'open'→]

modelling a car sequence in a train cannot be denoted by a catenation-word that uses these nonstandard-constants. If, in contrast, one chooses shortest nonstandard-constants 'h', 't', 'o' instead, the catenation [→'h'→'h'→'t'→'o'→] can more concisely be written as the catenation-word `"hhto"`. The reason for distinguishing nonstandard-constants is that it is anticipated that in many applications one will have to deal with character strings in the UoE, and that very often it will be most natural to model characters in the UoE by corresponding IMCL characters. Thus, if the UoE contains, say, letters **A, a, B, b** and **-**, one may find it convenient to use nonstandard-constants `'A'`, `'a'`, `'B'`, `'b'` and `'-'` for them. A word **Aab-ba** of the UoE could then be written as the catenation-word `"Aaab-ba"` in IMCL.

VALUATION-TERM ::=
(VARIABLE =) (TERM) |
(TERM) (= VARIABLE) |
(VARIABLE =) (TERM) (= VARIABLE)

Syntax (VARIABLE =) is called a **left valuation**, (= VARIABLE) is called a **right valuation**, VARIABLE is called the **valuation variable** of the valuation. If the valuation-term has a left and a right valuation, both must have the same variable. The use of both a left and a right valuation is redundant. It can be used to improve readability. An occurrence of a valuation has associated a subject term and a scope of the valuation variable in its syntactic environment. The **subject term** of a left (right) valuation is the immediately right (left) adjacent term in parentheses. The valuation variable must not occur freely in the subject term. The **scope** of the valuation variable is the entire expression in which the valuation occurs, unless the subject term has free variables. In this case, the smallest scope of the variables occurring freely in the subject term is the scope of the valuation variable. The valuation variable is bound in its scope.

Semantics In its scope, the valuation variable is assigned the value of its subject term (with exemptions for nested scopes of homonymous variables in the usual way, see VARIABLE). Left valuations and right valuations are semantically equivalent.

Example Assume an unordered table *payroll* to have among its attributes the names `'empname'`, `'sal'` and `'mgr'` (for an employee's name, salary and manager). The term

```
COLC (0 rows
        ⟨1 sub ||
           C sub.'sal' ≥
           C (^payroll.)(=rows)
             ⟨mgr|| C mgr.'empname' = C sub.'mgr'⟩.'sal' 1⟩ .
        'empname' 0)
```

denotes the collection of those employees who earn at least as much as their managers.

Example That the value of the valuation variable is dependent on the subject term only should in particular be clear when considering conditional-terms. Thus, in

$$\text{IF } a{>}0 \text{ THEN } (b{+}x)/a \text{ ELSE } (c)(=x)$$

the value of x does not depend on a. Consequently, the conditional-term evaluates to $(b+c)/a$ for $a>0$.

Semantics The value of a valuation variable may be dependent on the variable of another valuation, as in $3*(x)(=y)+(\mathsf{C}\ s)(=x)$. This kind of dependency may be continued in an arbitrary number of steps, it must, however, not be circular.

Syntax The valuation-term is a syntactic device for avoiding repetition of subterms. For example, if one wants to take an alternative value a for a term **t** if it is undefined, one can write

$$\mathsf{IF}\ \mathbf{t}{=}\mathsf{UNDEF}\ \mathsf{THEN}\ a\ \mathsf{ELSE}\ \mathbf{t}$$

If **t** is a complex term, this becomes unwieldy. By means of a valuation, the conditional-term can be written without repeating **t**:

$$\mathsf{IF}\ (x{=})(\mathbf{t}){=}\mathsf{UNDEF}\ \mathsf{THEN}\ a\ \mathsf{ELSE}\ x$$

or, alternatively

$$\mathsf{IF}\ x{=}\mathsf{UNDEF}\ \mathsf{THEN}\ a\ \mathsf{ELSE}\ (x{=})(\mathbf{t})$$

Valuations must, however, not be confused with textual substitution. If an occurrence of the valuation variable is substituted by the subject term, the result may be quite different due to different variable bindings in the context.

Syntax Note that the scope of a valuation variable is syntactically not so obvious as for other variable bindings because the binding specification (i.e., the valuation) may appear anywhere within the scope, rather than heading it. Thus, a valuation may be within the scope of some other variable, although the scope of the valuation variable embraces the latter (see Fig. 3.8). In particular, there is considerable danger of confusion if homonymous variables are used. It is strongly recommended not to use homonymous variables for valuations.

$$\underbrace{\ldots\ \underbrace{\exists x(\ \ldots\ (a{=})(\ \ldots\ )\ \ldots\ )}_{\text{scope of } x}\ \ldots}_{\text{scope of } a}$$

Figure 3.8 : The scope of a quantification nested in the scope of a valuation variable

Example Assume an unordered table *emp* to have among its attributes the names `'sal'` and `'dep'` (for an employee's salary and department). The following term denoting a nomination of two collections (departments with an average salary <1200 and employees of those departments) gives an example of mixed scope nesting and valuation scope restriction by a free variable (*dname*) in the subject term. The scopes are $\ulcorner_0 \cdots {}_0\urcorner$ for *dnames* and $\ulcorner_2 \cdots {}_2\urcorner$ for *dname* and *dspots*.

```
[₀'departments':
  (₁[₂dname|
     (₃(₄TOTAL (+) WITH C(x.'sal') FOR ALL x OF
        (^emp.⟨ C(xs.'dep')=dname⟩) (=dspots) ₄)/CARD dspots ₃)
     < 1200 ₂]
  ₁)(=dnames);
  'personnel':
  COLC(^emp.⟨C(xs.'dep')∈dnames⟩) ₀]
```

Syntax As for scopes in general, the scopes of homonymous valuation variables must not coincide. Thus, "x*x + IF a>0 THEN $(b/a)(=x)$ ELSE $(0)(=x)$" is not admissible because the entire term is the scope of both valuations.

Syntax Scope conflict of valuations with homonymous variables can always be avoided by renaming one of the variables. There may, however, be cases where one does not want to rename a variable, notwithstanding the above warning against homonymous valuation variables. For these, a way out is sometimes to restrict the scope of one or both of the valuation variables. This can be done by employing an extra free variable to force a scope restriction. Thus, the scope of the valuation variables in $(h)(=x)+(g)(=x)$ is the entire term, which is not admissible. In $(h)(=x)+$ THAT z $(g=(z)(=x))$ the scopes are properly nested, since for the latter valuation the scope is that of z only, i.e., THAT z $(g=(z)(=x))$.

PARAMETER-PART ::=
  TERM | (TERM [, TERM] ...)

Syntax A parameter-part is a single term or a list of terms. To avoid ambiguity, a list of terms is enclosed in parentheses. Parameter-parts are used in prime-formulae and operator-terms. The terms constituting the parameter-parts of a prime-formula or an operator-term are called its **parameter terms**.

Semantics The entities denoted by the parameter terms are called **parameters**. They are those entities for which the predicate denoted by the predicate symbol of the prime-formula is claimed to hold or on which the operator denoted by the operator symbol of the operator-term is applied, respectively. For operator-terms, parameters are also called **operands** to emphasize the transformational character of operators.

Semantics When we talk about **parameter positions**, positions of parameter terms, not of parameter-parts, in a prime-formula or an operator-term are meant. One parameter-part may contribute to several parameter positions. Thus, in t_1 OP (t_2,t_3), there are three parameter positions, occupied by the terms t_1, t_2 and t_3.

CHARACTER ::=
  LETTER | DIGIT | PREDICATE-CHARACTER | OPERATOR-CHARACTER |
  OTHER-CHARACTER

LETTER ::=

UPPERCASE-LETTER | LOWERCASE-LETTER

UPPERCASE-LETTER ::=

A | B | C | D | E | F | G | H | I | J | K | L | M | N | O | P | Q | R | S | T | U | V | W | X | Y | Z

LOWERCASE-LETTER ::=

a | b | c | d | e | f | g | h | i | j | k | l | m | n | o | p | q | r | s | t | u | v | w | x | y | z

DIGIT ::=

0 | 1 | 2 | 3 | 4 | 5 | 6 | 7 | 8 | 9

PREDICATE-CHARACTER ::=

CHARACTERISTIC-PREDICATE-CHARACTER | DIGIT | OTHER-CHARACTER

Syntax Predicate-characters are those admissible in a predicate-symbol-part characterized by a characteristic-predicate-character.

CHARACTERISTIC-PREDICATE-CHARACTER ::=

= | ≠ | < | ≤ | > | ≥ | ∈ | ∉ | $\hat{\in}$ | ⊂ | ⊆ | ⊃ | ⊇

Syntax Characteristic-predicate-characters characterize predicate-symbol-parts.

OPERATOR-CHARACTER ::=

CHARACTERISTIC-OPERATOR-CHARACTER | DIGIT | OTHER-CHARACTER

Syntax Operator-characters are those admissible in an operator-symbol-part characterized by a characteristic-operator-character.

CHARACTERISTIC-OPERATOR-CHARACTER ::=

^ | + | − | * | / | ∩ | ∪ | \ | // | . | · | ↓ | ↑

Syntax Characteristic-operator-characters characterize operator-symbol-parts.

OTHER-CHARACTER ::=

-. any character in the character set available, which is not a LETTER, a DIGIT, a CHARACTERISTIC-PREDICATE-CHARACTER or a CHARACTERISTIC-OPERATOR-CHARACTER .-

3.2.2 Standard predicate symbols

This section contains the syntax and semantics for standard predicate symbols. They are given in natural language terms. In this section, italic letters (possibly with indices) stand for arbitrary terms.

True	means	the valid fact (see Sec. 3.1.2.1 and Sec. 3.1.2.2)
False	means	the invalid fact (see Sec. 3.1.2.1 and Sec. 3.1.2.2)
IsConstruct t	means	t is a construct
IsAtom t	means	t is an atom
IsNat t	means	t is a natural number (zero excluded)
IsInt t	means	t is an integer
IsNumber t	means	t is a number
IsBin t	means	t is a binary atom (i.e., $t \in$[YES ;NO])
IsCompound t	means	t is a compound construct
IsCol t	means	t is a collection
IsNom t	means	t is a nomination
IsCat t	means	t is a catenation
IsSpotset t	means	t is a spotset
IsSingle t	means	t is a singleton spotset
IsRootset t	means	t is a nonempty set of rootspots
$t_1 = t_2$	means	t_1 is equal to t_2
$t_1 \neq t_2$	means	t_1 is not equal to t_2
$t_1 \leq t_2$	means	t_1 and t_2 are numbers and t_1 is not greater than t_2
$t_1 < t_2$	means	the same as $t_1 \leq t_2$ and $t_1 \neq t_2$
$t_1 \geq t_2$	means	the same as $t_2 \leq t_1$
$t_1 > t_2$	means	the same as $t_2 < t_1$
$t_1 \in t_2$	means	t_2 is a collection and t_1 is an immediate component construct of t_2
$t_1 \notin t_2$	means	the same as $\neg(t_1 \in t_2)$
$t_1 \hat{\in} t_2$	means	t_2 is a spotset and t_1 is a singleton subset of t_2
$t_1 \subseteq t_2$	means	t_2 is a collection or spotset and t_1 is a subset of t_2
$t_1 \subset t_2$	means	$t_1 \subseteq t_2$ and $t_1 \neq t_2$
$t_1 \supseteq t_2$	means	the same as $t_2 \subseteq t_1$
$t_1 \supset t_2$	means	the same as $t_2 \subset t_1$
t_1 Prec t_2	means	t_1 and t_2 are nonempty spotsets and t_1 precedes t_2 (for details see below)

The unary predicate symbols denote predicates for stating that an entity belongs to a certain class or "type" of entity. The listed binary predicate symbols mean what they usually do in mathematics (with the exception of $\hat{\in}$ and Prec). Natural numbers are considered integers, which in turn are considered numbers. All numbers are atoms. Numbers are rational numbers only. $=$ and $\neq$ denote identity or difference, respectively, in the strict sense. In particular, UNDEF =UNDEF is interpreted to be "true", while for any not undefined term t the formula UNDEF $=t$ is interpreted to be "false".

The nonconventional binary predicate symbols $\hat{\in}$ and Prec concern spotsets. $\hat{\in}$ denotes inclusion of a singleton spotset in another spotset and could be defined by

$$\forall x,y(x\hat{\in}y \iff \textsf{IsSingle}\ x \wedge x\subseteq y).$$

The decision for IMCL to represent spots as singleton spotsets (see Sec. 3.1.2.4) makes it necessary to provide a convenient way for dealing with singleton spotset inclusion. The symbol $\hat{\in}$ is chosen to allude to the close kinship with $\in$, where the circumflex ^ is at the same time a warning not to take the $\in$ literally. It is also intended to invoke associations with the angle brackets used to denote spotsets (see EXTENSIONAL-SPOTSET-TERM and SPOT-SELECTION-CLAUSE) and the circumflex used for the singleton spotset containing the ownspot of a construct (see Sec. 3.2.3, Standard operator symbols).

t_1 Prec t_2 holds if for any $s_1\hat{\in}t_1$ and $s_2\hat{\in}t_2$, s_1 precedes s_2 in a sense that generalizes the sequence of catenation member spots (see Fig. 3.9): s_1 precedes s_2 if there is an r_1 outward of s_1 and an r_2 outward of s_2 such that r_1 and r_2 are from a common neighborhood immediately inward of a catenation spot, and if r_1 is "left of" r_2 (i.e., if PF(r_1)<PF(r_2); for PF see Sec. 3.2.3). The spot r_i may already belong to s_i (remember that "outward" includes equality). The simplest and perhaps most common case is that t_1 and t_2 are subsets of the immediate component spots of one catenation. In that case, r_1=s_1 and r_2=s_2, and t_1 Prec t_2 simply means that t_1 is entirely "left of" t_2. For a formal definition of Prec and additional considerations see Sec. 3.3.2.1.

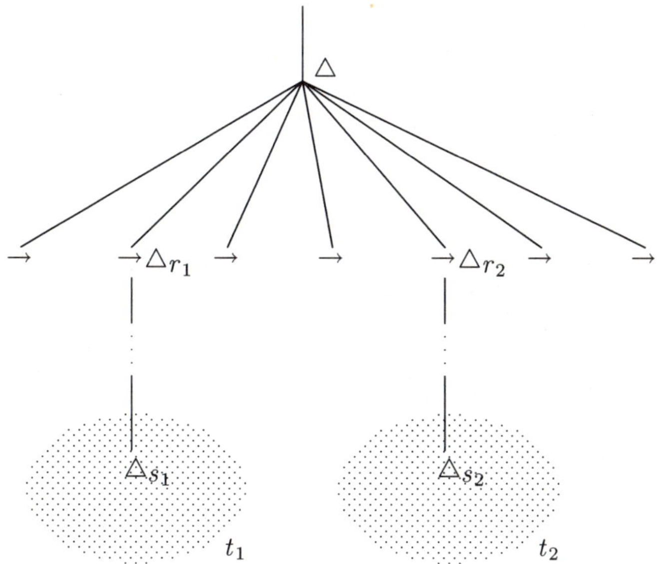

Figure 3.9: Spotset t_1 precedes spotset t_2

3.2.3 Standard operator symbols

This section contains the syntax and semantics for standard operator symbols. They are given in natural language terms. Standard nullary operator symbols are treated as constants and thus not included in the following list (see STANDARD-CONSTANT in Sec. 3.2.1). In this section, italic letters (possibly with indices) stand for arbitrary terms.

$\hat{}t$	If t denotes a construct, $\hat{}t$ (read "ownspot of t") denotes the singleton spotset containing the ownspot of t.
$t_1 + t_2$	Standard arithmetic operator (see below).
$t_1 - t_2$	Standard arithmetic operator (see below).
$t_1 * t_2$	Standard arithmetic operator (see below).
t_1 / t_2	Standard arithmetic operator (see below).
$t_1 ** t_2$	Standard arithmetic operator. Operators $+$, $-$, $*$, $/$ and $**$ apply to numbers and yield numbers in the usual way ($**$ is exponentiation). The usual precedence is assumed for the five basic arithmetic operators (see EXPRESSION in Sec. 3.2.1).
$t_1 \cap t_2$	Standard set operator (see below).
$t_1 \cup t_2$	Standard set operator (see below).
$t_1 \setminus t_2$	Standard set operator. For the purpose of IMCL, applicability of set operators $\cup$, $\cap$, $\setminus$ is restricted to collections and spotsets. Since sets containing both spots and constructs are not IMCL entities (not even IMC objects), these operators cannot be employed for combining collections with spotsets. Hence they yield "undefined" whenever not both of the operands are collections or not both are spotsets.
$t_1 /\!/ t_2$	If t_1 and t_2 denote catenations, $t_1 /\!/ t_2$ is the catenation obtained by concatenating t_1 and t_2, i.e., it is $t_1 {}^\frown t_2$ in terms of the notation introduced in Chap. 1. (Note that "$^\frown$" does not belong to the language IMCL.)
$t_\bullet$	If t denotes a spotset no spot of which is an atom spot, $t_\bullet$ (read "t next inward") is the set of all spots *immediately inward* of some spot of t. Spots in t the constructs at which are empty do not contribute to the resulting spotset. Thus, the resulting spotset may be empty even if t is not empty.
$t^\bullet$	If t denotes a spotset no spot of which is an ownspot, $t^\bullet$ (read "t next outward") is the set of all spots *immediately outward* of some spot of t. A useful relation between next inward and next outward spots is given by $\forall s,t\,(\mathsf{IsSingle}\ s \wedge \mathsf{IsSingle}\ t \Longrightarrow (s \hat{\in} t^\bullet \Longleftrightarrow t \hat{\in} s_\bullet))$, which also holds for exceptional cases.

$t(\textbf{.})$ — If t denotes a spotset, $t(\textbf{.})$ (read "t all inward") is the set of all spots *inward* of some spot of t. Remember that a spot is always inward of itself. Thus $t \subseteq t(\textbf{.})$.

$t(^{\bullet})$ — If t denotes a spotset, $t(^{\bullet})$ (read "t all outward") is the set of all spots *outward* of some spot of t. Remember that a spot is always outward of itself. Thus $t \subseteq t(^{\bullet})$.

$t\downarrow$ — If t denotes a spotset, $t\downarrow$ (read "t most inward") is the set of all leafspots of $t(\textbf{.})$.

$t\uparrow$ — If t denotes a spotset, $t\uparrow$ (read "t most outward") is the set of all rootspots of $t(^{\bullet})$. Note that, if all spots are in the same construct, the result is the singleton spotset containing the ownspot of that construct.

C t — If t denotes a singleton spotset, C t denotes the construct at the spot given by t. For any construct g holds C $\hat{}g = g$.

N t — If t denotes a singleton spotset immediately inward of a nomination spot, N t denotes the name at the spot given by t.

NAMESET t — If t denotes a nomination, NAMESET t denotes its name set.

F t — If t denotes a set of exactly one spot immediately inward of a catenation spot, F t denotes the initial part of this catenation up to but excluding the member denoted by t. F t is referred to as the **front part with respect to** t.

R t — If t denotes a set of exactly one spot immediately inward of a catenation spot, R t denotes the final part of this catenation up to but excluding the member denoted by t. R t is referred to as the **rear part with respect to** t.

DEPTH t — If t denotes a nonempty spotset the spots of which are all of the same depth, DEPTH t denotes this depth. (In terms of Sec. 2.3.4, the depth of a spot (q,g) is the length of the sequence q. It is the same as the number of spots outward of and different from the given spot.)

EMBED s AT t — If t denotes a singleton spotset, and if s denotes a spotset the spots of which have the construct at t as their common reference construct, EMBED s AT t denotes the embedding of s at the spot t in the reference construct of t. (In terms of Sec. 2.3.4, the "embedding" of $s=\{(q_i,g_i)\,|\,i=1,...,n\}$ at $t=\{(q_0,g_0)\}$ is $\{(q_0 \frown q_i,g_i)\,|\,i=1,...,n\}$, requiring g_0=REFCON$((q_i,g_i))$.)

CARD t — If t denotes a finite collection or spotset, CARD t denotes its cardinality, i.e., the number of component constructs or the number of spots.

LENGTH t — If t denotes a catenation, LENGTH t denotes the number of its members, counted by occurrences. That is, it is the cardinality of the set of spots immediately inward of the ownspot of the catenation. Thus
LENGTH(t)=IF IsCat t THEN CARD(^t.) ELSE UNDEF.

PF t
PR t — PF and PR mean "Position from Front end" and "Position from Rear end", respectively. t is required to denote a set of exactly one spot immediately inward of a catenation spot. PF t and PR t are position numbers of the indicated component spot, the count beginning with the first or last component, respectively, and ending at and including the component. Thus, for

$$[\rightarrow a \rightarrow \underset{\triangle}{b} \rightarrow c \rightarrow a \rightarrow]$$

and t denoting the singleton set containing the indicated spot, we have PF $t = 2$ and PR $t = 3$.

t FIRST — If t denotes a (possibly empty) spotset the spots of which are immediately inward of catenation spots, t FIRST denotes the set of those spots of t which in the sense of Prec are the first ones in their neighborhoods.

t LAST — If t denotes a (possibly empty) spotset the spots of which are immediately inward of catenation spots, t LAST denotes the set of those spots of t which in the sense of Prec are the last ones in their neighborhoods.

COLC t — If t denotes a (possibly empty) spotset, COLC t denotes the collection of the component constructs at the spots given by t.

COLN t — If t denotes a (possibly empty) spotset, COLN t denotes the collection of names at the spots given by t. These spots have to be immediately inward of nomination spots.

NOMC t — t is required to denote a (possibly empty) spotset the spots of which are immediately inward of nomination spots such that for any two spots s_1, s_2 of this spotset holds: if the names at s_1 and s_2 are equal, the constructs at s_1 and s_2 are also equal. NOMC t denotes the nomination the name set of which is the set of all names at the spots of t, mapping the name at each spot of t onto the construct at that spot.

CATC t — If t denotes a (possibly empty) spotset for which the singleton spotsets included in it are totally ordered with respect to the spotset precedence relation Prec, CATC t denotes the catenation the members of which are the constructs at the spots of t in the sequence of that order.

Fig. 3.10 gives a systematic arrangement of most, but not all, elementary IMCL terms to show the inherent "typing" associated with frequently used IMCL operators.

yields: / applied to:		non-std. atom, binary atom	number	collection	nomination	catenation	spotset: arbitrary	spotset: singleton
spotset	singleton	C N	C N PF PR	C N	C N	C N F R	⟨| ⟩ EMBED	
spotset	arbitrary		CARD DEPTH	COLC COLN	NOMC	CATC	. (.) ↓ · (·) ↑ ⟨ ‖ ⟩ ∪ ∩ \\ FIRST LAST	
non-std. atom, binary atom				[;] [|]	[: ; :]	[→ → →]		^
number			+ - * \\ **	[;] [|]	[: ; :]	[→ → →]		^
collection			CARD	[;] [|] ∪ ∩ \\	[: ; :]	[→ → →]		^
nomination				[;] [|]	[: ; :]	[→ → →]		^
catenation			LENGTH	[;] [|]	[: ; :]	[→ → →] //		^

Figure 3.10: Survey of elementary IMCL terms

Fig. 3.11 gives a survey of elementary IMCL operators which "shift" spotsets in the inward or outward direction. It is applicable to "pure" spotsets only, that is, spotsets the spots of which are all of the same kind (one of the six kinds given in the legend). However, since the considered operators obey the distributivity law with respect to the union operator ∪, it is very easy to derive the result for a mixed spotset by first partitioning it into "pure" subsets (e.g., singleton subsets), then applying the table, and finally joining the results.

To determine the result of operator application for a "pure" spotset, select from the middle row of the table the symbol for the kind common to the spots in the spotset (e.g., $\triangle$). In fields with two symbols take the upper one for an outward operator and the lower one for an inward operator. From there proceed upwards or downwards onto the row for the considered operator (e.g., from △ upwards, if $(^{\bullet})$ is your operator). The area where you have stopped has an inscription which indicates the result: either the (original) spotset s (as in the example), or the empty spotset, or the entity "undefined", or one of six possible spotsets depending on s.

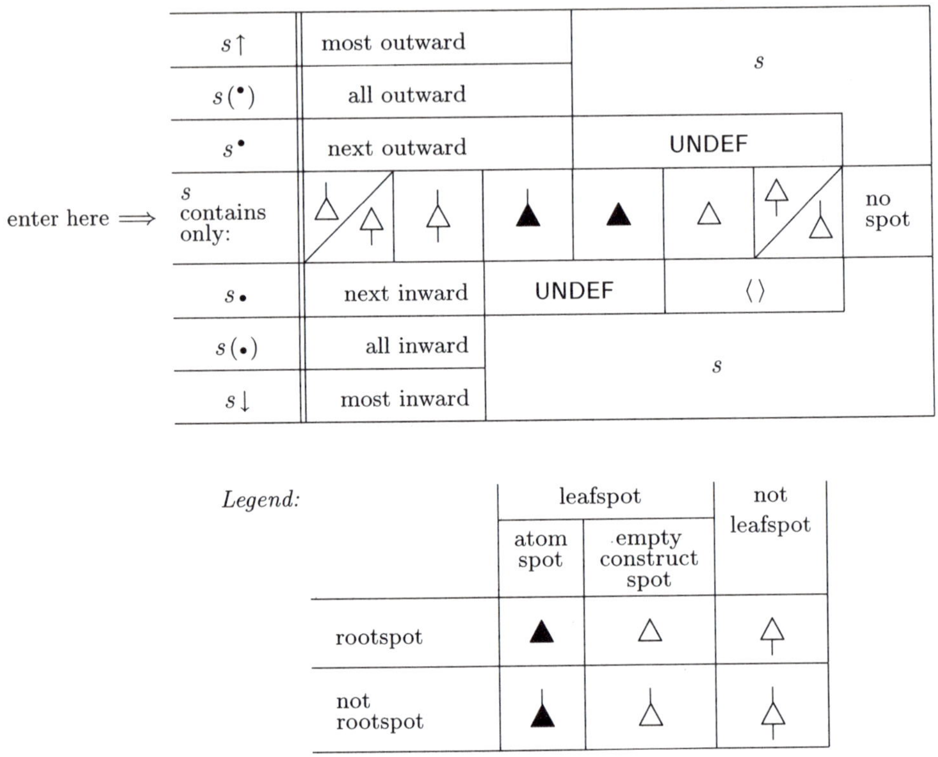

Figure 3.11: Elementary IMCL operators on spotsets

3.2.4 Complete syntax overview

EXPRESSION ::=
  FORMULA | TERM

FORMULA ::=
  PRIME-FORMULA |
  ¬ FORMULA | FORMULA { ∧ | ∨ | ⟹ | ⟺ | ⇎ } FORMULA |
  ∃ VARIABLE (FORMULA) | ∀ VARIABLE (FORMULA) |
  (FORMULA)

PRIME-FORMULA ::=
[PARAMETER-PART] PREDICATE-SYMBOL-PART ...
[PARAMETER-PART PREDICATE-SYMBOL-PART ...] ... [PARAMETER-PART]

PREDICATE-SYMBOL-PART ::=
[PREDICATE-CHARACTER ≡] ... CHARACTERISTIC-PREDICATE-CHARACTER
[≡ PREDICATE-CHARACTER] ... |
UPPERCASE-LETTER [≡ LETTER | ≡ DIGIT | ≡ _] ... ≡ LOWERCASE-LETTER
[≡ LETTER | ≡ DIGIT | ≡ _] ...

TERM ::=
VARIABLE |
CONSTANT |
OPERATOR-TERM |
SPOT-SELECTION-TERM |
ELLIPTIC-COMPONENT-SELECTION-TERM |
SUBSTITUTION-TERM |
AUGMENTATION-TERM |
DELETION-TERM |
TOTAL-OPERATOR-TERM |
CONDITIONAL-TERM |
PARTICULARIZATION-TERM |
EXTENSIONAL-COLLECTION-TERM |
EXTENSIONAL-SPOTSET-TERM |
EXPLICIT-COMPOSITION-TERM |
VALUATION-TERM |
(TERM)

VARIABLE ::=
LOWERCASE-LETTER [≡ LETTER | ≡ DIGIT | ≡ _] ...

CONSTANT ::=
STANDARD-CONSTANT |
NONSTANDARD-CONSTANT

STANDARD-CONSTANT ::=
UNDEF | YES | NO |
EMPTY-CONSTANT |
NUMBER-ATOM-CONSTANT

EMPTY-CONSTANT ::=
[ ] | [:] | [→] | ⟨ ⟩

NUMBER-ATOM-CONSTANT ::=
[+ ≡ | − ≡] DIGIT [≡ DIGIT] ... [≡ . ≡ DIGIT [≡ DIGIT] ...]

```
NONSTANDARD-CONSTANT ::=
    ' ≡ CHARACTER [ ≡ CHARACTER ] ... ≡ '          -. apostrophes must be paired .-

OPERATOR-TERM ::=
    [ PARAMETER-PART ] OPERATOR-SYMBOL-PART ...
    [ PARAMETER-PART   OPERATOR-SYMBOL-PART ... ] ... [ PARAMETER-PART ]

OPERATOR-SYMBOL-PART ::=
    [ OPERATOR-CHARACTER ≡ ] ... CHARACTERISTIC-OPERATOR-CHARACTER
    [ ≡ OPERATOR-CHARACTER ] ... |
    UPPERCASE-LETTER [ ≡ UPPERCASE-LETTER | ≡ DIGIT | ≡ _ ] ...

SPOT-SELECTION-TERM ::=
    TERM SPOT-SELECTION-CLAUSE |
    ELLIPTIC-SPOT-SELECTION-TERM

SPOT-SELECTION-CLAUSE ::=
    ⟨ VARIABLE || FORMULA ⟩ |
    ⟨ FORMULA ⟩ |
    ⟨ NAME-SPECIFICATION [ , NAME-SPECIFICATION ] ... ⟩

NAME-SPECIFICATION ::=
    NONSTANDARD-CONSTANT | VARIABLE

ELLIPTIC-SPOT-SELECTION-TERM ::=
    TERM SHIFT-OPERATOR-SYMBOL NAME-SPECIFICATION

SHIFT-OPERATOR-SYMBOL ::=
    . | ˙ | (.) | (˙) | ↓ | ↑

ELLIPTIC-COMPONENT-SELECTION-TERM ::=
    VARIABLE . NAME-SPECIFICATION [ . NAME-SPECIFICATION ] ...

SUBSTITUTION-TERM ::=
    SUBSTC WITH TERM FOR ALL [ VARIABLE ] OF TERM [ IN TERM ] |
    SUBSTN WITH TERM FOR ALL [ VARIABLE ] OF TERM [ IN TERM ]

AUGMENTATION-TERM ::=
    AUGCOL     WITH TERM FOR ALL [ VARIABLE ] OF TERM [ IN TERM ] |
    AUGNOM     WITH TERM FOR ALL [ VARIABLE ] OF TERM [ IN TERM ] |
    AUGCAT     WITH TERM FOR ALL [ VARIABLE ] OF TERM [ IN TERM ]
                                                        [ ACC TERM ] |
    AUGBEFORE  WITH TERM FOR ALL [ VARIABLE ] OF TERM [ IN TERM ] |
    AUGAFTER   WITH TERM FOR ALL [ VARIABLE ] OF TERM [ IN TERM ]

DELETION-TERM ::=
    DELETE FOR ALL OF TERM [ IN TERM ]
```

TOTAL-OPERATOR-TERM ::=
  TOTAL (OPERATOR-SYMBOL-PART ...) WITH TERM FOR ALL OF TERM |
  TOTAL (OPERATOR-SYMBOL-PART ...) WITH TERM
      FOR ALL VARIABLE OF TERM [ALL VARIABLE OF TERM] ...

CONDITIONAL-TERM ::=
  IF FORMULA THEN TERM ELSE TERM

PARTICULARIZATION-TERM ::=
  THAT VARIABLE (FORMULA)

EXTENSIONAL-COLLECTION-TERM ::=
  [VARIABLE | FORMULA]

EXTENSIONAL-SPOTSET-TERM ::=
  ⟨ VARIABLE | FORMULA ⟩

EXPLICIT-COMPOSITION-TERM ::=
  [TERM [; TERM] ...] |
  [TERM : TERM [; TERM : TERM] ...] |
  [→ TERM [→ TERM] ... →] |
  CATENATION-WORD

CATENATION-WORD ::=
  " ≡ CHARACTER [≡ CHARACTER] ... ≡ " -. quotes must be paired .-

VALUATION-TERM ::=
  (VARIABLE =) (TERM) |
  (TERM) (= VARIABLE) |
  (VARIABLE =) (TERM) (= VARIABLE)

PARAMETER-PART ::=
  TERM | (TERM [, TERM] ...)

CHARACTER ::=
  LETTER | DIGIT | PREDICATE-CHARACTER | OPERATOR-CHARACTER |
  OTHER-CHARACTER

LETTER ::=
  UPPERCASE-LETTER | LOWERCASE-LETTER

UPPERCASE-LETTER ::=
  A | B | C | D | E | F | G | H | I | J | K | L | M | N | O | P | Q | R | S | T | U | V | W | X | Y | Z

LOWERCASE-LETTER ::=
  a | b | c | d | e | f | g | h | i | j | k | l | m | n | o | p | q | r | s | t | u | v | w | x | y | z

DIGIT ::=
  0 | 1 | 2 | 3 | 4 | 5 | 6 | 7 | 8 | 9

PREDICATE-CHARACTER ::=
  CHARACTERISTIC-PREDICATE-CHARACTER | DIGIT | OTHER-CHARACTER

CHARACTERISTIC-PREDICATE-CHARACTER ::=
  $= \mid \neq \mid < \mid \leq \mid > \mid \geq \mid \in \mid \notin \mid \hat{\in} \mid \subset \mid \subseteq \mid \supset \mid \supseteq$

OPERATOR-CHARACTER ::=
  CHARACTERISTIC-OPERATOR-CHARACTER | DIGIT | OTHER-CHARACTER

CHARACTERISTIC-OPERATOR-CHARACTER ::=
  $\hat{} \mid + \mid - \mid * \mid / \mid \cap \mid \cup \mid \setminus \mid /\!\!/ \mid . \mid \cdot \mid \downarrow \mid \uparrow$

OTHER-CHARACTER ::=
  -. any character in the character set available, which is not a LETTER, a DIGIT, a CHARACTERISTIC-PREDICATE-CHARACTER or a CHARACTERISTIC-OPERATOR-CHARACTER .-

3.3 Examples

3.3.1 Construct manipulation

The following example shows an application of IMCL to a "data manipulation" problem. The construct to be manipulated is intended to model a tour description as might be used in a travel agency. Fig. 3.12 shows the model in some particular state. We assume that the shown construct has been obtained through a sequence of modifications starting from the "blank" construct b_0:

b_0 = ['code':'unspecified';'route':[:];'participants':[];'itinerary':[→]]

In the next two steps we transform b_0 into a model which contains the code and the starting point of the tour:

b_1 = SUBSTC WITH 'T-4-2' FOR ALL OF ^b_0.'code' IN b_0
b_2 = AUGNOM WITH ['from':'Lisboa'] FOR ALL OF ^b_1.'route' IN b_1

The same result is obtained by either of the following expressions:

```
b2 = AUGNOM WITH ['from':'Lisboa']
            FOR ALL OF ^x.'route'
            IN (x=)(SUBSTC WITH 'T-4-2'
                              FOR ALL OF ^b0.'code' IN b0 )
b2 = SUBSTC WITH 'T-4-2' FOR ALL OF ^y.'code'
           IN (y=)(AUGNOM WITH ['from':'Lisboa']
                              FOR ALL OF ^b0.'route' IN b0 )
```

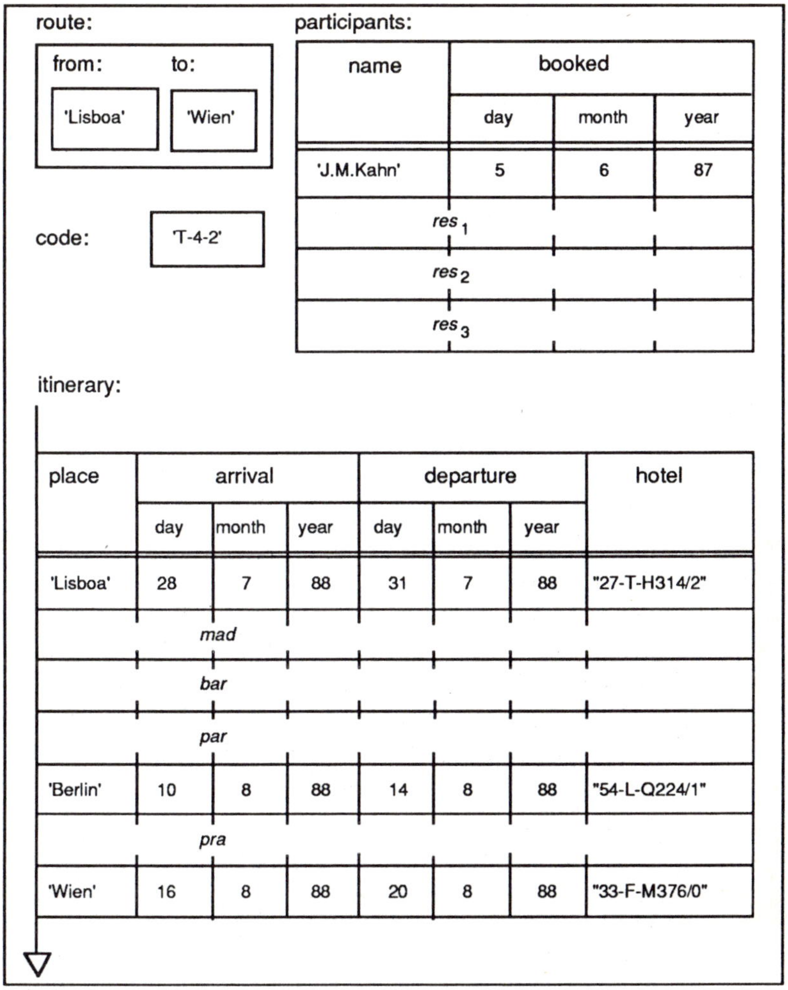

Figure 3.12: Compositional model of a tour description

Note that we made use of valuation terms for enhancing readability of the nested terms. Because we are sure that the sets of modification spots are nonempty, we may omit the IN-parts. Thus an alternative for the latter two formulae is:

```
b2 = AUGNOM WITH ['from':'Lisboa'] FOR ALL OF
        ^(SUBSTC WITH 'T-4-2'
                FOR ALL OF ^b0.'code').'route'
b2 = SUBSTC WITH 'T-4-2' FOR ALL OF
        ^(AUGNOM WITH ['from':'Lisboa']
                FOR ALL OF ^b0.'route').'code'
```

An alternative way that directly composes the desired construct is

```
b2 = NOMC(^b0.⟨N xs ≠'code' ∧ N xs ≠'route'⟩)
     :U ['code': 'T-4-2'; 'route': ['from': 'Lisboa']]
```

The latter method works well for spots that are not too far inward. For the operator :U ("nomination union" or "merge") see Sec. 3.3.2.3.

We proceed by inserting the final point of the tour:

```
b3 = AUGNOM WITH ['to':'Wien'] FOR ALL OF ^b2.'route'
```

which yields

```
b3 = ['code':'T-4-2';
      'route':['from':'Lisboa';'to':'Wien'];
      'participants':[];
      'itinerary':[→]]
```

A next step in the development towards the full tour description could be to insert the initial and the final point into the itinerary, yielding the construct b_4:

```
b4 = AUGCAT
     WITH [0→[1'place':'Lisboa';
                 'arrival':['day':28;'month':7;'year':88];
                 'departure':['day':31;'month':7;'year':88];
                 'hotel':"27-T-H314/2" 1]→
               [2'place':'Wien';
                 'arrival':['day':16;'month':8;'year':88];
                 'departure':['day':20;'month':8;'year':88];
                 'hotel':"33-F-M376/0" 2]→ 0]
     FOR ALL OF ^b3.'itinerary'
```

In a later stage of planning, the itinerary of b_4 might be augmented by the entry for Praha, which is assumed to be given by the variable *pra*. This yields b_5:

```
b5 = AUGAFTER WITH [→pra→] FOR ALL OF (^b4.'itinerary'.FIRST)
```

Assuming *pra*.'arrival'=['day':14;'month':8;'year':88], the tour description with the entry for Berlin is given by

```
b6 = AUGBEFORE
     WITH [0→[1'place':'Berlin';
                 'arrival':['day':10;'month':8;'year':88];
                 'departure':(['day':14;'month':8;'year':88])(=d);
                 'hotel':"54-L-Q224/1" 1]→ 0]
     FOR ALL OF ^b5.'itinerary'.⟨C xs.'arrival'= d⟩
```

where the variable *d* is introduced in a right valuation for easy reference to the spot before which the catenation with the new entry is to be linked into the itinerary. Note that the scope of *d* extends over the whole augmentation-term since no subterm containing the valuation-term is used as a parameter term in a prime-formula.

Finally, the missing entries may be inserted into the itinerary of b_6 using the ordering by (say) the arrival date:

b_7 = AUGCAT WITH [$\rightarrow$ *mad* $\rightarrow$ *bar* $\rightarrow$ *par* $\rightarrow$] FOR ALL OF ^b_6.'itinerary'
ACC [q | AscendingByArrival(q)]

where *mad*, *bar*, *par* are variables for the entries of Madrid, Barcelona and Paris, and where [q |AscendingByArrival(q)] denotes the order pattern, i.e., the reference set of catenations in which the itinerary of b_7 has to be contained. If we want the itinerary-rows be ordered by their arrival dates (excluding duplication of arrival dates), we can do this by defining AscendingByArrival as follows:

$\forall q$ ($_0$AscendingByArrival(q) $\Longleftrightarrow$
IsCat(q) $\wedge$
$\forall l,m \hat{\in}$^q.(PF(l)<PF(m)$\Longrightarrow$ (C l.'arrival') EarlierThan (C m.'arrival')) $_0$)

The components at the spots ^q..'arrival' are expected to be calendar dates for which the predicate EarlierThan is assumed to be defined.

To complete the construct obtained to that shown in the figure, the component under 'participant' has still to be established. An entry for a particular reservation is inserted by

b_8 = AUGCOL WITH [['name': 'J. M. Kahn';
'booked': ['day':5;'month':6;'year':87]]]
FOR ALL OF ^b_7.'participants'

Let res_1, res_2 and res_3 denote the other three reservations contained in the tour description. Their inclusion into b_8 is specified by:

b_9 = AUGCOL WITH [res_1;res_2;res_3] FOR ALL OF ^b_8.'participants'

Assume now that for some reason the constructs which model the month of a reservation are to be changed from numbers to corresponding special atoms. This is achieved by

b_{10} = SUBSTC WITH C ^'translation table'.$\langle$C xs.'num'=C $m\rangle$.'name'
FOR ALL m OF ^b_9.'participants'..'booked'.'month'

where the nonstandard-constant 'translation table' denotes an unordered table according to

'translation table' = [$_0$['num':1;'name':'Jan']; ['num':2;'name':'Feb'];
['num':3;'name':'Mar']; ['num':4;'name':'Apr'];
['num':5;'name':'May']; ['num':6;'name':'Jun'];
['num':7;'name':'Jul']; ['num':8;'name':'Aug'];
['num':9;'name':'Sep']; ['num':10;'name':'Oct'];
['num':11;'name':'Nov']; ['num':12;'name':'Dec']$_0$]

This is an example of defining a semantic mapping from a nonstandard-constant to a non-atom (see Sec. 3.1.2.1).

Just to demonstrate also the use of DELETE, let the resulting construct b_{10} finally be modified by deleting those entries of the itinerary, which have "-L-" in their hotel codes:

DELETE FOR ALL OF

$$\hat{}b_{10}.\texttt{'itinerary'}.\langle\, x \parallel \exists f,r \ (\mathsf{C}\ x.\texttt{'hotel'} = f /\!/ \texttt{"-L-"} /\!/ r)\rangle \ \mathsf{IN}\ b_{10}$$

3.3.2 Predicate and operator definition

For various reasons one might wish to introduce predicates and operators which are not included in plain IMCL. Two common such reasons are application-specific concepts and structured organization of a body of formal definitions.

In a large application, it could be desirable to reflect its terminology through suitably defined language elements which are formal counterparts of properties, relationships and operations familiar to the experts of the application area. Consider, for example, a document processing environment: a predicate IsParagraph(c) or an operator EXTRACT (s)—with c denoting a construct modelling text and s a spotset with text fragments—could intuitively reflect aspects of a document processing reality.

To structure a body of formal definitions, it may be practical to enrich IMCL to improve conciseness of expression and "mental economy". A frequently used pattern of IMCL expressions can be used for defining a new predicate or operator which becomes an element of IMCL in the considered context.

The following examples are to illustrate the technique of defining IMCL *extensions*. They are more or less grouped by functionality. Note that they do not go beyond IMCL, because they only use the definitional extension mechanism provided with IMCL. Some of the examples given in this section provide formal definitions for predicates and operators described in Sections 4.2.2 and 4.2.3.

3.3.2.1 Elementary and ancillary definitions

Predicates for "empty" and "nonempty"

Readability of formal definitions is often enhanced by using special predicates for empty or nonempty entities.

IsEmpty(e) means e is the empty spotset or an empty compound:

$\forall e\ (\mathsf{IsEmpty}\ c \iff e = [\,] \lor e - [:] \lor e = [\rightarrow] \lor e = \langle\,\rangle)$

IsNe...(g) means g is a nonempty compound:

$\forall g\ (\mathsf{IsNeCol}\ g \iff \mathsf{IsCol}\ g \land g \neq [\,])$

$\forall g\ (\mathsf{IsNeNom}\ g \iff \mathsf{IsNom}\ g \land g \neq [:])$

$\forall g\ (\mathsf{IsNeCat}\ g \iff \mathsf{IsCat}\ g \land g \neq [\rightarrow])$

Predicate "precedes"

Recall from Sec. 3.2.2 that a spotset t_1 precedes a spotset t_2 if for any two spots drawn from t_1 and t_2, respectively, there are two outward spots r_1 and r_2 which are immediately inward of the same catenation spot such that $\mathsf{PF}\,(r_1)<\mathsf{PF}\,(r_2)$. Fig. 3.9 in Sec. 3.2.2 gives a visual representation thereof.

$$\forall t_1, t_2 \;(_1\; t_1 \,\mathsf{Prec}\, t_2 \iff t_1 \neq \langle\rangle \wedge t_2 \neq \langle\rangle \wedge \\ \forall s_1 \hat{\in} t_1, s_2 \hat{\in} t_2\; \exists r_1 \hat{\in} s_1(^\bullet), r_2 \hat{\in} s_2(^\bullet) \\ (\, r_1{}^\bullet = r_2{}^\bullet \wedge \mathsf{PF}\, r_1 < \mathsf{PF}\, r_2 \,)\; _1)$$

The relation Prec is transitive and asymmetric, and it carries over to subsets:

$$\forall s_1, t_1, s_2, t_2\, (\, s_1 \;\mathsf{Prec}\; s_2 \wedge t_1 \subseteq s_1 \wedge t_2 \subseteq s_2 \implies t_1 \;\mathsf{Prec}\; t_2)$$

Note that different pairs of spots (t_1, t_2) can have different neighboring outward spots r_1 and r_2. This is obvious in the case of relating two sets of immediate component spots of a given catenation, say "abbabce":

$$\hat{}\texttt{"abbabce"}.\langle\mathsf{C}\,xs{=}\texttt{'a'}\rangle \;\mathsf{Prec}\; \hat{}\texttt{"abbabce"}.\langle\mathsf{C}\,xs{=}\texttt{'e'}\rangle$$

The pairs of neighboring spots can even be from different levels of composition, i.e. from different catenations. For the catenation $g{=}[\rightarrow\texttt{'a'}\rightarrow[\rightarrow\texttt{'b'}\rightarrow\texttt{'c'}\rightarrow]\rightarrow]$, for instance, we have $\hat{}g(.)\langle\mathsf{PF}\,xs{=}1\rangle$ Prec $\hat{}g{\downarrow}\langle\mathsf{PF}\,xs{=}2\rangle$. By contrast, $\hat{}g(.)\langle\mathsf{PF}\,xs{=}1\rangle$ Prec $\hat{}g(.)\langle\mathsf{PF}\,xs{=}2\rangle$ does not hold.

Operators for "counting"

If x denotes a finite collection or spotset, $\mathsf{CARD}\,(x)$ denotes its cardinality, i.e. the number of immediate component constructs or the number of spots:

$$\forall x \;(_1\; \mathsf{CARD}\, x \;=\; \mathsf{THAT}\, z \;(_2((x{=}[\,] \vee x{=}\langle\rangle) \wedge z{=}0) \vee \\ (\mathsf{IsCol}\, x \wedge \exists y\; (y \in x \wedge z = 1{+}\mathsf{CARD}\,(x \setminus [y]))) \vee \\ (\mathsf{IsSpotset}\, x \wedge \exists y\; (y \hat{\in} x \wedge z = 1{+}\mathsf{CARD}\,(x \setminus y))\; _2)\; _1)$$

If g denotes a catenation, $\mathsf{LENGTH}\,(g)$ denotes the number of its immediate component spots:

$$\forall g\; (\mathsf{LENGTH}\, g{=}\mathsf{THAT}\, z\; (\mathsf{IsCat}(g) \wedge z{=}\mathsf{CARD}\,(\hat{}g\,.)))$$

If s denotes a spotset whose spots are all of the same depth, $\mathsf{DEPTH}\,(s)$ denotes this depth:

$$\forall s\; (\mathsf{DEPTH}\, s{=}\mathsf{THAT}\, z\; ((\mathsf{IsRootset}\, s \wedge z{=}0) \vee \exists t\; (s \subseteq t\,. \wedge z = 1{+}\mathsf{DEPTH}\, t)))$$

Operator "multiple-inward"

We define two versions of a binary operator $(t).{*}(l)$ for denoting all spots which are l levels inward of some spot of a given spotset t. The "hard" version of $.*$ applies the $.$-operator l times:

$$\forall t, l \;(_1\; t.{*}l \;=\; \mathsf{THAT}\, z\; (_2 \mathsf{IsSpotset}\, t \wedge l{\geq}0 \wedge \\ (l{=}0 \implies z{=}t) \wedge \\ (l{>}0 \implies z{=}t.{*}(l{-}1).)\; _2)\; _1)$$

This version yields UNDEF if there is at least one path in the spot tree which does not allow one to step l levels inwards from t. The "soft" version of $.*$ ignores such paths:

$\forall t,l\ (t.{*}l = t(.)\langle s\,||\,\mathsf{CARD}\,(s(^\bullet)\backslash t(^\bullet))=l\rangle)$

If there are no such paths, the versions of `.*` are not different.

For the following example, the soft version is preferable to the hard one. Consider the task of selecting in each row of a table all spots of a given depth, where the depth varies with the row and is given as an immediate component of the row under the name `'lev'`. The spots to be selected are component spots of another immediate component of the same row named `'body'`. The set of all these spots is denoted by:

TOTAL (∪) WITH $((x.$'body'$)$.* C $(x.$'lev'$))$ FOR ALL x OF ^g.

Remember that the object term of TOTAL may also denote a spotset (see TOTAL-OPERATOR-TERM in Sec. 3.2.1).

Operators "common name/component construct"

It sometimes occurs in an application that the same name or the same component construct appears at all spots of a spotset s, for example, in a column of a table. To obtain this name or component, the operator N or C cannot be applied to s because this would yield UNDEF if the cardinality of s were not 1. The following definitions introduce operators COMN (s) and COMC (s) which yield respectively the COMmon Name or the COMmon Component at all spots of s:

$\forall s$ (COMN (s)=C ^(COLN s).)

$\forall s$ (COMC (s)=C ^(COLC s).)

Under the assumption made, COLN and COLC yield singleton collections, so that C is applied to singleton spotsets. If the assumption is violated, the result is UNDEF.

An example of applying COMC is a query against an unordered table which models students attending courses: "get the courses which are attended by students who are older than student John Smith." The table t has the attributes `'student'` and `'course'`, the `'student'` components are nominations with components `'name'` and `'age'`. The age of a student is assumed to be functionally dependent on the name of the student. So the query is answered by the term

```
COLC ^t
      .⟨C xs.'student'.'age' >
        COMC ^t.⟨C (xs.'student'.'name') = "John Smith"⟩.'age'⟩
      .'course'
```

3.3.2.2 Boolean algebra for binary atoms

It may be convenient to deal with truth values as entities (see Sec. 3.1.2.2). For this, operator counterparts to logical connectives may be defined. The operator symbols NOT, AND, OR, IMPL, EQUIV, XOR denote the usual Boolean operators applied to the binary atoms YES and NO. The following two examples show how such binary operators can be defined by directly specifying the "truth tables".

$\forall g$ (NOT g = THAT z $((g$=YES $\wedge$ z=NO$)$ $\vee$ $(g$=NO $\wedge$ z=YES$)))$

$$\forall g,h\ (_1 g \text{ AND } h = \text{THAT}\, z\ (_2(g{=}\text{YES} \wedge h{=}\text{YES} \wedge z{=}\text{YES}) \vee (g{=}\text{YES} \wedge h{=}\text{NO} \wedge z{=}\text{NO}) \vee (g{=}\text{NO} \wedge h{=}\text{YES} \wedge z{=}\text{NO}) \vee (g{=}\text{NO} \wedge h{=}\text{NO} \wedge z{=}\text{NO})\ _2)\ _1)$$

It should be noted, that if not all of the operands denote binary atoms, the result is UNDEF.

3.3.2.3 Dealing with nominations

Nominations can be seen as mathematical sets of ordered pairs, although these pairs are not constructs and a nomination is therefore not a collection of pairs. Handling nominations can be made easier with special predicates and operators which draw on the resemblance to mathematical sets.

Nomination x is a proper subnomination of nomination y iff the name set of x is contained in the name set of y and the components with the same name are equal.

$$\forall x,y\ (_1 x :\subset y \iff \text{NAMESET}\, x \subset \text{NAMESET}\, y \wedge \forall n \in \text{NAMESET}\, x\ (x.n{=}y.n)\ _1)$$

The nomination union or *merge* of two nominations x and y is given by the union of their (name, component)-pairs. Components with the same name have to be equal. The operator AUGNOM (see Sec. 3.2.1) is based on the merge operator.

$$\forall x,y\ (_1 x :\cup y = \text{THAT}\, z\ (_2 \text{NAMESET}\, x \cup \text{NAMESET}\, y = \text{NAMESET}\, z \wedge \forall n \in \text{NAMESET}\, x\ (x.n{=}z.n) \wedge \forall n \in \text{NAMESET}\, y\ (y.n{=}z.n)\ _2)\ _1)$$

The nomination intersection of two nominations x and y is given by the intersection of their (name, component)-pairs. Components with the same name have to be equal.

$$\forall x,y\ (_1 x :\cap y = \text{THAT}\, z\ (_2 \text{NAMESET}\, x \cap \text{NAMESET}\, y = \text{NAMESET}\, z \wedge \forall n \in \text{NAMESET}\, z\ (x.n{=}z.n \wedge y.n{=}z.n)\ _2)\ _1)$$

Despite their similar designations the notions of subobject, object union and object intersection introduced in [BaKh86] are quite different from the ones defined here.

Nomination difference is of no practical interest. Instead, a nomination restriction (in a sense, a "single row projection") seems to be more useful. RESTRICT x TO y denotes the nomination with only those components of x whose names are in y:

$$\forall x,y\ (_1 \text{RESTRICT}\, x \text{ TO } y = \text{NOMC}\,(\hat{}x.\langle \text{N}\,(xs) \in y\rangle)\ _1)$$

3.3.2.4 Dealing with catenations

A catenation g is a **subcatenation** of h iff g can be obtained by cutting off appropriate front and rear parts from h:

$$\forall x,y\ (x \text{ Subcat } y \iff \exists f,r\ (f \mathbin{/\!/} x \mathbin{/\!/} r = y))$$

Among the spots of a spotset s, which are immediate component spots of catenations, those spots are the **first** ones which in the sense of Prec are the first ones in their neighborhoods, i.e. are closest to the front ends:

$$\forall s\ (_1\ s\ \mathsf{FIRST} = \mathsf{THAT}\ z\ (_2 \forall t \hat{\in} s\ (\mathsf{IsCat}(\mathsf{C}\ t^\bullet)) \wedge$$
$$z = \langle t \mid t \hat{\in} s \wedge (t = s \cap (t^\bullet .) \vee t\ \mathsf{Prec}\ s \cap (t^\bullet .) \setminus t) \rangle\ _2)\ _1)$$

Similarly, for the **last** spots:

$$\forall s\ (_1\ s\ \mathsf{LAST} = \mathsf{THAT}\ z\ (_2 \forall t \hat{\in} s\ (\mathsf{IsCat}(\mathsf{C}\ t^\bullet)) \wedge$$
$$z = \langle t \mid t \hat{\in} s \wedge (t = s \cap (t^\bullet .) \vee s \cap (t^\bullet .) \setminus t\ \mathsf{Prec}\ t) \rangle\ _2)\ _1)$$

As an example, if

t = (^["London";["Paris";"Berlin"]])↓ ∪ ^"Belfast".⟨C $xs \notin$ ['f';'t']⟩

(a spotset containing 22 character spots), then (t)FIRST is a set of four spots leading to 'L', 'P' and twice to 'B', (t)LAST is a set of four spots leading twice to 'n' and twice to 's'. Note that the spots of t do not have the same depth nor a common rootspot.

The operator CATC (s) defines the catenation of component constructs which are at the spots of s, if they are totally ordered with respect to the spotset precedence relation Prec:

$$\forall t\ (_1\ \mathsf{CATC}\ s =$$
$$\mathsf{THAT}\ z\ (_2 (s = \langle\rangle \wedge z = [\rightarrow]) \vee$$
$$(\mathsf{IsSingle}\ s \wedge z = [\rightarrow \mathsf{C}\ s \rightarrow]) \vee$$
$$\exists p, q\ (p \cup q = s \wedge p \cap q = \langle\rangle \wedge p\ \mathsf{Prec}\ q \wedge z = \mathsf{CATC}\ p /\!/ \mathsf{CATC}\ q)\ _2)\ _1)$$

3.3.2.5 Dealing with unordered tables

The **projection** of a relation r (in the sense of an unordered table) on a set of attributes a can be defined by the following formula:

$$\forall r, a\ (\mathsf{PROJECT}\ r\ \mathsf{ON}\ a = [p \mid \exists t\ (t \in r \wedge p = \mathsf{RESTRICT}\ t\ \mathsf{TO}\ a)])$$

Note that this is a very liberal definition: for the term to be defined the elements of r need not have the same name sets nor need the set a be included in one of the name sets.

When dealing with nested relations in the sense of tuple valued attributes (as opposed to relation valued attributes), one sometimes needs to **unnest** a column. Let r be an unordered ("relational") table and p a nomination valued attribute of r. All nominations with name p have the same name set. This name set shall become a subset of the table's attributes, i.e. the attribute p shall be discarded. We define a binary operator "unnest r in column p":

$$\forall r, p\ (\mathsf{UNNEST}(r, p) = [l \mid \exists x\ (_1\ x \in r \wedge l = (x.p) :\cup (\mathsf{NOMC}\ \hat{}x.\langle \mathsf{N}(xs) \neq p \rangle)\ _1)\ ])$$

The most widespread approaches to information modelling are known as data models, in particular the hierarchical, the network and the relational data models. Usually they are presented in a compositional manner. This applies even to the relational data model, where databases are seen as consisting of relations, relations of tuples, and tuples of attribute values. A possible (complete) description of the relational model in terms of IMC is given in Sec. 3.3.3 below. From the very beginning of its development, operations were always associated with relational structures: INSERT, SELECT, JOIN, to name only a few. Among them, the **join operator** is certainly the most interesting one. Essentially, it serves to define an unordered table whose rows are obtained from a specified merge of two input rows from given tables. The selection of input rows from the input tables depends on a criterion (equi-join, theta-join). From a more general point of view, a join of two tables is only a special case of a set operator which allows one to process all combinations of elements drawn from the operand sets. Roughly speaking, this is the functionality of the total operator (see Sec. 3.2.1 TOTAL-OPERATOR-TERM). The following term shows an application of TOTAL to specify a quite general join:

```
TOTAL(∪) WITH (IF f THEN [nom] ELSE [])
          FOR ALL var₁ OF tab₁
          FOR ALL var₂ OF tab₂
```

where tab_1 and tab_2 are terms for two (not necessarily different) unordered tables, var_1 and var_2 are variables for their rows, and *nom* is a term which defines the rows of the resulting unordered table. var_1 and var_2 occur as free variables in the term *nom* as well as in the formula **f**. The formula gives the selection criterion ("join predicate").

As an example, think of a table tab_1 with attributes 'A', 'B' and a table tab_2 with attributes 'A', 'F'. Let their values be numbers.

```
TOTAL(∪) WITH (IF x.'A' = y.'F' ∧ (2*x.'B'+y.'A') < 8
                 THEN [['A':x.'A'; 'B':2*x.'B'; 'C':y.'A']]
                 ELSE [])
          FOR ALL x OF tab₁
          FOR ALL y OF tab₂
```

specifies the desired table with attributes 'A', 'B', 'C', where columns 'A' and 'B' have their values from tab_1 and column 'C' contains values from column 'A' of tab_2. Since IMCL does not provide a possibility of passing a formula as a parameter in an operator term, a general join operator with the selection criterion as a parameter would require an augmentation beyond the built-in extension mechanism of IMCL.

3.3.2.6 Spot manipulation

A construct transformation operator which makes reference to several spots in an argument construct (as do SUBST..., AUG... or DELETE) cannot easily be described by specifying its effect on each single spot because a change at any one spot renders invalid all other spots for the changed construct, in particular those not yet exploited in the evaluation. Thus, one would have to "transfer" the spots still to be used to an intermediate construct resulting from such a partial change. This can be rather cumbersome. Alternatively, one can encode the spots of the argument construct as constructs, perform an analogous transformation on these and finally decode these to obtain the desired result. One possible encoding and decoding is described below. Note, however, that the details of encoding are irrelevant for its usage. What matters, is the fact that there is a one-to-one correspondence between a spot and its encoded counterpart.

If s denotes a singleton spotset, SPOTENCODE s denotes a construct such that for any two different singleton spotsets s_1 and s_2, the constructs denoted by SPOTENCODE s_1 and SPOTENCODE s_2 are also different. Basically, SPOTENCODE s mimics the mathematical definition of the spot in s as a sequence (q, g) (see Section 2.3.3), where q is the sequence of immediate context shells (ics) and g is the construct at the spot. SPOTENCODE is structurally very similar to the mathematical definition, except that it cannot use @ for a placeholder. Instead, it marks the "holes" by an appropriate compositional structure: a hole in a collection is simply ignored, because there is only one way in which it can be there; a hole in a nomination is represented by saving its name as the name of the rest; a hole in a catenation is given by cutting the catenation at the position of the hole into two parts.

$$
\begin{array}{l}
\forall s\ (_1\ \mathsf{SPOTENCODE}\, s = \\
\quad \mathsf{THAT}\ z\ (_2 \mathsf{IsSingle}\ s\ \wedge \\
\qquad\qquad (_3 (_4\ \mathsf{DEPTH}\, s{=}0\ \wedge\ z{=}[\ 1{:}\,[\rightarrow];\, 2{:}\, \mathsf{C}\, s]\ _4)\ \vee \\
\qquad\qquad\ (_5\ \mathsf{DEPTH}\, s{>}0\ \wedge \\
\qquad\qquad\quad \exists ics\ (_6 z{=}[\ 1{:}\, (\mathsf{C}\,((\hat{}\mathsf{SPOTENCODE}\,(s^{\bullet})).\ 1) /\!/\ [\rightarrow ics \rightarrow]);\, 2{:}\, \mathsf{C}\, s]\ \wedge \\
\qquad\qquad\qquad (_7 (\mathsf{IsCol}(\mathsf{C}\, s^{\bullet})\ \wedge\ ics{=}(\mathsf{C}\, s^{\bullet})\backslash[\mathsf{C}\, s])\ \vee \\
\qquad\qquad\qquad\ (\mathsf{IsNom}(\mathsf{C}\, s^{\bullet})\ \wedge\ ics{=}[\mathsf{N}\, s{:}\, \mathsf{NOMC}\,(s^{\bullet}.\backslash s)])\ \vee \\
\qquad\qquad\qquad\ (\mathsf{IsCat}(\mathsf{C}\, s^{\bullet})\ \wedge\ ics{=}[\rightarrow \mathsf{F}\, s \rightarrow \mathsf{R}\, s \rightarrow])\ _7)\ _6)\ _5)\ _3)\ _2)\ _1)
\end{array}
$$

If g denotes a construct obtained by applying SPOTENCODE to a singleton spotset, SPOTDECODE (g) denotes this singleton spotset:

$$\forall g\ (\mathsf{SPOTDECODE}\, g = \mathsf{THAT}\ z\ (\mathsf{SPOTENCODE}\, z{=}g))$$

Henceforth, with SPOTENCODE and SPOTDECODE available, the details of encoding can be forgotten. In the next step towards defining construct transformation operators based on spotsets, an entire function from spots to constructs is encoded as a single construct. "SPOTMAP WITH object term FOR ALL ⌊VARIABLE⌋ OF range term" will be defined as to denote such a function-representing construct. The range term must denote a (not necessarily finite) spotset. The object term must denote a construct if the variable assumes any value of its range. (For an explanation of the words "object term", "range term" and "range" see Sec. 3.2.1, preamble for common features of SUBSTITUTION-TERM, AUGMENTATION-TERM, DELETION-TERM and TOTAL-OPERATOR-TERM). In the following definition, it should be noted that *var* is a bound variable. Thus, the formula is actually a definition *schema* since there is one such definition for each bound variable.

$$
\begin{array}{l}
\forall g, s\ (_1\ \mathsf{SPOTMAP\ WITH}\ g\ \mathsf{FOR\ ALL}\ var\ \mathsf{OF}\ s = \\
\qquad [\ h \mid \exists var \hat{\in} s\ (h{=}[\ 1{:}\,\mathsf{SPOTENCODE}\, var;\, 2{:}\, g])]\ _1)
\end{array}
$$

SPOTMAP WITH g FOR ALL *var* OF s is a table the rows of which represent an (argument, value)-pair for each spot from the range.

If f denotes a construct representing in the sense of SPOTMAP a function from spots to constructs, and s denotes a singleton set of a spot on which this function is defined, SMVALUE (f, s) denotes the construct which is the value of this function for the spot in s:

$\forall f, s$ (SMVALUE $(f, s) =$ THAT z ([1: SPOTENCODE s; 2: z]$\in f$))

If f denotes a construct representing in the sense of SPOTMAP a function from spots to constructs, SMDOMAIN (f) denotes the set of all spots from the domain of this function:

$\forall f$ (SMDOMAIN f = $\langle s \mid \exists h$ ([1: SPOTENCODE s; 2: h]$\in f$)$\rangle$)

If s denotes a construct representing a function from spots to constructs in the sense of SPOTMAP and if s denotes a singleton spotset, SMCLIP (f, s) denotes the SPOTMAP representation of a function defined as follows: the domain of the function is the set of all spots which, embedded into s, yield a spot in the domain of f and inward of s. The value of the function for a spot is the value of f for the same spot embedded in s.

$\forall f, s$ ($_1$ SMCLIP (f, s) =
SPOTMAP WITH SMVALUE $(f,$ EMBED x AT $s)$
FOR ALL x OF $\langle x \mid$ EMBED x AT $s \hat{\in}$ SMDOMAIN $f \rangle$ $_1$)

Fig. 3.13 illustrates the clipping of a SPOTMAP function. A solid triangle denotes a spot from SMDOMAIN (f). A hollow triangle denotes the spot which, when embedded at s, yields the spot denoted by the solid triangle next to it. The connecting broken lines indicate the inward-relation (not necessarily next inward).

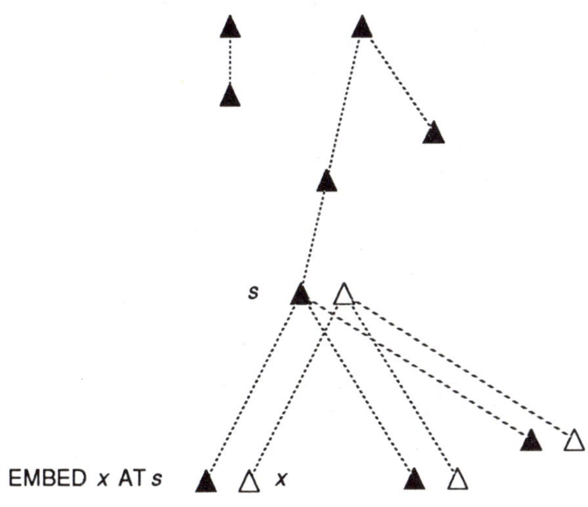

Figure 3.13: Clipping of a SPOTMAP function

We are now ready to define complex built-in operators of plain IMCL with spotset parameters. SUBSTC is taken as an example. In a preparatory step, the substitution spots are singled out and related to their respective object constructs (the constructs to be inserted). This is achieved by making the substitution spots (or, rather, their encodings) the domain, and the object constructs the codomain of a function. For SUBSTC WITH g FOR ALL var OF s IN h, the function is represented by the expression

SPOTMAP WITH g FOR ALL var OF s. This can be considered a "substitution table".

Assume CODEDSUBSTC(f, h) to perform the substitution in construct h according to a substitution table f. Then SUBSTC is easily defined by

$\forall g, s\ (_1$ SUBSTC WITH g FOR ALL var OF s IN $h =$
CODEDSUBSTC(SPOTMAP WITH g FOR ALL var OF $s, h)\ _1)$

The remaining task is to define CODEDSUBSTC. In the following definition, CODEDSUBSTC(f, h) recursively dismantles the construct h, thereby constructing the result construct from outside. On each level, it retains the component constructs that are not affected by the substitution. Those affected are substituted by components given by a reduced CODEDSUBSTC-expression. A spot is *affected* by f if the spot itself or any of its inward spots is in the domain of the substitution table f.

```
∀fs, h (₁
CODEDSUBSTC(fs, h) = THAT z (₂
SMDOMAIN fs⊆^h(.) ∧
(₃(₄SMDOMAIN fs=⟨⟩ ∧ z=h ₄) ∨
  (₅^h ∈̂ SMDOMAIN fs ∧ z=SMVALUE(fs, ^h) ₅) ∨
  (₆¬(SMDOMAIN fs=⟨⟩ ∨ ^h ∈̂ SMDOMAIN fs) ∧
   ∃fc (₇fc= SPOTMAP WITH
                    THAT zz (₈(¬ x∈̂ (SMDOMAIN fs)(˙) ∧ zz=C x) ∨
                              (x∈̂ (SMDOMAIN fs)(˙) ∧
                               zz= CODEDSUBSTC(SMCLIP(fs, x), C x)) ₈)
                    FOR ALL x OF ^h. ∧
       (₉(₁₀IsCol h ∧ z=[g| ∃t∈̂^h.(g=SMVALUE(fc, t))] ₁₀) ∨
         (₁₁IsNom h ∧ NAMESET z=NAMESET h ∧
                    ∀t∈̂^h. (C(^z.⟨N xs=N t⟩)=SMVALUE(fc, t)) ₁₁) ∨
         (₁₂IsCat h ∧ LENGTH z=LENGTH h ∧
                    ∀t∈̂^h. (C(^z.⟨PF xs=PF t⟩)=SMVALUE(fc, t)) ₁₂)
       ₉) ₇) ₆) ₃) ₂) ₁)
```

Some comment on this somewhat lengthy definition may be helpful. If the substitution table fs is empty, h itself is the result of the substitution, cf. $(_4 \cdots _4)$. If the ownspot of h is among the substitution spots, the value of fs for the ownspot of h is the new construct z, cf. $(_5 \cdots _5)$. In this case, no further dismantling needs to be done and the recursion stops. If neither is the case, a "composition table" fc is introduced for composing the result construct from the immediate component spots x of h, cf. $(_6 \cdots _6)$. (Note that in this case h is neither an atom nor an empty construct.) The bound variable fc is merely an abbreviation for the expression SPOTMAP WITH THAT zz $(_8 \cdots _8)$ FOR ALL x OF $\hat{}h$. referred to in subexpression $(_9 \cdots _9)$. The value of fc for a spot x is either the original component at x (if x is not affected by fs), or the construct resulting from a local substitution at x (if x is affected). The affected spots are sufficiently characterized by $x\hat{\in}$(SMDOMAIN fs)$(^\bullet)$ since the variable

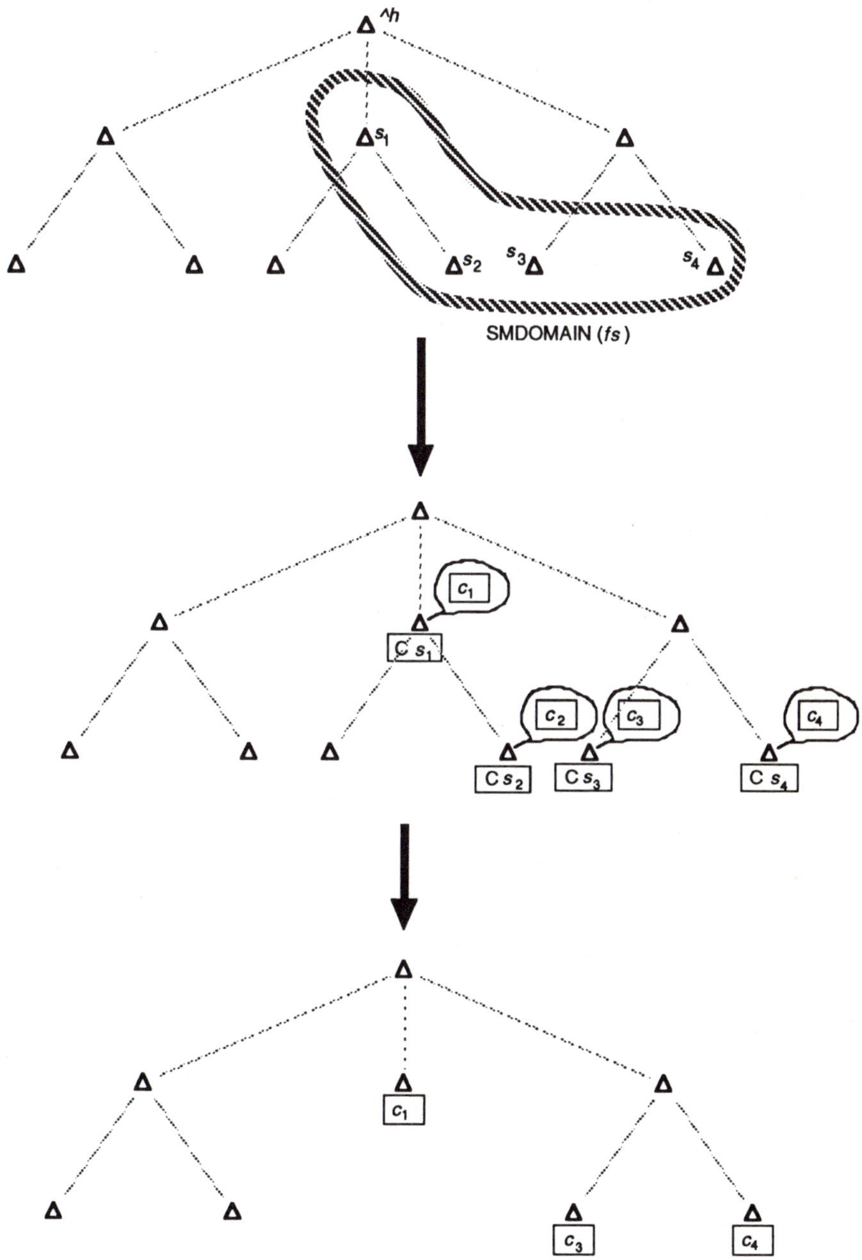

Figure 3.14 : Substitution of components

x is already restricted to the correct level (^h.). (Otherwise $x \hat{\in}$ (SMDOMAIN fs)↑. would additionally have to be required.) A local substitution at x is performed by applying CODEDSUBSTC to the construct at spot x with a substitution table for the "clipped" spot tree of this construct (SMCLIP (fs, x) in subexpression $(_8 \cdots _8)$).

Given the composition table *fc*, the new construct is assembled from the values of *fc*, cf. $(_9 \cdots _9)$. Three cases are distinguished: if h is a collection, the new construct z is the collection of all values of *fc*, cf. $(_{10} \cdots _{10})$; if h is a nomination, the name set of the new construct z is the same and the components of z are the values of *fc*, cf. $(_{11} \cdots _{11})$; if h is a catenation, the components of z are the values of *fc* at the same positions as the original component spots in h, cf. $(_{12} \cdots _{12})$.

Note that in the definition SPOTMAP-functions are used in two very different roles. The substitution table *fs* is in the focus of interest as the real subject of CODEDSUBSTC. Also, in its reduced form SMCLIP (fs, x), it plays this role for the next recursion step. In contrast, the composition table *fc* is used as a descriptional device local to each recursion step.

The two steps for substitution are illustrated in Fig. 3.14. In the first step, the object constructs, denoted c_1, c_2, c_3 and c_4, are "attached" to the spots from the substitution range. In the second step, the original components are actually substituted. The figure does not express that this substitution takes place in the encoded counterpart.

3.3.3 A relational data model as a construct type

The relational data model (RDM) is very simple in its basic principles, but its elaboration in detail for practical application introduces significantly more complexity. Already the traditional constraints of the RDM lead to a fairly involved definition for the type "relational database". An attempt to define this type of information object with VDM can be found in [BjJo82]. In the following, we present a type definition in IMCL capturing the typical constraints for relational databases. Apart from minor deviations, this view relies on the description given in [Date90], and some supplementary assumptions. It can be summarized as follows:

- Only simple domains (atomic values) are considered.
- Domains are considered conceptual parts of a relational database: a *domain catalog* comprises all domains of the database.
- Domain names, relation names and attribute names are arbitrary constructs (atoms, strings, or something else).
- Apart from its *body*—an unordered table, a relation has two further components which characterize its type: the *heading* indicates for each attribute the corresponding domain, the *primary key* indicates the attributes which form the (only) key of the body.
- There are two general "relational integrity rules": the *entity integrity* rule (no null values for key attributes) and the *referential integrity* rule (foreign key values actually occur as primary key values). Referential integrity is expressed by means of a table of *references* as a further component of a relational database (self-referencing is regarded as an intra-relational constraint and hence does not appear in the *references*-component). Other constraints (e.g., those in connection with views) are not considered.
- There is no more than one relation over each set of attributes [Kane90].

We will now give a general definition of the relational database architecture, i.e., a formal specification of the "structural" and the "integrity" part of the RDM as an IMCL-formula $\mathbf{f}_{RDM}$. This is a definition for a predicate IsRelationalDatabase in the sense that a construct denoted by **t** has the properties required of a relational database if and only if IsRelationalDatabase **t** holds. $\mathbf{f}_{RDM}$ consists of the definition for IsRelationalDatabase plus two auxiliary definitions. It has the form

$$\mathbf{f}_{RDM} \equiv \mathbf{f}_{IsRelationalDatabase} \wedge \mathbf{f}_{IsDomainCatalog} \wedge \mathbf{f}_{IsRelation}$$

The auxiliary definitions are concerned with the type of the two main components of a relational database construct. The type of constructs which satisfy $\mathbf{f}_{RDM}$ is illustrated by the box diagram in Fig. 3.15. In the diagram, a generic box notation for construct types is employed. This notation is explained in Appendix A, Sec. A.3.1.

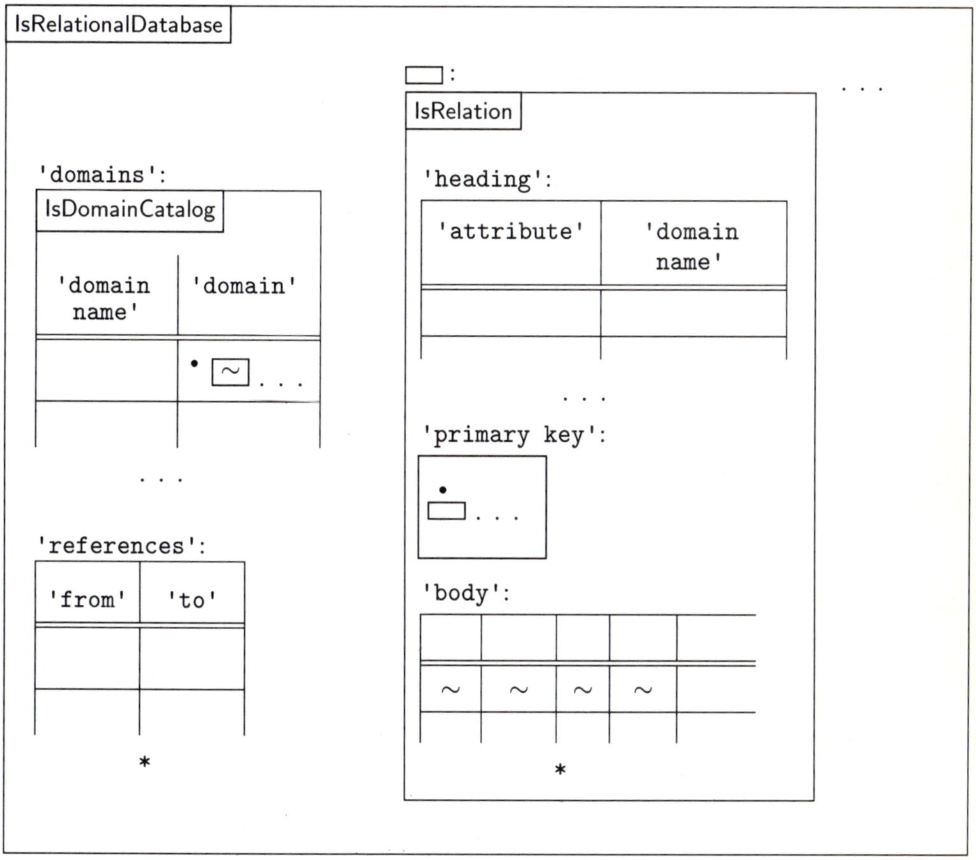

Figure 3.15: Generic box diagram for relational databases

We consider the auxiliary definitions first.

The component `'domains'` is the domain catalog of the relational database. It is an unordered table where each component is a nomination of a (unique) domain name and a nonempty domain (collection of atoms). A special atom which stands for the "null value" (say, `'null'`) is required not to belong to any domain. A construct which satisfies these constraints is an instance of the type IsDomainCatalog:

$$
\begin{array}{l}
\mathbf{f}_{IsDomainCatalog} \equiv \\
\forall g \\
(_1\,\mathsf{IsDomainCatalog}(g) \iff \\
\quad \mathsf{IsCol}(g) \wedge \\
\quad \forall d{\in}g\ \exists n, values \\
\quad (d = [\texttt{'domain name'}{:}\, n;\ \texttt{'domain'}{:}\, values] \wedge \mathsf{IsNeCol}(values) \wedge \texttt{'null'} \notin values) \wedge \\
\quad \forall d,e{\in}g\ (d.\texttt{'domain name'} = e.\texttt{'domain name'} \implies d = e)\ _1)
\end{array}
$$

A relation, i.e., a construct of type IsRelation is defined to be a nomination with three components, namely, the heading where the attribute names and their associated domain names are listed, the collection of primary key attributes and the body which contains the relational tuples. Between the three components, integrity constraints are to be established. They are expressed in the formula $\mathbf{f}_{IsRelation}$ and explained below.

$$
\begin{array}{l}
\mathbf{f}_{IsRelation} \equiv \\
\forall r \\
(_1\,\mathsf{IsRelation}(r) \iff \\
\quad \exists h, k, b \\
\quad (_2\, r = [\texttt{'heading'}{:}\, h;\ \texttt{'primary key'}{:}\, k;\ \texttt{'body'}{:}\, b] \wedge \\
\quad\quad \mathsf{IsNeCol}(h) \wedge \\
\quad\quad \forall p{\in}h\ \exists a, d\ (p = [\texttt{'attribute'}{:}\, a;\ \texttt{'domain name'}{:}\, d]) \wedge \\
\quad\quad \forall p,q{\in}h\ (p.\texttt{'attribute'} = q.\texttt{'attribute'} \implies p = q) \wedge \\
\quad\quad k \subseteq \mathsf{COLC}\ \hat{}\, h..\texttt{'attribute'} \wedge \\
\quad\quad \mathsf{IsCol}(b) \wedge \\
\quad\quad \forall t{\in}b\ (\mathsf{NAMESET}(t) = \mathsf{COLC}\ \hat{}\, h..\texttt{'attribute'} \wedge \forall n{\in}k\ (t.n \neq \texttt{'null'})) \wedge \\
\quad\quad \forall u,v{\in}b\ (\forall n{\in}k\ (u.n = v.n) \implies u = v)\ _2)\ _1)
\end{array}
$$

The constraint $k \subseteq \mathsf{COLC}\ \hat{}\, h..\texttt{'attribute'}$ makes sure that the primary key is composed from attributes of the relation in question only. The last two lines say that the attributes of the body are exactly those listed in the heading, that no component of the primary key is `'null'` and that the primary keys are unique. The definition also caters for the minimality of primary keys. As this minimality must be understood relative to a relation *type*, rather than to a single relation, it is sufficient that the type definition admits at least one relation in which the key is minimal. This is obviously the case for IsRelation.

The notion of primary key deserves some comment. Usually it is claimed, that several *candidate* keys may exist for a given relation type. One of them is arbitrarily designated as the *primary* key. Then the remaining candidate keys are called *alternate* keys [Date90]. The terminology is not quite to the point: the primary key is not merely a key (i.e., has the uniqueness property), but also serves to establish continuance for tuple spots in changing relations (see Appendix A, Sec. A.2.3) and thus to define tuple *locations*.

The foreign key feature is modelled by references collected under the name `'references'` as a further standard component of a relational database. It is an unordered table with two columns of relation names. The formal definition of this component type is given within the definition of the predicate IsRelationalDatabase below.

So far, domain catalog and relation have been defined as isolated construct types. If they are to form component types of a relational database ("aggregation"), they are combined and furnished with relational integrity rules. Thus, $\mathbf{f}_{IsRelationalDatabase}$, the definition of the predicate IsRelationalDatabase, not only exhibits the (simple) compositional properties, but also the (less simple) "integrity constraints" on the relationships between the domain catalog and each relation as well as between the referential catalog and each pair of relations for which a foreign-to-primary-key match exists.

$$
\begin{array}{l}
\mathbf{f}_{IsRelationalDatabase} \equiv \\
\forall db \\
{(}_0\,\mathsf{IsRelationalDatabase}(db) \iff \\
\quad [\texttt{'domains'};\texttt{'references'}] \subseteq \mathsf{NAMESET}\,(db) \wedge \\
\quad \forall f \hat{\in} \,\hat{}\,db\,\texttt{.} \\
\quad {(}_1{(}_2\,\mathsf{N}f{=}\texttt{'domains'} \Longrightarrow \mathsf{IsDomainCatalog}(\mathsf{C}f)\,{}_2{)} \wedge \\
\qquad {(}_3\,\mathsf{N}f \not\in [\texttt{'domains'};\texttt{'references'}] \Longrightarrow \\
\qquad\quad \mathsf{IsRelation}(\mathsf{C}f) \wedge \\
\qquad\quad \mathsf{COLC}\ (f\texttt{.'heading'..}dn) \subseteq \mathsf{COLC}\ (\hat{}\,db\texttt{.'domains'..}dn) \wedge \\
\qquad\quad \forall p \in \mathsf{C}\,f\texttt{.'heading'} \\
\qquad\quad {(}_4\,\mathsf{COLC}\,(f\texttt{.'body'..}\langle \mathsf{N}\,xs{=}p\texttt{.'attribute'}\rangle) \subseteq \\
\qquad\qquad \mathsf{C}\,(\hat{}\,db\texttt{.'domains'.}\langle \mathsf{C}\,xs\texttt{.}dn{=}p\texttt{.}dn\rangle\texttt{.'domain'}) \cup [\texttt{'null'}]\,{}_4{)}\,{}_3{)} \wedge \\
\qquad {(}_5\,\mathsf{N}f{=}\texttt{'references'} \Longrightarrow \\
\qquad\quad \mathsf{IsCol}(\mathsf{C}f) \wedge \\
\qquad\quad \forall r \in \mathsf{C}f\ \exists s,t \\
\qquad\quad {(}_6\,r{=}[\texttt{'from'}{:}\,s;\texttt{'to'}{:}\,t] \wedge \\
\qquad\qquad \exists k \\
\qquad\qquad {(}_7\,k{=}db\texttt{.}t\texttt{.'primary key'} \wedge \\
\qquad\qquad\quad k \subseteq \mathsf{COLC}\,(\hat{}\,db\texttt{.}s\texttt{.'heading'..'attribute'}) \wedge \\
\qquad\qquad\quad \forall ls \in db\texttt{.}s\texttt{.'body'} \\
\qquad\qquad\quad (\forall n \in k\ (ls\texttt{.}n{=}\texttt{'null'}) \vee \exists\, lt \in db\texttt{.}t\texttt{.'body'}\ \forall n \in k\ (ls\texttt{.}n{=}lt\texttt{.}n))\,{}_7{)}\,{}_6{)}\,{}_5{)}\,{}_1{)} \wedge \\
\quad \forall f,g \hat{\in} (\hat{}\,db\texttt{.}\langle \mathsf{N}\,xs \not\in [\texttt{'domains'};\texttt{'references'}]\rangle) \\
\quad {(}_8\,\mathsf{COLC}\,(f\texttt{.'heading'..'attribute'}) = \mathsf{COLC}\,(g\texttt{.'heading'..'attribute'}) \Longrightarrow \\
\qquad f{=}g\ {}_8{)}\ {}_0{)}
\end{array}
$$

In this formula, we have abbreviated `'domain name'` by *dn* for layout reasons.

For an entity *db* to be a relational database it must be a nomination with at least `'domains'` and `'references'` among its component names where the component `'domains'` has to be a domain catalog, cf. $({}_2 \cdots {}_2)$, and the component `'references'` has to be a referential catalog, as defined in $({}_5 \cdots {}_5)$. A construct at any other immediately inward spot f has to be a relation, cf. $({}_3\cdots{}_3)$. For any two different relation spots f and g, the attribute sets are different, cf. $({}_8\cdots{}_8)$.

A relation is required to refer only to domains which are provided in the domain catalog. The values of each attribute (column) are drawn from the corresponding domain or are `'null'`, cf. $({}_4\cdots{}_4)$. The referential catalog of a relational database is a (possibly empty) unordered table with two columns `'from'` and `'to'`. A row r in the referential catalog requires that the primary key attributes k of the target relation t are a subset of the attributes of the source relation s and that for each row ls of the source relation the foreign key is either wholly `'null'`-valued or is equal to the primary key of some row lt in the target relation, cf. $({}_7\cdots{}_7)$.

A database type for a particular application can now be defined with respect to the predicate IsRelationalDatabase by providing only the additional constraints which characterize the desired subtype. Let the predicate IsBoringDatabase specify relational databases with at least three relations named `'S'` for suppliers, `'P'` for kinds of parts and `'SP'` for shipments and with two entries in the table of references:

$\forall d$
$({}_0$IsBoringDatabase$(d) \iff$
  IsRelationalDatabase$(d) \wedge$ `['S';'P';'SP']` $\subset$ NAMESET $d \wedge$
  IsSupplierRelation$(d$`.'S'`$) \wedge$
  IsKindOfPartRelation$(d$`.'P'`$) \wedge$
  IsShipmentRelation$(d$`.'SP'`$) \wedge$
  d`.'references'` = `[['from':'SP';'to':'S']; ['from':'SP';'to':'P']]` ${}_0) \wedge$
$\forall b$ (IsSupplierRelation$(b) \iff \ldots \wedge b$`.'primary key'=['S#']`$) \wedge$
$\forall b$ (IsKindOfPartRelation$(b) \iff \ldots \wedge b$`.'primary key'=['P#']`$) \wedge$
$\forall b$ (IsShipmentRelation$(b) \iff \ldots \wedge b$`.'primary key'=['S#';'P#']`$)$

The two entries in the referential catalog define foreign-to-primary-key matches from shipments to suppliers and to kinds of parts. The three relation types are assumed to be suitably defined.

Although, in the present context, we are not concerned with the question as to what is a "relational system", it has to be mentioned that other data structures than the ones defined above can occur as intermediate results, without being explicitly introduced in the RDM as relational data structures. As an example take a so-called multiple-record INSERT in SQL ([Date90]). Assume that for a database d of type IsBoringDatabase a temporary relation `'TEMP'` is asked for, which gives for each part kind the total number of shipped parts. `'TEMP'` shall have two attributes: `'P#'` (part number) and `'TOTQTY'` (total quantity supplied for that part). The SQL instruction

```
INSERT
INTO   TEMP (P#,TOTQTY)
       SELECT P#, SUM(QTY)
       FROM SP
       GROUP BY P#;
```

specifies the insertion of tuples ['P#':...;'TOTQTY':...] into the relation 'TEMP', where the total quantity is the sum calculated for each part number P# on an intermediate construct resulting from GROUP BY. This construct is a "partitioned relation" which is not a construct of the RDM, but a set of equally structured tuple sets called *groups*.

The IMCL-term

$[_1\, t \mid \exists p, q\, (_2\, t=[\texttt{'P\#'}: p; \texttt{'TOTQTY'}: q] \wedge$
$\quad p \in \mathsf{COLC}\ \hat{}d.\texttt{'SP'}.\texttt{'body'}..\texttt{'P\#'} \wedge$
$\quad q=\mathsf{TOTAL}(+)\,\mathsf{WITH}\ (\mathsf{C}\, x)$
$\quad\quad \mathsf{FOR\ ALL}\, x\ \mathsf{OF}\ (\hat{}d.\texttt{'SP'}.\texttt{'body'}.\langle \mathsf{C}\ xs.\texttt{'P\#'}=p\rangle.\texttt{'QTY'})\ _2)\ _1]$

yields the body of the corresponding relation 'TEMP'. It makes explicit the implicit complexity of the above SELECT clause. In the term, no intermediate set of groups (one for each part number) is used. The individual sums (for each part number) are calculated directly from the relation 'SP'.

3.3.4 Predicates and integrity constraints

The following type definitions serve to demonstrate generalization, specialization and inheritance when defining construct types with IMCL. We start with a construct type for calendar dates where the components modelling the attributes *day*, *month* and *year* appear in consistent combinations only. Any instance of this type, called a *strict date*, is thus a correct calendar date, leap-years not taken into account.

$\forall x\, (_0\, \mathsf{IsStrictDate}(x) \iff$
$\quad \mathsf{NAMESET}(x)=[\texttt{'day'};\texttt{'month'};\texttt{'year'}] \wedge$
$\quad \mathsf{IsNat}(x.\texttt{'year'}) \wedge x.\texttt{'year'} \leq 2999 \wedge$
$\quad \mathsf{IsNat}(x.\texttt{'month'}) \wedge x.\texttt{'month'} \leq 12 \wedge$
$\quad \mathsf{IsNat}(x.\texttt{'day'}) \wedge$
$\quad (x.\texttt{'month'} \in [1;3;5;7;8;10;12] \Longrightarrow x.\texttt{'day'} \leq 31) \wedge$
$\quad (x.\texttt{'month'} \in [4;6;9;11] \Longrightarrow x.\texttt{'day'} \leq 30) \wedge$
$\quad (x.\texttt{'month'}=2 \Longrightarrow x.\texttt{'day'} \leq 29)\ _0)$

By introducing a further integrity constraint we define a specialization which is neither a horizontal nor a vertical subtype in the object-oriented terminology [Wegn87], because we neither add new components nor do we restrict any component type.

$\forall x\, (_0\, \mathsf{IsOurCenturyDate}(x) \iff$
$\quad \mathsf{IsStrictDate}(x) \wedge 1900 \leq x.\texttt{'year'} \wedge x.\texttt{'year'} \leq 1999 \wedge$
$\quad (_1\, (x.\texttt{'day'}=29 \wedge x.\texttt{'month'}=2) \Longrightarrow$
$\quad\quad \exists n (\mathsf{IsNatOrZero}(n) \wedge (x.\texttt{'year'}=4*n))\ _1)\ _0),$

where IsNatOrZero is defined by $\forall x (\mathsf{IsNatOrZero}\ x \iff \mathsf{IsNat}\ x \vee x=0)$.

A supertype with respect to IsStrictDate results from relaxing the integrity constraint for the 'day' component of a strict date. Alluding to its reduced complexity we call an instance of this type a *plain date*. It is like a strict date but also has day/month combinations not corresponding to real dates (e.g., February 31). It is basically the full Cartesian product of the component types. This could also be directly constructed from the component types, the point here, however, is to demonstrate how a given type can be generalized. A plain date inherits all component types from its reference type IsStrictDate.

$$\begin{aligned}&\forall x\ ({}_0\,\mathsf{IsPlainDate}(x) \iff\\ &\quad \exists s(\mathsf{IsStrictDate}(s) \wedge \mathsf{NAMESET}\,(s)=\mathsf{NAMESET}\,(x)) \wedge\\ &\quad \forall y{\in}\mathsf{NAMESET}\,(x)(\exists s(\mathsf{IsStrictDate}(s) \wedge x\,.\,y=s\,.\,y))\ {}_0)\end{aligned}$$

Another generalization of strict dates is obtained by admitting dates with unspecified attributes, for example, for an application where dates are used in planning activities. Let a *deficient date* be a possibly not completely specified strict date. That is, one or more components may still be `'unspecified'`. However, all integrity constraints of IsStrictDate shall hold for components different from `'unspecified'`.

$$\begin{aligned}&\forall x\ ({}_0\,\mathsf{IsDeficientDate}(x) \iff\\ &\quad \exists s\ ({}_1\,\mathsf{IsStrictDate}(s) \wedge \mathsf{NAMESET}\,(s)=\mathsf{NAMESET}\,(x) \wedge\\ &\qquad \forall y{\in}\mathsf{NAMESET}\,(x)(x\,.\,y=s\,.\,y \vee x\,.\,y=\texttt{'unspecified'})\ {}_1)\ {}_0)\end{aligned}$$

A slightly different form of the same generalization is a *loose date*, which is like a strict date with some combination of components possibly missing (instead of being `'unspecified'`).

$$\begin{aligned}&\forall x\ ({}_0\,\mathsf{IsLooseDate}(x) \iff\\ &\quad \exists s\ ({}_1\,\mathsf{IsStrictDate}(s) \wedge\\ &\qquad ({}_2\,x=s \vee\\ &\qquad\ x=\mathsf{RESTRICT}\ s\ \mathsf{TO}\ \mathsf{NAMESET}\,(s)\backslash\texttt{['day']} \vee\\ &\qquad\ x=\mathsf{RESTRICT}\ s\ \mathsf{TO}\ \mathsf{NAMESET}\,(s)\backslash\texttt{['day';'month']}\ {}_2)\ {}_1)\ {}_0)\end{aligned}$$

Up to this point we have defined three types of date which are supertypes of IsStrictDate, inheriting different shares of its properties: IsPlainDate, IsDeficientDate and IsLooseDate. Note that the direction of inheritance is opposite to the direction of subsetting.

We now want to show that properties can be transferred by inheritance to models with a quite different compositional structure. According to the standard ISO notation, the identification of date components is given by their position in a sequence. We call an *international date* a catenation of five components (three natural numbers, two hyphens) where the same integrity constraints apply as with strict dates.

$$\begin{aligned}&\forall x\ ({}_0\,\mathsf{IsInternationalDate}(x) \iff\\ &\quad \exists s\ ({}_1\,\mathsf{IsStrictDate}(s) \wedge\\ &\qquad x=\texttt{[}\rightarrow s\,.\,\texttt{'year'} \rightarrow \texttt{'-'} \rightarrow s\,.\,\texttt{'month'} \rightarrow \texttt{'-'} \rightarrow s\,.\,\texttt{'day'} \rightarrow \texttt{]}\ {}_1)\ {}_0)\end{aligned}$$

This is a kind of inheritance, where only the component types and their possible combinations are inherited, but not the compositional structure. So the construct types are disjoint, whereas the set of modelled objects (dates) is the same.

To prepare for a demonstration of "horizontal subtyping", let us now introduce a new type, called *time of day*, which is a compositional model of the hour as shown by a clock.

$\forall x\ ({}_0\ \mathsf{IsTimeOfDay}(x) \iff$
$\quad \mathsf{NAMESET}\,(x){=}[\texttt{'hour'};\texttt{'minute'}] \land$
$\quad \mathsf{IsNatOrZero}(x.\texttt{'hour'}) \land x.\texttt{'hour'}{\leq}23 \land$
$\quad \mathsf{IsNatOrZero}(x.\texttt{'minute'}) \land x.\texttt{'minute'}{\leq}59\ {}_0)$

Adding a new component for the seconds yields a "horizontal subtype" of IsTimeOfDay. We call an instance of this subtype an *exact time of day*. Formally it is defined as a time of day with an additional component `'second'`.

$\forall x\ ({}_0\ \mathsf{IsExactTimeOfDay}(x) \iff$
$\quad \exists t,s\ ({}_1\ \mathsf{IsTimeOfDay}(t) \land \mathsf{IsNatOrZero}(s) \land s{\leq}59 \land x{=}t{:}\mathsf{U}[\texttt{'second'}{:}s]\ {}_1)\ {}_0)$

In this case, the specialization does not correspond to subsetting, although the instances of IsExactTimeOfDay inherit all properties of the parent type IsTimeOfDay.

Next, we define a type that inherits properties from two predefined types. Let a *point of time* be a merge of a strict date with a time of day.

$\forall x\ ({}_0\ \mathsf{IsPointOfTime}(x) \iff$
$\quad \exists d,t\ ({}_1\ \mathsf{IsStrictDate}(d) \land \mathsf{IsTimeOfDay}(t) \land x{=}d{:}\mathsf{U}t\ \ {}_1)\ {}_0)$

A point of time has thus inherited its attributes from IsStrictDate and from IsTimeOfDay, inclusive of their integrity constraints. While the two reference types are used as sources for attribute inheritance, the sets of their instances have no elements in common with the set of instances of IsPointOfTime.

A comprehensive supertype can be obtained by simply taking all components as being optional. We define a *point of time fragment* the instances of which are nonempty nominations which have one or several components of a point of time and no other components.

$\forall x\ ({}_0\ \mathsf{IsPointOfTimeFragment}(x) \iff \mathsf{IsNeNom}(x) \land \exists p\ ({}_1\ \mathsf{IsPointOfTime}(p) \land x{:}{\subseteq}p\ \ {}_1)\ {}_0)$

This type includes all other ones defined so far except deficient dates, international dates and those plain dates which are not strict dates.

Finally we generalize various forms of time information to a *usual time reference* which is a strict date, a time of day or an exact time of day.

$\forall x\ ({}_0\ \mathsf{IsUsualTimeReference}(x) \iff$
$\quad \mathsf{IsStrictDate}(x) \lor \mathsf{IsTimeOfDay}(x) \lor \mathsf{IsExactTimeOfDay}(x)\ {}_0)$

The instances of this type form a superset of the instances of the three reference types.

3.3.5 Recursive construct type definition

Use of recursive construct types can be demonstrated with a bill of materials application: parts include other parts, which themselves can have other parts as components, and so on (a simpler variant of this problem is also specified in [Jone80] and [Dill90]). As usual, the term "part" means "part type" rather than an individual piece of such a type. A compositional model of parts is defined by the following predicate:

$$
\begin{aligned}
\forall e\,({}_0\,\mathsf{Part}(e) \iff\; & \mathsf{NAMESET}\,e = \texttt{['part name';'composition']} \wedge \\
& \mathsf{Partname}(e\texttt{.'part name'}) \wedge \mathsf{IsCol}(e\texttt{.'composition'}) \wedge \\
& \forall p{\in}e\texttt{.'composition'}\,({}_1\,\mathsf{NAMESET}\ p = \texttt{['quantity';'part']} \wedge \\
& \qquad\qquad\qquad\quad \mathsf{IsNat}(p\texttt{.'quantity'}) \wedge \\
& \qquad\qquad\qquad\quad \mathsf{Part}(p\texttt{.'part'})\,{}_1) \wedge \\
& \forall x, y\hat{\in}\hat{\ }e(\texttt{.})\texttt{'part name'}(\mathsf{C}\,x{=}\mathsf{C}\,y \Longrightarrow \mathsf{C}\,x^{\bullet}{=}\mathsf{C}\,y^{\bullet}) \wedge \\
& \forall x, y{\in}e\texttt{.'composition'}\,(x\texttt{.'part'}{=}y\texttt{.'part'} \Longrightarrow x{=}y\ )\,{}_0)
\end{aligned}
$$

For basic parts (i.e. parts without components) the collection e`.'composition'` is empty. The last two lines specify uniqueness of part names in the entire bill of materials, and that in one composition the same part may occur only once. Note that uniqueness of part names does not preclude parts from occurring at several spots within a given composite part. However, since a construct cannot be a component of itself, uniqueness of part names excludes cycles in the composition graph: a part cannot occur within itself. A construct satisfying the predicate Part can be viewed as the bill of materials for the part it describes. Fig. 3.16 shows a pictorial representation of the construct type Part in the notation explained in Appendix A, Sec. A.3.1.

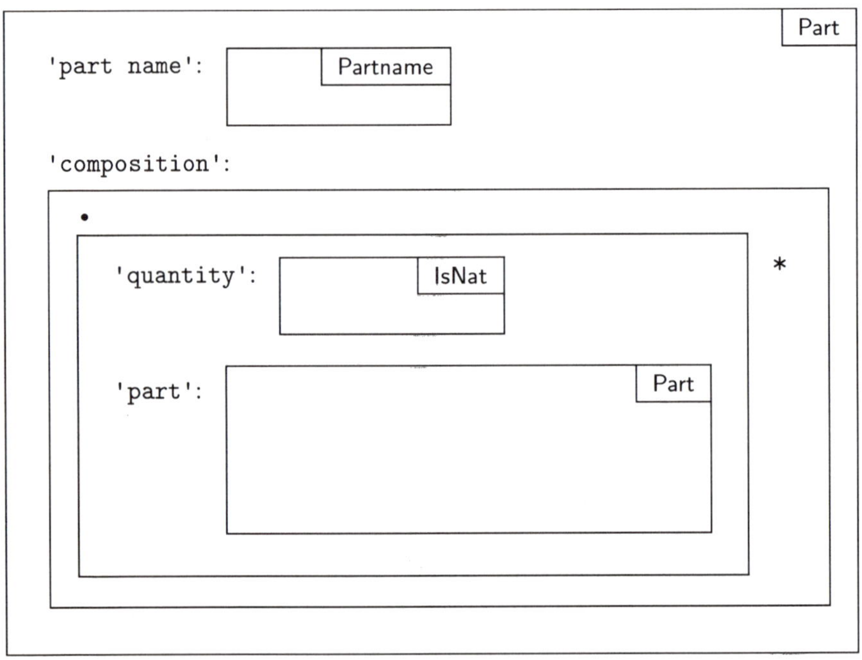

Figure 3.16 : Generic box diagram for parts and their bill of materials

A few examples shall illustrate how queries against a given part *bom* can be formulated taking advantage of spots.

Example 1. The collection of all component parts of *bom* (all-level part explosion) is

$\mathsf{COLC}\ (\hat{}\,bom(\mathtt{.})\langle \mathsf{Part}(\mathsf{C}\ xs)\rangle)$

This collection also contains *bom* itself. If *bom* is to be excluded, this can be expressed by

$\mathsf{COLC}\ (\hat{}\,bom\mathtt{.}(\mathtt{.})\langle \mathsf{Part}(\mathsf{C}\ xs)\rangle)$

Example 2. The component part with name m contained in *bom* is given by

$\mathsf{THAT}\ g\ ({}_1\exists s\ ({}_2\ s\hat{\in}({}_3\hat{}\,bom(\mathtt{.})\langle \mathsf{Part}(\mathsf{C}\,xs) \wedge \mathsf{C}\,(xs\mathtt{.'part\ name'})=m\rangle\ {}_3) \wedge g=\mathsf{C}\,s\ {}_2)\ {}_1)$

or, using the operator COMC defined in Sec. 3.3.2.1:

$\mathsf{COMC}\ \hat{}\,bom(\mathtt{.})\langle \mathsf{Part}(\mathsf{C}\,xs) \wedge \mathsf{C}\,(xs\mathtt{.'part\ name'})=m\rangle$

If we use this to define

$\forall m, bom\ ({}_0\mathsf{THEPART}\,(m, bom)=$
$\qquad \mathsf{COMC}\ \hat{}\,bom(\mathtt{.})\langle \mathsf{Part}(\mathsf{C}\,xs) \wedge \mathsf{C}\,(xs\mathtt{.'part\ name'})=m\rangle\ {}_0),$

Example 1 can easily be modified to render the collection of component parts for a part with a given name m:

$\mathsf{COLC}\,(\hat{}\,\mathsf{THEPART}\,(m, bom)\mathtt{.}(\mathtt{.})\langle \mathsf{Part}(\mathsf{C}\ xs)\rangle)$

Note that $\mathsf{THEPART}\,(m, bom)$ yields UNDEF if a part with name m does not occur in the construct *bom*.

Example 3. The collection of parts (sub-assemblies) with more than n immediate component parts is:

$\mathsf{COLC}\ \hat{}\,bom(\mathtt{.})\langle_1\ x||\ \mathsf{Part}(\mathsf{C}\,x) \wedge$
$\qquad \mathsf{CARD}\,({}_2\ x\mathtt{.'composition'.}\ {}_2) > n\ {}_1\rangle$

Example 4. The collection of parts with more than n component parts is:

$\mathsf{COLC}\ \hat{}\,bom(\mathtt{.})\langle_1\ x||\ \mathsf{Part}(\mathsf{C}\,x) \wedge$
$\qquad \mathsf{CARD}\,({}_2\ \mathsf{COLC}\ x\mathtt{.'composition'(.)'part\ name'}\ {}_2) > n\ {}_1\rangle$

Example 5. The collection of all parts which have a part with name m at depth d (d = levels of explosion to arrive at m) is:

$\mathsf{COLC}\ \hat{}\,bom(\mathtt{.})\langle_1\ s||\ \mathsf{Part}(\mathsf{C}\,s) \wedge$
$\qquad \exists t\hat{\in}(s(\mathtt{.})\ \langle \mathsf{Part}(\mathsf{C}\,xs)\rangle)\ (\mathsf{C}\,(t\mathtt{.'part\ name'})=m \wedge$
$\qquad\qquad \mathsf{EXPLEV}\,(t)\ \mathsf{IN}\,(s)=d)\ {}_1\rangle$

The operator $\mathsf{EXPLEV}\,(t)\mathsf{IN}\,(s)$ is defined to yield the explosion level of the part at spot t with respect to the part at spot s:

$\forall t,s\ ({}_0\mathsf{EXPLEV}\,(t)\mathsf{IN}\,(s)=\ \mathsf{CARD}\,({}_1\,(t(^\bullet)\backslash s(^\bullet))\langle \mathsf{Part}(\mathsf{C}\ xs)\rangle\ {}_1)\ {}_0)$

Example 6. The total quantity of a part with name m needed for a part *bom* is given by a recursively defined operator $\mathsf{TOTQ}\,(m,bom)$ which, on each level of part explosion, sums up the quantities needed for the parts occurring on that level. These values are obtained by applying TOTQ (m, bom) to each corresponding (sub-)bill of materials.

```
∀m, bom (₀TOTQ (m, bom)=
        IF bom.'part name'=m THEN 1
        ELSE
            IF bom.'composition'=[] THEN 0
            ELSE
                TOTAL (+) WITH cp.'quantity'* TOTQ (m, cp.'part')
                        FOR ALL cp OF bom.'composition' ₀)
```

Note that there is no need to look into a part with name m for further parts with name m, since a part cannot occur within itself.

Chapter 4

The development of IMC/IMCL in perspective

Introductory statement

IMC/IMCL is the result of almost two decades of observation and analysis of information structure description needs and information structure modelling, initially in the database world, but then also in other fields like conceptual modelling, information system design (including conceptual schema design), and document architectures. In concluding this book it seems appropriate to give an account of the background on which it was developed and from which it received its inspiration. An outline of this has already been given in the preface. The present chapter briefly reviews the general background and the history of IMC/IMCL development, and for selected aspects discusses the relation of IMC/IMCL to other work. The chapter closes with some thoughts on future development.

The general background of IMC/IMCL development

There are three major principles for information structure modelling: composition, pointers and operations. The pure method of abstract data types is a prominent example of exploiting exclusively one of these principles. Normally, a mixture of all three is employed, although with differing distribution of emphasis.

In the early days of information structure description, a compositional view of data objects prevailed, using pointers on top to describe additional structure. Files were considered to be composed of records, records of fields, and these, in turn, consisted iteratively of subfields. Linkages, as in index files, were shown as pointers. A well-known example of combining compositional with pointer structure was the DBTG data model ([CODA73a] and predecessor).

In the relational approach [Codd70], the situation was not much different in principle. However, because now the compositional structure was homogeneous and very restricted, it became a matter of relatively little concern. The demanding issue was the integrity of intra-relation and inter-relation connections as constituted by functional dependencies and user-defined linkages (foreign keys).

The trend away from compositional structure was reversed when it was felt that the "flat" relational structure was inappropriate for applications with rich, inhomogeneous and deeply nested information structure, as was the case, for example, for geographic and materials databases. Proposals for "nonconventional" data models or, more specifically, "non-first-normal-form" (NF^2) relations were made, which tried to provide more structure while retaining the advantages of the relational view. They resulted in data models with complex compositional structure, even with indefinite depth of nesting.

While the extensions originating from and dedicated to the relational view still impose overall compositional constraints, there have been other approaches to a more general compositional view, imposing as few compositional restrictions as possible (e.g., STDS [Chil68], VDL [LuLaSt70], VDM [BjJo78], Z [Dill90], SETL [ScDeDuSc86]). They offer the advantage that complex structures can be represented directly, rather than having to be mapped onto lower level relational structure [Banc88]. This allows one to think in terms of structures best suited to the problem at hand (in [Dill90] it is called "representational abstraction"). IMC/IMCL belongs to this class of developments. With respect to information structure, it bears closest relationship to SETL, VDM and Z.

In parallel to the composition- and pointer-centred strain of data modelling, which is located mainly in the information systems area, the operational view was pursued particularly in the programming language field. Abstract data types were extensively studied, starting with the seminal work of [GoThWaWr75]. VDM, although using a compositional setup for its basic constructs, is strongly oriented toward an operational view. Presently, the object-oriented programming paradigm is a much discussed way of dealing with the operational view, but it also accommodates compositional and pointer-oriented ideas for object as well as message representation. Though still lacking a solid and generally accepted conceptual basis ([Banc88], [Kim90]), it bears the promise of reconciliation for the programming world and the database world.

Object-orientation does, however, not go unchallenged. The absence of a theoretical basis is held responsible for a lack of consensus for the data model, and deficiencies in dealing with complex data and complex queries are deplored [Banc88]. In recent work, the so-called *value-oriented* approach is defended against the object-oriented approach ([Ullm87], [LeRi89], [Scio91]). The main advantages claimed are that value-orientation (i) encourages the use of declarative programming, (ii) does not restrict queries to predefined access paths, and (iii) enables more natural manipulation of complex information objects. These are, in fact, advantages also claimed for IMC/IMCL, which is clearly on the value-oriented side, if one insists on the distinction.

Third generation database systems are presently one of the challenges faced by the DBMS community ([Comm91], [SiStUl91]). They will have to provide advanced data management capabilities such as rich type systems, (integrity) rules not bound to functions, non-procedural high-level data access languages and updatable views. IMC/IMCL is a reasonable candidate for a formal description tool to specify solutions which are based on a compositional or structural [Otis91] view of information modelling.

General outline of IMC/IMCL development

IMC started from quite specific descriptional needs when an attempt was made to put CODASYL's Feature Analysis ([CODA73b] and predecessor) on a solid conceptual basis [DuRi72]. It was originally intended for this and some related work only, but it proved to be helpful also in the analysis of various other data models then under discussion, and as a conceptual tool for discussing information structure in applications like file systems, information retrieval systems or message structures. Naturally, IMC application was focussed on inherently compositional information structure, but an analysis of the data definition and the data manipulation language of the DBTG model [CODA73a] in IMC terms showed that a strongly pointer-oriented model could adequately be treated, too.

Although its principles were published quite early (e.g., [DuRi74], [DuRi76]), IMC was used more privately by its originators. In the meantime, it was not pursued continuously, but rather at irregular intervals, as required by occasional description tasks. Yet, gradually IMC matured. Meanwhile, there was a renaissance of the compositional paradigm that was all the time present both in data processing practice and as an undercurrent of information structure research. In its wake, old descriptional problems reappeared. They could adequately be treated and a number of misunderstandings could be avoided by using IMC concepts. Thus it seemed desirable to make IMC publicly available.

However, to make IMC attractive to others, suitable languages had to be provided. Pictorial languages (box and tree notation) were used right from the inception of IMC, but a textual language was still lacking. There was some ad-hoc notation, but this had to be developed into a systematic language design. In addition, the pictorial languages had to be reconciled with it to make mixed representation possible. Thus, the language IMCL was inaugurated. Its design principles were selected according to its intended use as a language for humans to deal with IMC concepts. As there was no need to restrict its expressive power for reasons of implementability, full first-order predicate logic was admitted. In accordance with IMC's basic goals, procedural notions have been carefully avoided, so that IMCL became a strictly term-oriented language.

While still in experimental and preliminary stages, IMC/IMCL has been applied in a number of examples and case studies (e.g., [Rich79], [Rich81a], [RiDu82], [DuSi83], [Rich84], [HeRi86], [PiHe89]). When IMCL was just about to take its final shape, the formal specification of an office document architecture (ODA) was undertaken as a major application in standardization ([ApCaTe90], [Rugg90], [ISO91]). In this application, it helped to express the underlying model of the standard and to detect deficiencies and inconsistencies in its highly complex information structures [BlBoRuTe90]. In parallel with the specification, a subset of IMCL was implemented for conformance analysis of (electronic) ODA documents [Kara90].

Compositionality

There are a number of proposals for "composite", "complex", "molecular" or "highly structured" objects, in particular in the context of "nonconventional" database applications (in [Kim90] collectively referred to as CAx applications, see also [BaBu84],

[Lame85], [ScSc86], [Daya87], [Mits88], [KiBeGa89], [PaSp89], [Ditt90]). They share the common feature that complex objects are built from atomic ones by iteratively applying very few (typically two or three) composition operators. Not all models which start from composition principles really exploit compositional properties.

The proposed models can be subdivided into two classes: those with general compositional constraints and those that allow unlimited iterative nesting. The traditional data models and the E/R model are examples of the former, SETL [ScDeDuSc86], VDM [BjJo78], Z [Dill90] and also IMC/IMCL belong to the latter.

There is a striking similarity in the choice of basic composition operators in different approaches, although there are differences in detail, concerning, for example, types of atoms, cardinality of constructs, or empty constructs. Fig. 4.1 gives an overview for some of these approaches. The entries in the table show the term used in the respective model. The ∞-symbol indicates that countably many components are admitted if so stated explicitly.

	set	function	sequence
IMC/IMCL	collection (∞)	nomination (∞)	catenation
SETL	set	single-valued map	tuple
"data abstraction"[1]	set (∞)	mapping	list (∞)
VDM	set (∞)	function (∞), map	list/tuple
RDM	relation	–	tuple
GSM[2]	grouping	–	aggregation
"complex objects"[3]	set object	tuple object	–
"complex structures"[4]	set value	tuple value	–

[1] [Jone80], [2] [HuKi87], [3] [BaKh86], [Hull89], [KhFrCa90], [4] [LeRi89]

Figure 4.1 : Basic composition operators

The choice of fundamental constructors is a matter of opinion on adequacy. It can be justified only by the success it has in actual usage. Nonetheless, the independent selection of an almost identical operator base can be taken as a confirmation that a common need is addressed.

General compositional constraints are of three kinds. (i) Restriction on applicability of composition operators. The relational model, for example, admits collections only for aggregating tuples into relations. (ii) Restriction on cardinality of the number of immediate components. Most models assume finitely many immediate components. (iii) Restriction on the depth of nesting. For example, [PaSp89] does not allow relationships to be defined on relationships, nor entities to be used as attributes of other entities. IMC/IMCL is unrestricted in all respects, except for finiteness requirements for catenations and the depth of nesting. There seemed to be no obvious need in information structure description to introduce the additional complexity resulting from infinity in these respects.

According to [KiBeGa89], models of composite objects should have three features in order to support general information modelling, database design and database usage. First, the model should not restrict a composite object to a strict hierarchy of *exclusive* component objects, where a component object may be part of one object only. In IMC/IMCL, multiple occurrence of the same construct in other constructs is standard. The spot concept allows one to distinguish occurrences formally. Second, the model should not force a top-down creation of a composite object, because this would prevent a bottom-up creation of objects by assembling already existing objects. IMC/IMCL postulates no particular direction of construction. For information system design, it allows one to deal with models containing incomplete specifications on all levels of aggregation, even with respect to the depth of aggregation. Third, a model should not require the existence of a component object to depend on the existence of the parent object. This feature is closely related to the first one, because a component of several objects can be deleted only if they are not claimed by other parents, a problem well-known from the DBTG owner-member relationship. In IMC/IMCL, deletion of a component deletes any subcomponents *in this particular context*. The deleted components continue to exist in all other contexts. Note, however, that persistence is a dynamic aspect that cannot really be treated in plain IMC, but must also include systems considerations (cf. Appendix A, in particular Sec. A.2.3).

Structural expressiveness

In comparison with other data models, IMC has occasionally been called a hierarchical data model (e.g., in [KeKlTs77]), probably due to its emphasis on the spot concept. The spots of a construct do, in fact, form a strict hierarchy. The component constructs, however, do not, since the same component construct may occur at several component spots. With respect to the model class (hierarchical, network, relational or other), IMC is neutral and IMCL may be specialized to any of them by additionally introducing appropriate operators and predicates.

In IMC/IMCL, the structure of a single construct is solely given by its composition. Structure, in a wider sense, also refers to the variety of objects that may occur in a given context (i.e., a type). This is handled in IMC/IMCL by use of predicates with the expressiveness of the first-order calculus on the basis of explicitly given operators and predicates.

Specification of an admissible variety is sometimes done on a lower level of composition than is actually affected, because the underlying data model is too specific for dealing with constructs on the appropriate level. In the relational model, for example, *constraints* are made responsible for referential integrity. These constraints address lower level components (relations), though they restrict a higher level construct only (the database) that contains the addressed components. In contrast, IMCL allows one to deal with compositional properties of any size and complexity, and hence provides a means to address the affected construct at the correct level.

Sometimes, structure resulting from constraints is sharply distinguished from structure obtained by composition only. The distinction between structure and constraint may even be taken as fundamental ([AbHu87], [HuKi87]). In IMC/IMCL, no such distinction is made. The structure of a construct (or, more typically, a class of constructs) may be specified by composition or by constraining a given class to those constructs satisfying a given condition. It is a matter of convenience rather than of principle how they are combined.

Closely related to the issue of constraints for the generation of structure is that of "more semantics", also often referred to as "semantic constraints". Lack of expressive power in structurally more specialized approaches fostered a call for "data semantics" in the sense of providing richer data structuring capabilities [Codd79], which finally led to semantic data modeling as a research activity in its own right [HuKi87]. Typically, its data structuring principles are non-compositional, though the additional structure could well be expressed as a compositional constraint on a comprising construct, for example, the entire database. Thus, the same structure is easily expressible in the IMC/IMCL-framework. Recently, the call for more semantics was reinforced in the context of database interoperability. "Dramatic progress on semantic issues" is called for in [SiStUl91]. Such progress can certainly not be based on a proliferation of add-ons to existing data models but must reconsider the principal frame for further development. IMC/IMCL could serve as an input to such a debate.

Types and instances

In information systems design, types are of more concern than individual objects. Not surprisingly, most data models focus primarily on types. With respect to the conceptual setup, however, it seems preferable to define a universe of objects before types are considered at all, rather than to start with types without knowing exactly the objects to which they may apply. This is particularly true for compositional models. If composition is considered on the type level, it is not always clear what composition of types means and how it is related to the composition of individual objects.

IMC/IMCL first defines the universe (called "universe of entities"). Subsequently, predicates can be used for the definition of types. In contrast, the *declaration* of types is not dealt with, but is considered to pertain to the system environment in which IMC/IMCL is used. Although an outline is given of how types in a system can be seen (Appendix A, Sec. A.3.1), it is not an issue of IMC/IMCL proper.

Composition of new types from given ones may be envisaged as resulting from the application of type operators (as with E/R-diagrams and other graphical languages, also as in [LeRi89]), or as the generation of instances from instances of the given types. The latter means that the instances of the new type are produced by composing instances of the constituent types, as illustrated by the diagram in Fig. 4.2. In this case, the transition from constituent types to the composite type is achieved by taking all instances of the constituent types, forming composite objects from them and defining these to be the instances of the new type.

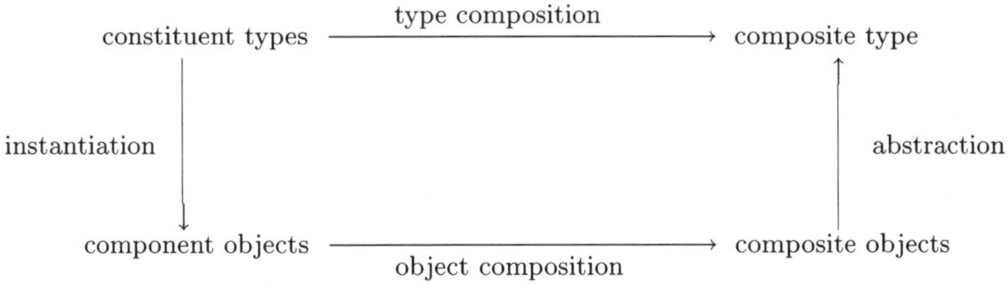

Figure 4.2 : Type composition based on object composition

With IMCL, the definition of new types from existing ones amounts to defining new predicates from predicates already available. For this, the general mechanisms of predicate logic may be used in conjunction with IMC-specific operators and predicates, in particular with composition operators, so that there is no need for a sharp distinction between the two ways of type composition. In the type language described in Appendix A, Sec. A.3.1, which is derived from IMC box notation, only particular kinds of instance composition can be depicted.

Spots

Spots are a unique feature of IMC. No other approach provides spots as a general and explicit concept, although the idea is sometimes present implicitly and for specialized application. Most naturally it is invoked in navigational database systems. For example, the DBTG currency indicator can be explained as a spotset-valued variable [Durc75]. Recently, in the context of object-oriented databases, a revival of navigation and access paths can be observed—even in a relational setting [Lori91]: in any database state, the unique object identifiers essentially represent those spots on which continuance (see Sec. A.2.3), and thus object persistence, is defined. From an IMC point of view, an object (in the sense of object-oriented databases) turns out to be a location, i.e., a trajectory of spots with the same object identifier through a series of database states.

A data model with a particular structure may provide means of identifying and handling selected spots. Thus, in the DBTG model, a database key is used to force a unique name for identifying all record spots of the database. In a relational database, the name of a relation and a key value identify a row spot. If in addition an attribute name is given, a spot for a field in a row is identified. VDL admits nominations as the only composition principle. Therefore, a spot can be identified by a fully qualified name. In VDM, there are no operators on spots, although specification of dynamic constraints and an emphasis on functional representation are clearly objectives of VDM. In [KhFrCa90] special spot selection terms ("paths") are provided which allow one to step inwards from a database root using key values (for selecting a component in a set object) and attribute names (for selecting a component in a tuple object).

Information structure and processes

In several approaches, information structure and process structure are more or less intertwined. VDM, for example, was designed as a conceptual and linguistic frame mainly for specifying sequential software architecture and hence is slanted towards procedural description of construct manipulation. Also, SETL relies heavily on procedural facilities. For object-oriented approaches, binding information to processes is a constituent idea.

In contrast, IMC/IMCL is made solely for information object description and consequently leaves out any aspects of processing, thus attempting a clean conceptual separation of concerns. This way, no bias is introduced as to whether processes have to be sequential, parallel, or concurrent. In fact, the authors regard IMC constructs an adequate choice for representing objects in concurrent systems (e.g., individual tokens in high-level Petri nets) when real-life applications are modelled, but there is no attempt to tie process concepts to IMC/IMCL, though a link between these worlds can readily be established (see also Appendix A).

Language, notation

Considerable effort has been spent on the concrete syntax of IMCL to make it obvious and consistent, and also to make it harmonize with the graphical languages that have been defined earlier. The graphical languages have a precise meaning and are sufficiently expressive to describe any individual construct and spot. From one of them, the box notation, a graphical language suitable for describing simple compositional properties of types has been derived. However, to develop this notation further to meet general requirements of applications would easily overload the symbolism and still never reach the expressiveness of IMCL.

IMCL's notation is not singular. Other approaches propose similar notation for object composition. However, no general consent has developed on how to write compositional expressions. Thus, there did not seem to be a strong argument for seeking compliance with other notation at the expense of compromises in the language itself. For instance, SETL and VDM use different kinds of parentheses to distinguish between different generic construct types. As parentheses don't appear in the graphical languages for IMC, it was preferable for IMCL to express the distinction by characteristic composition symbols ("→" and ":"), rather than by different parentheses. As another example, we wanted to use the arrow for catenations to convey the idea of direction. Therefore, the arrow could not be used for functional association (nominations, maps) as is done in VDM and [Jone80]. In more recent work ([BaKh86], [LeRi89], [KhFrCa90]), nominations (in specific use) are written almost exactly as in IMCL ([*name* : *object*, ...]).

Application as design language and meta-language

IMC was originally intended for discussing data structures, not for data structure design. Thus, it could be seen as a meta-language. As it turned out, however, it was also well suited to design applications. In this respect, it underwent a typical pragmatic metamorphosis also found in other conceptual systems (e.g., CDL, VDM, ML).

In the past, there was only relatively little interest in general conceptual systems for data model description. More recently, some attention was given to the issue in the context of relational systems ([BiDePaTh88], [DeTh89], and [Kane90] with a comprehensive bibliography), of the ER-approach ([Hain89], [Hohe90]) and of semantic data models ([AbHu87], [HuKi87], [PeMa88]). Thus, IMC/IMCL was more likely to be used in information structure design applications than in data model analysis. Some such applications have been mentioned above under *General outline of IMC/IMCL development*.

Outlook

The conceptual frame of IMC is considered by the authors to be completed. The language IMCL is, like any practical language, a compromise between conflicting goals such as conciseness, orthogonality, learnability, ease of writing and readability. It would therefore be hardly surprising if extensive use brought up new requirements and requests for practical improvements. In addition, IMCL is certainly not the only possible language for IMC. For particular applications it could be appropriate to develop specific alternatives. There may be more or less trivial syntactic variants, user group jargons and even augmentations of the expressive power, as well as entirely different IMC languages. The diagram in Fig. 4.3 shows the relations of such languages to one another and with respect to IMC. The lines indicate "... provides basis for ..." in top-down direction.

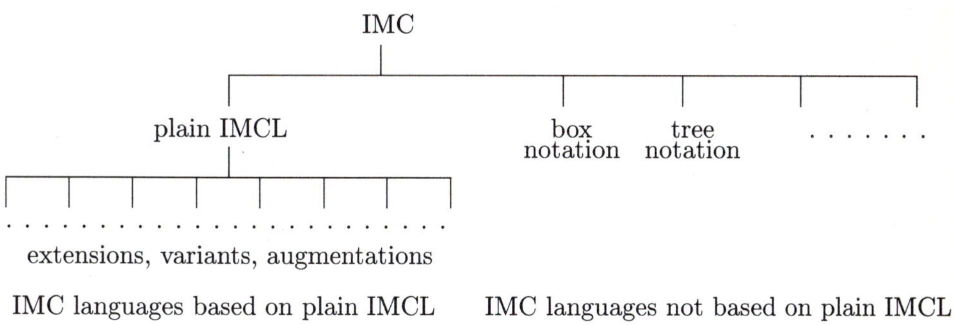

Figure 4.3: Relations between IMC languages

At first, IMCL was thought of as a language for human communication. However, to become fully effective as a specification language, it needs software support. Certainly, an implementation of IMCL would promote the idea of the general compositional information structure paradigm.

An implementation may be of two different kinds: (i) IMCL as a *sublanguage* in some information processing system, where a compiler or interpreter uses executable code to deal with IMC objects; (ii) an information modelling *environment* that interactively helps in handling IMCL language expressions, in particular in editing IMCL specifications, translating between graphical and textual language, transforming expressions, finding and verifying equality proofs, and checking whether a given construct is of a given type (satisfies a given predicate).

Implementation in the sense of (i) is impossible for full IMCL and will hardly be feasible with tolerable efficiency for a comprehensive subset, reduced only in predicate logic expressiveness. IMCL sublanguages, however, could well be implemented. Of course, finding an appropriate sublanguage for a specific application can be a nontrivial task.

An implementation in the sense of (ii) is indispensable for an efficient and secure treatment of IMCL expressions. It is also not a matter of all or nothing. There are many sensible levels of support that can be provided for the information structure designer, at the low end starting from interactive layout editing, proceeding to syntactic correctness checkers and transformation verifiers, and extending up to semi-automatic proof-finders at the high end. First steps towards software support in this sense have been made in the context of ODA development, as has been mentioned above under *General outline of IMC/IMCL development*.

Further work should also be done on theoretical aspects of IMC/IMCL. A formal calculus for the transformation of expressions would be desirable as a prerequisite for using computer-algebra based support tools. For this, a basis of elementary operations and predicates must be sifted out and formal definitions must be provided for all other operators and predicates.

Appendix A

Constructs and spots in systems

The main purpose of this manual is to present IMC and the language IMCL. However, in any application environment, additional concepts like "interface", "change" and "object identity" turn up, the relations of which to IMC must be established. This appendix introduces a few pertinent basic concepts and offers an outlook of how they can be handled in conjunction with IMC concepts.

A.1 Information objects at interfaces

Information structure modelling becomes operational in the context of information exchange. This involves two kinds of functional units: **agencies** which exchange information and **channels** through which information is exchanged. It also involves the concept of **interface**, which we take as all channels surrounding any one agency together with the totality of rules which govern information exchange through these channels. When we say (**information**) **system**, we mean a system of agencies and channels together with its interfaces.

Information structure considerations can be conducted in their own right. They are not necessarily tied to system concepts. IMC, as presented in this manual, does not deal with systems. However, when IMC is applied in a system design context, information structure description must be linked to system structure description. This entails inclusion of dynamic aspects. Beyond the mere structure of information objects, their use and effect within the system must be made explicit. A system model is required iwhich allows one to study or specify in an abstract (preferably mathematical) way system behavior in terms of information exchange.

In this appendix, we use Petri nets for talking about systems. We will explain concepts of net theory as far as they are needed, but we will rely on a more intuitive understanding, rather then giving a rigorous formal treatment. A detailed introduction into net theory can be found in [Reis85].

A key aspect of net theory is the distinction between **passive** and **active** system components. Consider a system where three agencies (active components) communicate via a central channel (passive component). Think, for example, of persons as agencies and of a mail system or a database as the channel. Fig. A.1 shows a net diagram which represents such a model: round symbols denote channels, rectangular symbols denote agencies. The arrows indicate which agencies act on which channels. Each channel is capable of assuming **local states**. A local state is modelled by **marking** the channel with entities of a given universe of information objects.

Fig. A.1 shows a very coarse model of an information system. The construct in channel `CurrentCon` (small rectangle) stands for an information object that is accessed by the three agencies called $\mathtt{AU}_i$ (access units). In this context, "access" is intended to mean seizing the construct for exclusive use and subsequently releasing it either in its original form or after some modification. Shared use is not considered in this model.

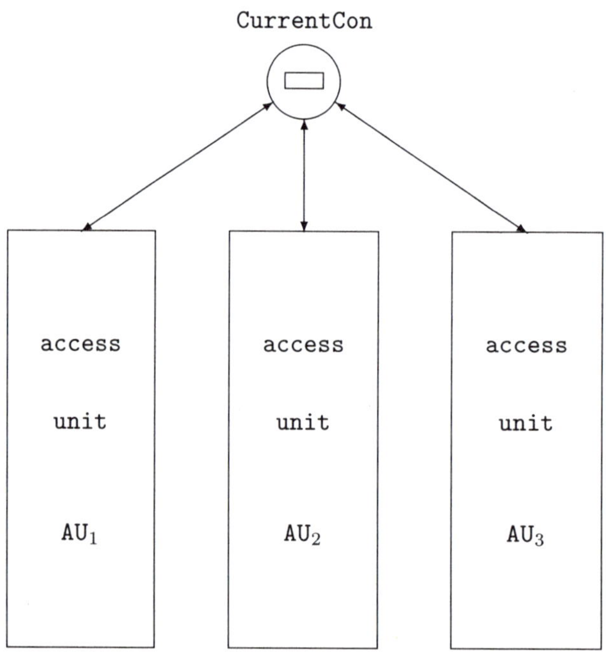

Figure A.1 : Petri net with one channel and three agencies

Where the communication interface is implemented on a computer, for instance as a centralized database, access to this interface is mediated by a software system. Fig. A.2 shows a model which results from refining each access unit into a user agency $\mathtt{U}_i$, a software agency $\mathtt{S}_i$ and a channel $\mathtt{I}_i$. The channels $\mathtt{I}_i$ together can be considered part of a distributed interaction interface `DI` (distributed interface) of an agency `CS` (computer system) composed of $\mathtt{S}_1$, $\mathtt{S}_2$ and $\mathtt{S}_3$, and having `CurrentCon` as an internal channel, i.e., a memory. The dashed lines in the figure relate the refined agencies to the former unrefined model. The dotted lines indicate coarsening by looking at `DI` as a single channel and `CS` as a single agency. Thus we have two different coarse models with a common refinement. (The common refinement is given by the diagram without the dotted and dashed lines.)

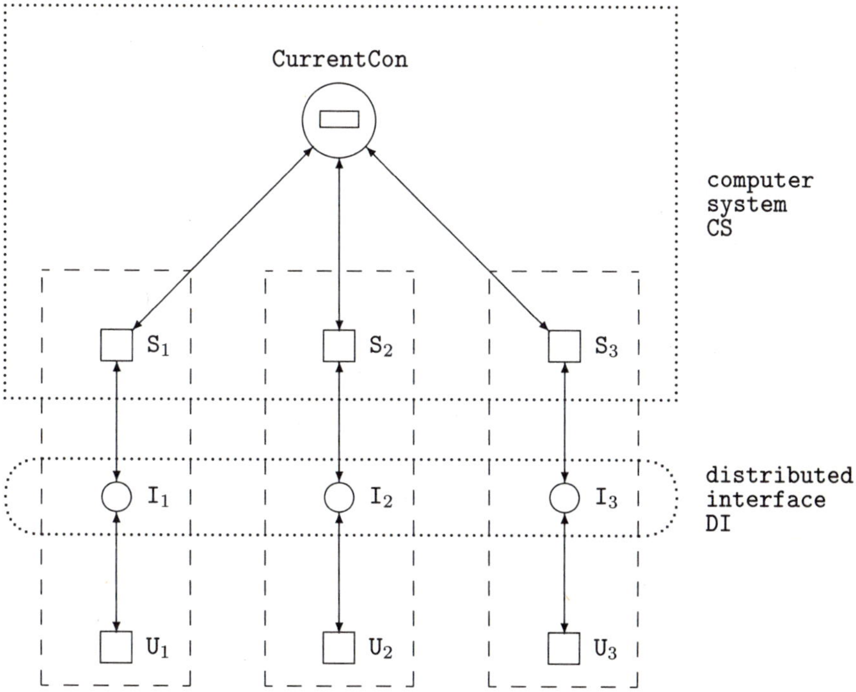

Figure A.2 : Two coarse models with a common refinement

Even the refined model is still coarse, because it is not specific about the kind of information exchange. In the proposed interpretation, it would be natural to assume for example that $\mathtt{U}_i$ causes an instruction to appear in $\mathtt{I}_i$, and that $\mathtt{S}_i$ models the transformation of the construct in `CurrentCon` according to this instruction and the return of a response in $\mathtt{I}_i$ indicating the end of the transaction. Ultimately we want an exact specification as to how the passive and active components represent states and changes-of-state.

Before we proceed from the overall model to more detailed ones, it is advisable to introduce *folding* for a more convenient and concise rendition of repeated substructures. In the above figure, there are three almost identical copies of access units. Such replication seems quite acceptable in a simple case, but it becomes a nuisance or even unmanageable when the substructures become sophisticated or copious. We can imagine all access units to be shuffled into one pile, where the topmost one is taken as a representative of all of them, properly parametrized. This leads to Fig. A.3.

In the folded representation, the index i, which distinguishes the units in one overlay pile, would reappear in a detail description of the interworkings of the units.

Note that folding is a representational gadget that *does not change* the model, as opposed to the coarsening we exerted above on the refined model by introducing channel `DI` and agency `CS`.

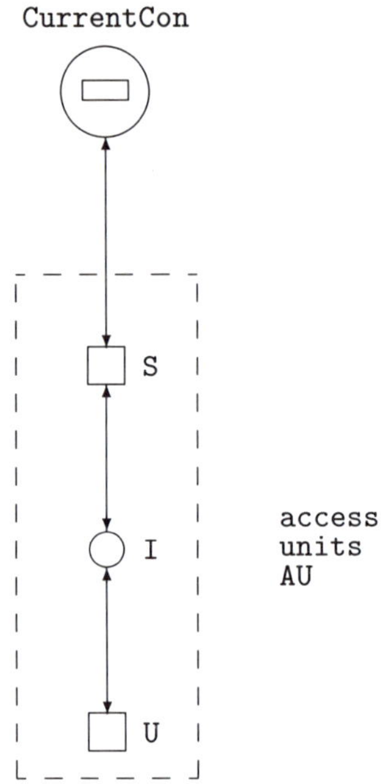

Figure A.3: Folded net diagram

Now we return to the issue of achieving detailed and exact models of information object handling. For this, we need more formal concepts and representational means for expressing the essence while abstracting from irrelevant detail, and doing this with sufficient precision. To this end, a new interpretation of the active and passive components of a net is used. Instead of a channel, we now consider its *state* only. That is, passive components are interpreted as representing local states. A local state is envisaged as the extension of a time-varying **predicate**: the predicate *holds* for exactly those objects that are in the current extension. Thus, channels are abstracted into (variable) predicates. Likewise, instead of agencies we consider their effects on the states of adjacent channels only, that is, the changes of predicate extensions. This abstraction of an agency is called a **transition**. Moreover, a transition is required to be *atomic* in the sense that no intermediate states are visible in the model chosen. Complex changes must be built from atomic ones. Thus, in general, an agency gives rise to several transitions together with new predicates (in addition to those representing channel states). A transition is specified by a **transition formula**, which is a truth-valued expression the free variables of which are associated with the arrows attached to the transition. These variables are local to the transition. A transition is **enabled** for given objects in the extensions of adjacent predicates, if the transition formula becomes true when these objects are assigned to the respective variables.

Nets of predicates and transitions are called PrT-nets. They have been introduced in [GeLa81]. Rules for PrT-nets will be introduced in an informal manner when and as far as they are needed.

The folded channel/agency-net above needs only slight modification to be interpretable as a PrT-net. The most prominent change is the distinction between directions and—as a consequence—the refinement into pairs of components (Fig. A.4).

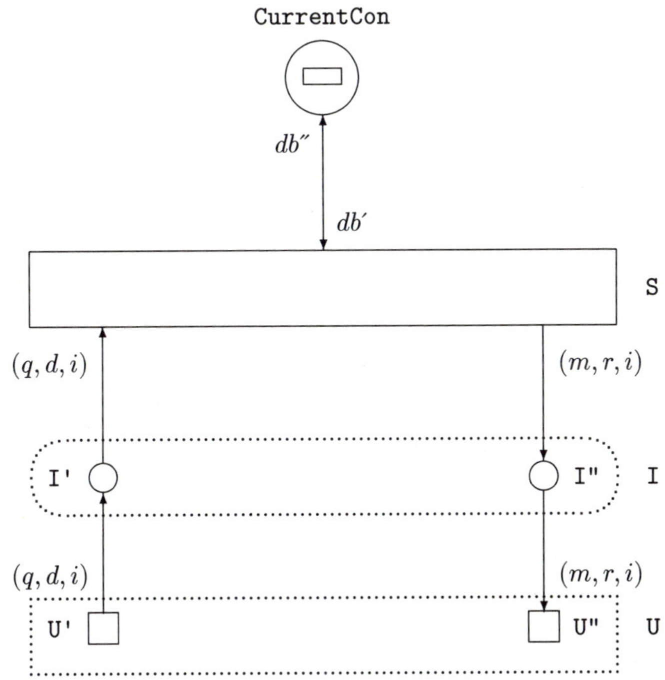

Figure A.4: PrT-net for one database and several access units

The diagram is interpreted as follows: occurrence of U′ means that an instruction to the database system is issued by some U_i. The instruction (q, d, i) is included in the extension of I′, where q stands for the requested service, d for data supplied as parameters to that service, and i for an identification of access unit U_i. After this, software agency S (the database management system) may act upon the instruction, thereby using the old database (variable db') and replacing it by a new version (variable db'').* S also generates in I″ a response (m, r, i), which echoes the access unit identifier i and consists otherwise of a response text m and a result r. Occurrence of U″ means that ultimately U_i absorbs the response (m, r, i) from I″.

* For a formal reason not relevant to the current discussion, we assume that any access to the database, that is, inclusive of rejected requests and pure queries, effects a change in the database. The change can be quite tiny, as incrementing an access counter.

As a further means of expression from net theory, **state assertions** are subsequently used to exclude specified local states. In net theory, they are called "facts" or "dead transitions". They are "dead" in the sense that they are required to be never enabled. In other words, in no case may the predicates adjacent to a dead transition have extensions such that the transition is enabled. This simply means that there is no marking admissible or possible for which the transition formula evaluates to true. In net diagrams, state assertions are distinguished by special rectangular symbols. As an example, think of two predicates on numbers, `High` and `Low`. Each number in `Low` is required to be less than each number in `High`, i.e., we want to exclude states where the extension of `High` contains a number which is less than or equal to a number in `Low` (Fig. A.5).

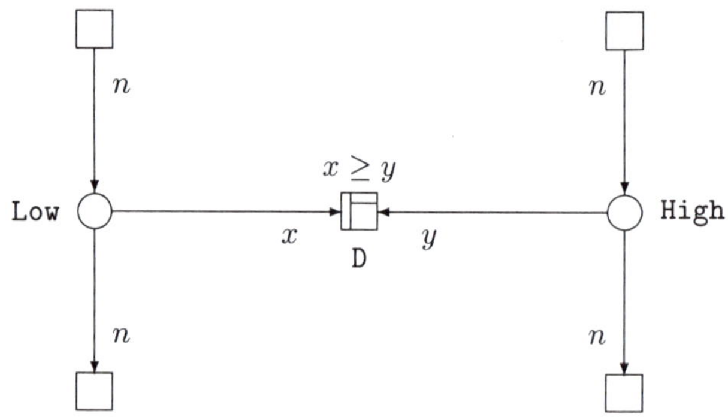

Figure A.5 : PrT-net with a dead transition

If there were a number x in `Low` and a number y in `High` such that $x \geq y$, the dead transition `D` would be enabled for those two numbers.

The curious thing about state assertions is that the transition formula expresses what is *not* wanted. Hence its negation specifies what is required. The reason for this is that the asserted property is an invariant of the system. As a transition cannot invariably (continuously) occur, an invariant can only be expressed by a transition that continuously does *not* occur. Hence the negation of the asserted property. To facilitate inspection of dead transition formulae, they better start with a negation symbol. By ignoring the negation symbol, one sees directly what is required. Thus, in the above example, $\neg(x<y)$ would reveal the intention more evidently.

A.2 Handling information objects at interfaces

A.2.1 Labelling spotsets

The purpose of introducing spots was to have a conceptual means for "pointing" to parts of a (large) construct (see also Sec. 2.3.1). To be able to refer to selected spots, spotset-valued variables can be used. We call such variables "labels". The spots in a label value can be thought of as being flagged with the label. The same spot may be flagged by several labels.

There are various occasions where one wants to refer to a previously selected spotset. Two important and well-known ones are navigation and locking. *Navigation* is used in network database systems, where labels are called *currency indicators*. In a navigation oriented database setting, specialized labels play a prominent role. They are restricted to spotsets the spots of which lead to constructs of a certain kind (for example, records of a given type). Such labels can be "moved" over the database to pinpoint the current component in a particular process (as, for example, the "current of run unit" in a network data manipulation language). For *locking*, spotsets are identified to evaluate access claims and to inherit access rights to subsequent versions of the (possibly modified) database. In this context, labels (together with associated claims and rights) are called *locks*.

Label is an undefined concept, as is "name". Thus, arbitrary things can be chosen for labels. In particular, it may be convenient at times to use names or constructs for labels. However, the same warning applies as for names (see Sec. 2.1.2.4).

A label may change its value. A **labelling** is a (time-varying) function which maps labels onto spotsets. Restrictions on labellings may be appropriate in a specific context, depending on the purpose of their use. In a database application, for example, one will probably require that all spots of all label values of a labelling are in one overall construct, the database. Thus it would be natural in this case to require that all spots of a labelling have a common rootspot.

At any one time, there is a **current labelling** for a construct under consideration at a given interface, which may change implicitly or by explicit instructions. To avoid undefined values, the labelling assigns a spotset to each label. As a default value, the assigned spotset is empty. Because processes are considered to start with finitely many nonempty label values (in fact, the initial value of *all* labels will normally be taken to be empty), only finitely many labels will have nonempty values. A label is said to **cover** a spot, if the spot is in the assigned set.

An interface for handling labellings can be modelled by a net comprising a predicate `CurrentCon` for the current reference construct, and a predicate `CurrentLab` representing the current labelling. Part of such a net is given in Fig. A.6.

Predicate `CurrentLab` means "is the current labelling". The predicates `CurrentCon` and `CurrentLab` are linked by a state assertion which says that the object *lg* from `CurrentLab` must be a labelling the spots of which all have the construct *g* from `CurrentCon` as their common reference construct.

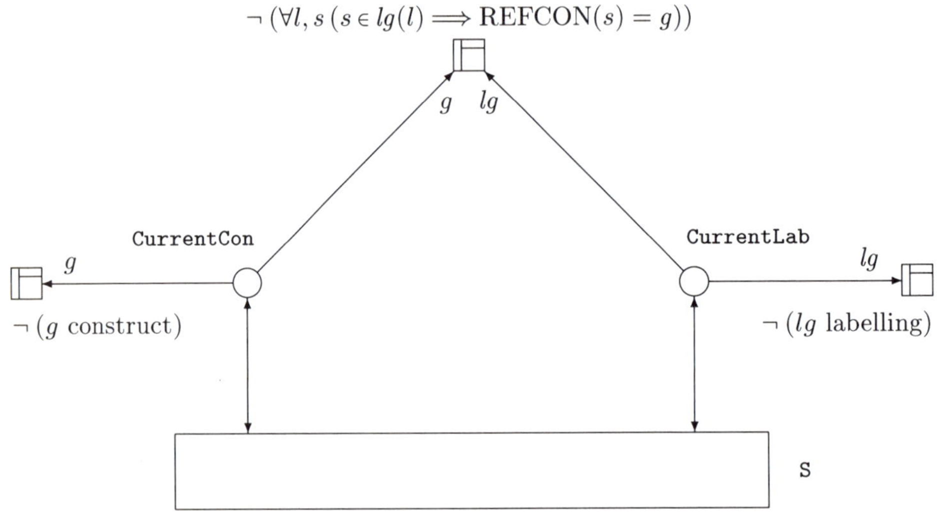

Figure A.6 : Dead transition for specifying labelling integrity

If a construct at an interface, say, a database, is changed, a problem of identity arises for spots. This question is pursued in Sec. A.2.3.

An IMC language which supports the use of labels would allow one to manipulate labels, to test whether a spot is covered by a label, and to use labels for spot selection. IMCL is not designed for dealing with labels.

A.2.2 Changing constructs

The notion of change not only involves operators performing transformations, but also the idea of the trajectory of an object considered to be the "same" in some sense through all evolutions within its given environment. Reference to the environment is essential for defining identity of a changing object, in recent literature also referred to as "persistence" of an object. We take the referential environment to be a *system* as introduced earlier.

In what follows we look at systems which are variations of the one modelled in Fig. A.4. To be definite in the examples, the case of a database is assumed, but the considerations are not restricted to databases.

In the first example, we ignore user interaction and let software agencies act all by themselves. Assume that the database is a collection of numbers and that the software is designed to discard all odd numbers. This is modelled by the net in Fig. A.7.

Note that the transformations effected by transition S are described by a formula rather than in procedural terms. The formula expresses the relationship between the (old) construct db' and the (new) construct db''. Thus, the values of the free variables db' and db'' are the constructs which will appear or disappear in the extension of the adjacent predicate `CurrentCon` when the transition occurs. The variables are local to the transition. For example, if the current object is the collection {3,2,5,8}, `S` is enabled with values

$$db' = \{3,2,5,8\}$$
$$db'' = \{2,8\}$$

In this example, the transition formula uniquely determines the value of db'' (new `CurrentCon`) from any given db' (old `CurrentCon`). Uniqueness is, however, not required. If, for example, a different transition formula

$$\exists n(db'{=}db''\cup\{n\})$$

is specified for `S`, an arbitrary set element is discarded from `CurrentCon`. This allows both {2} and {8} as values of db'' if db'={2,8}. The actual value is not determined.

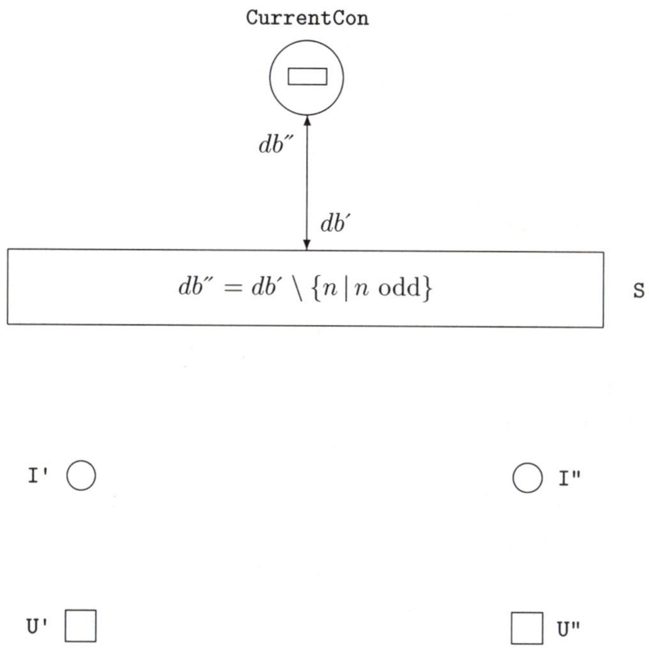

Figure A.7: Discarding all odd numbers from a collection of numbers

We extend the example by admitting *instructions from* and *responses to* the user. This could make the transition formula of `S` quite complex, because it has to take an entire instruction as a parameter, i.e., to include an interpreter capability for a command language. In the present context, we deal with this on an abstract level only, since we are interested in the dynamic aspects of a system, rather than in the details of construct transformation or instruction execution. We assume that we have a constant predicate exec(q, d, db', m, r, db'') available which says that request q with data d applied to the database db' may yield database db'' and response text m to the user together with result data r ("*may* yield" expresses that db'', r and m need not be functionally dependent on db', q and d). Of course, the entire operational power of the database software is conceptually crammed into this predicate. In Fig. A.8, the previous diagram (Fig. A.7) is modified to include user interaction.

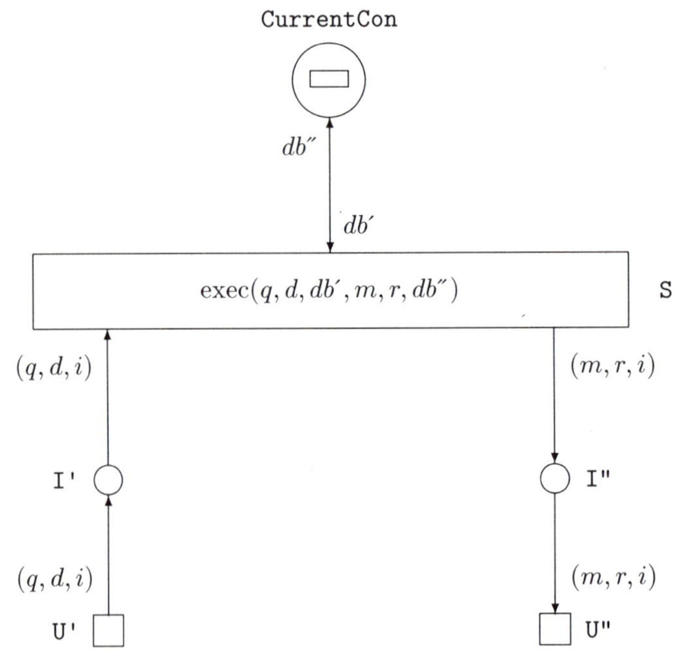

Figure A.8: General net model with instructions from and responses to the user

If, for example, q_0 is a request to increase each number in the database by the number given as the second parameter d of the instruction, then an exec for which

$$\text{exec}(q_0, d, c, \texttt{"number of updated items:"}, |c|, \{x+d \mid x \in c\})$$

holds for any number d and any collection of numbers c would lead to a proper response. Thus, a database $db'=\{2,8\}$ and an instruction $(q_0, 3, i)$ issued by user i would result in $db''=\{5,11\}$ as the new database and $(m, r, i)=(\texttt{"number of updated items:"}, 2, i)$ as response.

A.2.3 Continuing spots in a changing construct

Labels have been introduced as a means for remembering spotsets. However, a label value does not survive the tiniest change of the reference construct since, by definition, the changed construct ceases to be the reference construct of the original spots. At first sight, this might appear a minor technical slip, easy to correct, but it has quite profound aspects for object identity.

What we want is a way to say "this spot in the changed construct is the *same* as that spot in the previous construct". As just pointed out, we cannot literally say "same spot". Instead, we will say that spots in the old construct are **continued to** spots in the new construct.* The rest of this section explores the intuitive notion of **continuance** and seeks a formal counterpart.

For illustration, think of the example in Fig. A.9. It shows a construct with a spot marked by a triangle. The spot is formally represented by $s=(q,g)$, where

$q = (f_1,f_2)$
$f_1(SMALL)=\{2,11\}$, $f_1(BIG)=@$ (f_1 undefined otherwise)
$f_2 = \{12,26,@\}$
$g = 11$

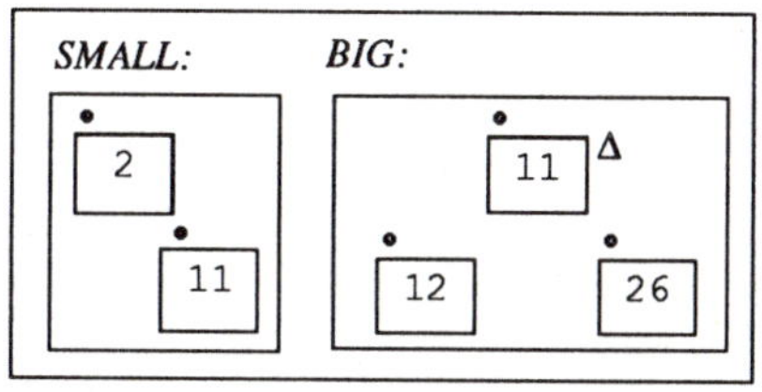

Figure A.9: A spot before construct modification

Now assume that the smaller collection is modified by inserting 15 as a further immediate component. This would result in the construct shown in Fig. A.10.

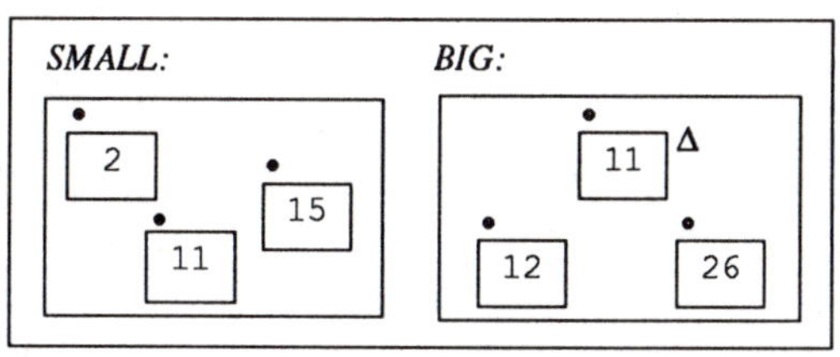

Figure A.10: A different spot after construct modification

The triangle in this figure indicates the spot which—we would intuitively say—is "s continued". Formally, the spot is represented by $s'=(q',g)$, where now

$q' = (f_1',f_2)$
$f_1'(SMALL)=\{2,11,15\}$, $f_1'(BIG)=@$ (f_1' undefined otherwise)
$f_2 = \{12,26,@\}$
$g = 11$

Intuitively, the atom 11 in the construct named *BIG* is not considered to have changed its "location" by this insertion, although it is surely no longer at the same

* The idea of continuance also turns up in [Vian87], restricted to the special case of relation tuples. Note that there a tuple spot is uniquely identified by the tuple, so that it is sufficient to talk about tuples instead of spots.

spot.

The problem of formally defining continuance would be solved if a *general* relation could be established which, given an "old" and a "new" construct, matches each spot in the old construct with its counterpart in the new construct, if possible. Fig. A.11 shows an obvious example.

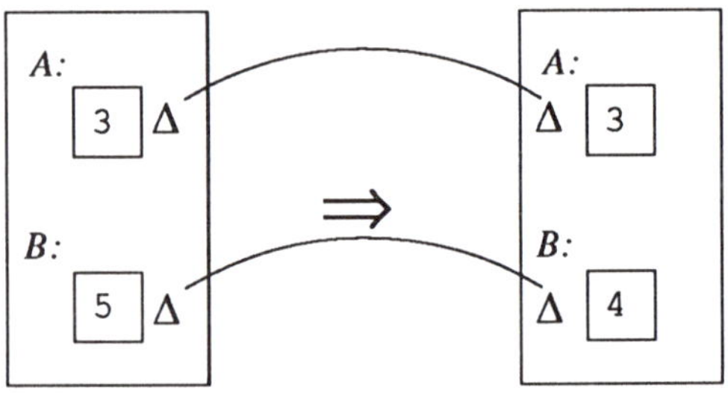

Figure A.11 : "Obvious" continuance

Unfortunately this does not work in general, because the intuitive idea of continuance depends on a wider context than just the before- and the after-state. This is demonstrated by the example in Fig. A.12, for which it is unclear, whether names have been exchanged or the components have been modified. In the first case, the continuance would be as in Fig. A.13, whereas in the second case it would be as in Fig. A.14

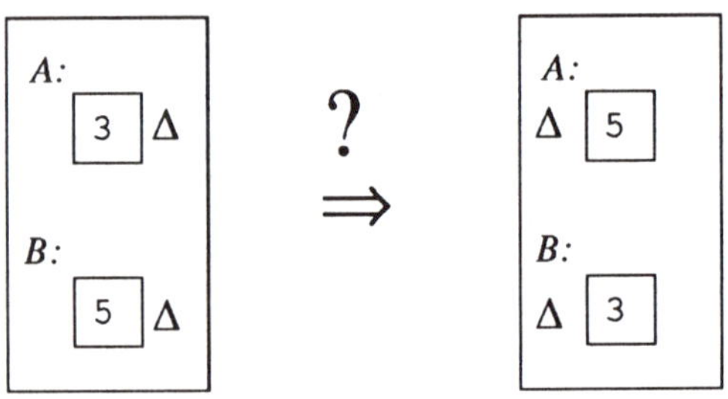

Figure A.12 : Unclear continuance

One can find many more examples, and also more sophisticated ones, to show that continuance cannot solely be based on a comparison of the constructs before and after the change. Rather, it needs additional information that has to be considered an integral part of the change request. For most kinds of change requests, this additional information is implicitly given. For example, a request to interchange names will normally be understood as continuing a spot onto an equal component under the new name. Similarly, a request to change components of a nomination will be expected to establish continuance between components with equal names. In principle, any language dealing conceptually with spots must semantically provide information on how spots are continued.

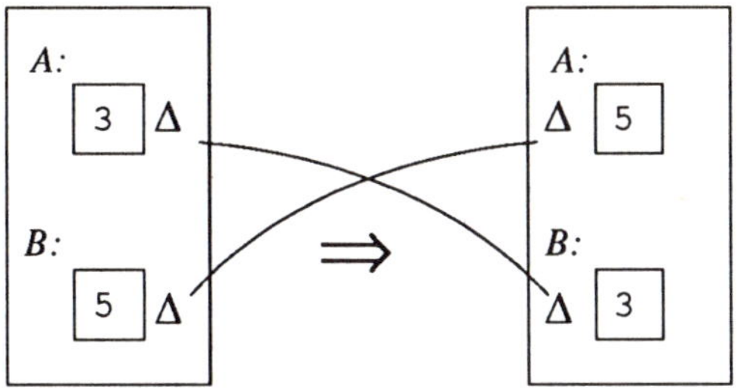

Figure A.13: Continuance by components

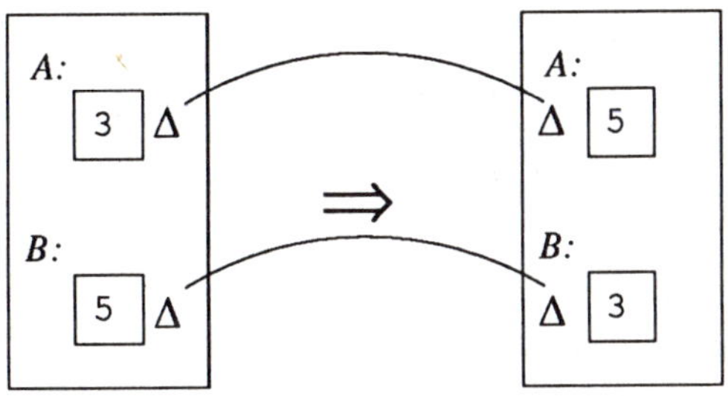

Figure A.14: Continuance by names

The relational data model provides a well-known example of a continuance that is established between user and system by declaring a primary key for tuple spots. Relational tuples are unnamed components of unordered relational tables. When a tuple is updated, the spot of the tuple in the old relation is continued to the spot of the tuple with the same primary key in the new relation. For this reason, primary keys cannot be updated.

It should be clear by now that continuance is not just between *spots*, but between *spots in a sequence of constructs* within a given context. Such a sequence is illustrated in Fig. A.15.

The topmost triangles stand for the ownspots of the constructs next to which they are drawn. In the lower part of the diagram the triangles are flagged with component information to make clear which spots they represent in the construct above. The dotted lines indicate some given continuance. The interesting point in this figure is that, although t_1 and t_4 are the same spot, they are considered as spots in different members of the sequence.

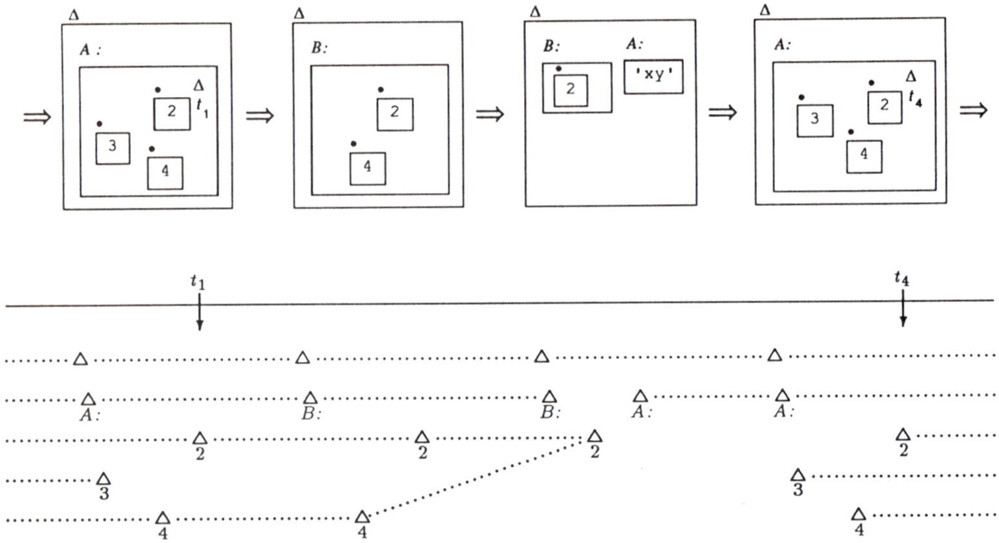

Figure A.15: Continuance in a sequence of constructs

To talk formally about continuance, a reference to the sequence must conceptually be made manifest. For ease of discussion, we make the simplifying assumption that the sequence is defined by a special component of each reference construct. Thus the considered reference constructs are "time-stamped" in a way. This implies in particular, that the reference constructs of any two considered spots are either equal or that one is "earlier" than the other. Fig. A.16 shows a time-stamped version of the above example.

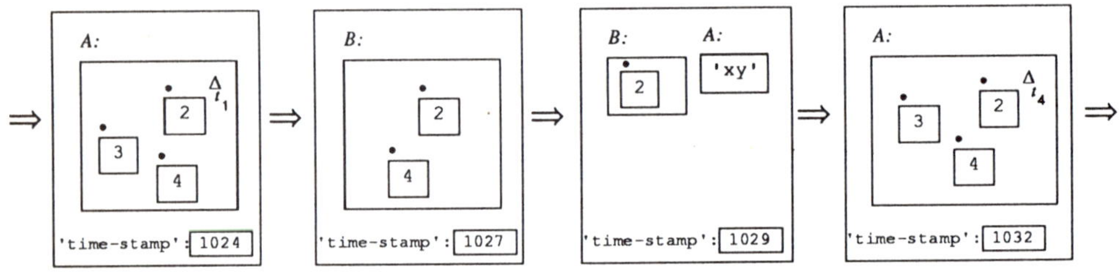

Figure A.16: Sequence of constructs induced by time-stamps

Up to now, continuance was understood as *immediate* continuance. However, more interesting is its transitive closure. It is more natural to pursue identity through an arbitrary number of steps, particularly if intermediate changes are not relevant for the considered spot. Also, this avoids the difficulties typical for "next"-semantics when refinement and abstraction are dealt with. (In addition, if transitive continuance is taken as the primary concept, the assumption of a "next" construct can be abandoned. A more general order structure (dense order) can be admitted for the development of a construct. This is, however, not further pursued here.)

We approach the initial question of object identity by defining a formal counterpart to the intuitive idea of "sameness" of a spot in a changing construct: a **location** is defined as a maximal set of spots any two of which are in the continuance relation one way or the other. In mathematical terms, a location is a *chain* in the partial order of continuance. It is now sensible to say, for instance, that a label remains at the "same location" when changes occur somewhere else in the construct. It is also sensible to say that two different spots "belong to the same location". However, since continuance may fork and join (see the above example), a spot may, in general, belong to several locations. Note also that a location may appear and disappear in the sequence. The same location may, however, not reappear.

To describe continuance it is helpful to have a number of prefabricated relations available, which represent ideas of "natural" continuance for various cases, and which can be customized for application to specific manipulation instructions. Such relations are called **affinities**. Some obvious affinities are:

component affinity	relating spots with equal components,
name affinity	relating spots with equal names,
front-part affinity	relating spots which lead to catenation members at the end of maximal identical front parts,
reduction affinity	relating spots on different compositional levels in a "natural" way.

Other affinities can be devised if convenient for a given purpose. In a relational setting, for example, tuple continuance based on primary keys and value continuance based on name affinity would be an obvious choice.

A.3 Constraints at interfaces

To be able to make assertions about a system's behavior, communication across its interfaces must adhere to explicitly stated rules. Some of the rules impose restrictions on the information objects exchanged and the order in which they are allowed to appear. Such restrictions are known as *constraints* [Grie82], in particular within the world of databases (see, for example, the discussion of "integrity constraints" in [Date90]).

Static constraints reduce the variety of states a particular channel may assume, for example, the entities which may occur in a database. *Dynamic constraints* reduce the variety of changes-of-state of a channel, for example, the transformations a database may undergo.

The notion of constraint is inextricably tied to the notion of interface. A constraint is established as a convention between communicating functional units and applies to their common interface. Thus, it relates to a particular communication situation [Durc77].

In the literature and in practical use words like *constraint*, *rule*, *type*, *law*, etc. are used in closely related ways, sometimes interchangeably, but frequently with more or less subtle variations in meaning. There is no commonly accepted agreement on the use of these words. In this section, a specific terminology is suggested.

A.3.1 Static constraints

A **static constraint** says which information objects are admissible in a given context. In our present conceptual setup we rather say: "which constructs are admissible in a given channel" or "for which constructs a given (variable) predicate may hold". All constructs which satisfy some static constraint form a set which can be seen as the extension of a (constant) unary predicate on entities of a given universe. In database parlance, the set as well as the predicate are usually called a *type*, each element of which is called an *instance* or *occurrence* of the type. Although a constraint is inherently tied to an interface, the sets or the predicates used in the constraint have an existence of their own. To account for this, a **type** is here taken as a set or a predicate defined *for the purpose of being used in a constraint.* Thus, the same type may be used in constraints for several interfaces. (If one wants to be very explicit, one can say a (static) type is a set or predicate handled in a meta-system in which constraints for an object-system are negotiated.)

Here, we have distinguished constant and variable predicates (i.e., predicates with constant and variable extensions). It is important to note that constant predicates play a quite different role in system description than variable ones. A constant predicate is one in the general sense of predicate logic. It is not specific to and can be defined independent of any particular system. In contrast, a variable predicate describes a time-varying local state in a system. It makes sense only as part of a particular system.

For illustration of the notions of *type* and *constraint*, imagine a static constraint which permits only triples of one even and two odd numbers to appear in a channel of a considered interface. Fig. A.17 shows a section of a system where the channel represents a predicate `CurrentTriple`. The type predicates even and odd are assumed to be defined elsewhere. The state assertion specifies that only constructs of the required type appear in the extension of `CurrentTriple`.

The state assertion could be simplified by explicitly introducing a type predicate limpingtriple predefined by the formula

$\forall p$ (p limpingtriple $\Longleftrightarrow$

$\quad \exists x,y,z$ ($p=(x,y,z)$ $\wedge$ $x+y+z$ even $\wedge$ (x odd $\vee$ y odd $\vee$ z odd)))

with the same types even and odd as in Fig. A.17. This would convert the figure to Fig. A.18.

The example demonstrates that in a net representation a constant predicate is in fact treated differently than a variable one. It is not considered a passive system component, since it does not model states and hence does not undergo changes. Rather, it appears most naturally as a system invariant expressed as a state assertion.

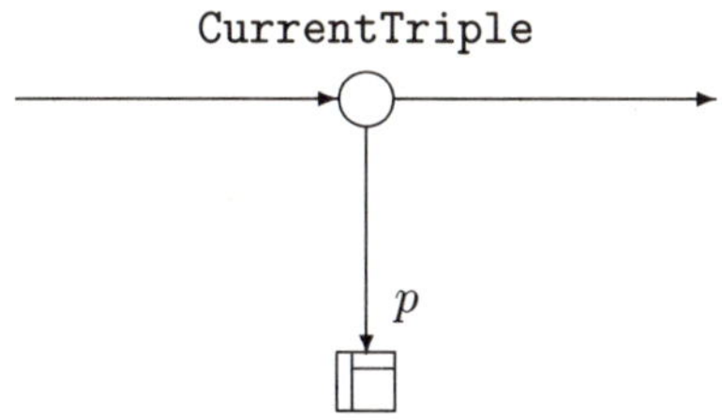

$$\neg \exists x, y, z \, (p = (x, y, z) \wedge \\ x + y + z \text{ even } \wedge \\ (x \text{ odd } \vee y \text{ odd } \vee z \text{ odd}))$$

Figure A.17 : State assertion for a variable predicate

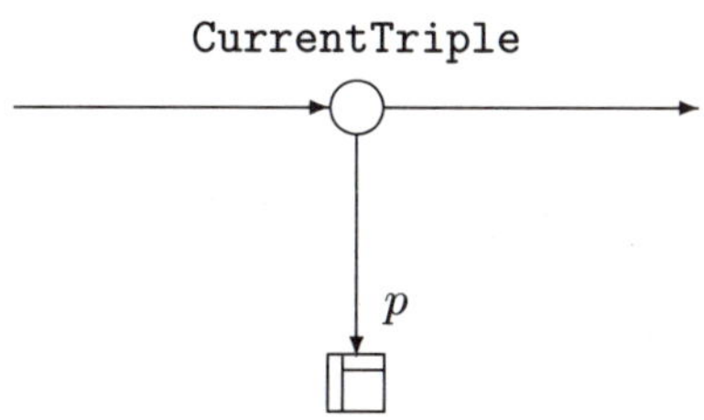

$\neg\,(p$ limpingtriple)

Figure A.18 : Concise inscription with a type predicate

It is appropriate to point out main differences between the terminology as suggested here and as is frequently used in the database world. In the latter, the intrinsic dependence of constraints on interfaces is rarely made explicit and it is unclear whether it is in fact assumed. Moreover, the word "constraint" is often used in a quite different and narrower sense, which refers to how something is *specified*, rather than what it *means*, and thus makes a language-dependent distinction that is semantically irrelevant. It refers to a commonly used method of defining types in programming languages as well as in database systems, which is to introduce in a first step all possible combinations of given component types, much like in a Cartesian product, and then, in a second step, excluding undesirable combinations. The type obtained in the first step is then said to be "constrained" by the second step. Thus, the word "constraint" refers to the process of type definition rather than to its result, much less to its role in a communication model. Calendar dates are a good example of a type that can be defined with and without "constraints" in this sense, requiring about the same descriptional effort: either by first allowing all combinations of {1,...,31} and {1,...,12}, and then "constraining" the result by excluding non-calendar combinations, or by allowing all combinations of {1,...,29} and {1,...,12}, and then adding the remaining dates by enumeration.

Thus, a "constraint" is often seen as something *additional* to a type definition, rather than part of it. This is particularly the case when properties involving several components of a relatively large construct are considered. A well-known such case is encountered in the definition of the concept of a key. A *key* is a construct seen as part of an object which is said to *have* the key. The characteristic feature of a key, however, its uniqueness, refers to a higher object, namely a set of such objects. Thus the object on which the constraint is imposed is the whole set. Or, in terms of type definition: first, the type of all sets of objects is considered. It is then restricted by an additional "uniqueness constraint" requiring that within each instance of the type, i.e., each such set, a key value must occur only once.

In our view, a "constraint" in this sense is conceptually just part of a type definition and does not in principle distinguish itself from other elements of the type definition. It is not a constraint in our sense, since it does not refer to a system context.

In practical data processing, predefining types independent of a particular interface is quite common. For example, in the Data Division of a COBOL program, record types are established that are valid for all program runs. The program runs may in turn occur at various interfaces. A still more remote predefinition of types is in a data dictionary the entries of which can be accessed by a COPY command.

In general, predefined types are very useful for the specification of constraints. For defining types, one can often take advantage of the particularly simple structure of Cartesian-product-like types. They are also quite frequently used, so that it makes sense to provide language elements for specifically this case. The pictorial box notation for individual IMC constructs lends itself to adaptation for describing types consisting of all combinations of given component types. Below we make some suggestions for conventions for a **generic box and table notation** which proved to be useful in practice. A kind of generic tree notation (for atoms, nominations and collections) is used in [HuKi87] and [Hull89].

A **construct template** is basically an incompletely specified box diagram. Thus, the symbols ▭ and [~] introduced in Sec. 2.1.2 can be considered construct templates. A less trivial example is given in Fig. A.19.

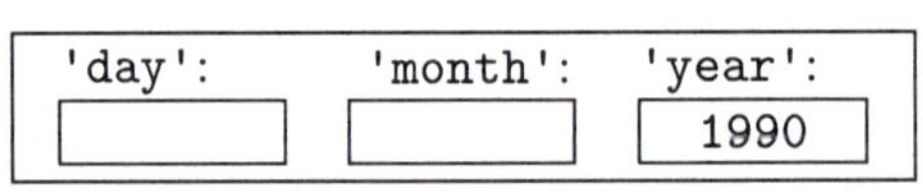

Figure A.19: Construct template for a nomination type

The idea is that a template specifies a type as given by all possible completions. Alternatively, one may take a template also as a representative of that type, that is, as standing for an arbitrary instance of the type. Thus, the example in Fig. A.19 means either the type of all calendar dates of the year 1990, or an arbitrary calendar date of the year 1990.

Incomplete construct specification can also be obtained by using a construct type specification instead of a component construct, by leaving out a name, or, if the name is itself a construct, by using again a construct type specification in its place. In the above example, the trivial type $\square$ ("any construct") has been used for incomplete construct specification.

Apart from incomplete construct specification, a few additional symbols may be convenient at times, for example, "..." for expressing one or more repetitions, or "*" for expressing zero or more (but finitely many) repetitions. Fig. A.20 illustrates the use of this symbolism. It describes the type of collections of zero or finitely many nonempty catenations of arbitrary length.

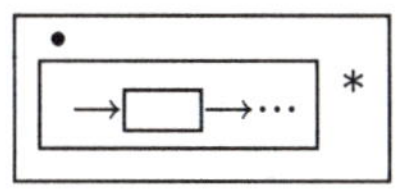

Figure A.20: Construct template describing repetitions

If we want to give the type a designation, a **type plate** with a predicate symbol may be attached (Fig. A.21).

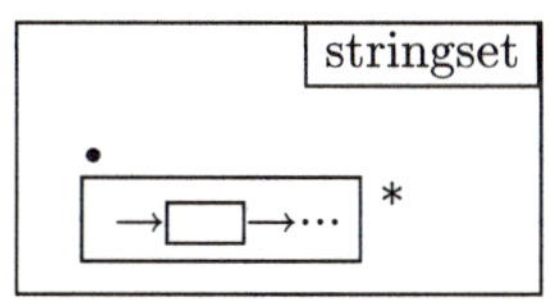

Figure A.21: Construct template with type plate

A construct of type stringset is a collection of catenations. Note that the type plate does not belong to the constructs of the type. The same construct may in fact belong to several types.

The type plate is useful for reference in other construct templates. Fig. A.22 specifies the type of nominations the components of which are arbitrary stringsets under arbitrary names, including the empty nomination.

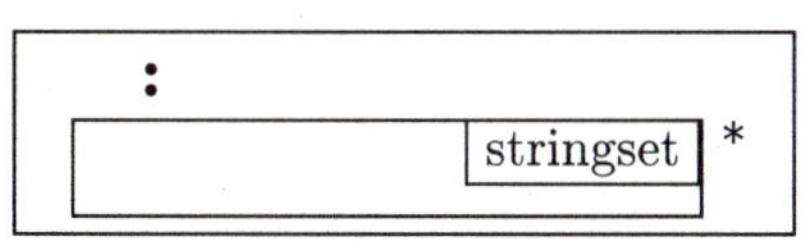

Figure A.22: Type plate used for reference

In our general understanding of *type*, a table type can contain any selection of tables, also tables with different attribute sets. If, however, all instances of a table type have the same attributes, a representation as shown in Fig. A.23 may be used. A tabular representation may also have a type plate attached.

'quantity'	'due'		
	'day'	'month'	'year'

Figure A.23 : Construct template for a type of unordered table

An elaborated example of pictorial construct type representation is shown in Sec. 3.3.3 (Fig. 3.15).

A.3.2 Dynamic constraints

A dynamic constraint says which transformations of information objects are admissible in a given context. In our present conceptual setup we rather say "in which way agencies are allowed to act upon channels" or "which transitions may occur for (variable) predicates".

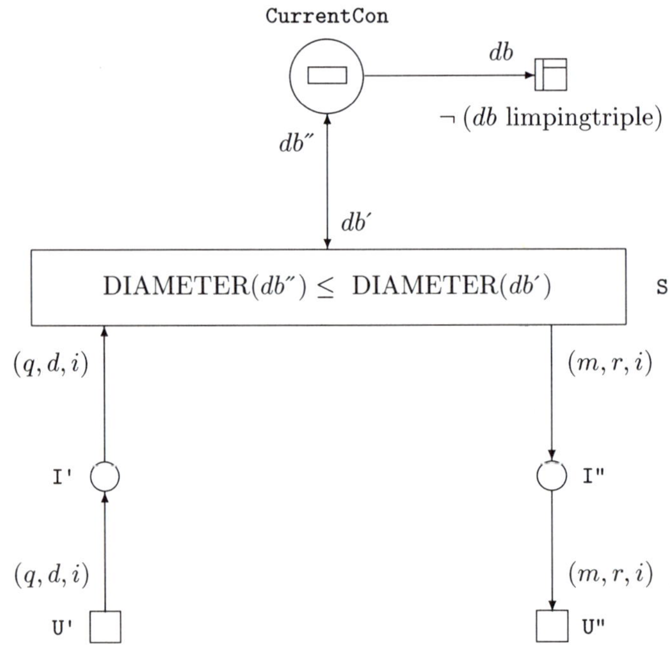

Figure A.24 : PrT-net expressing static and dynamic constraints

We have introduced net representations to describe the system context in which information handling is considered (Sec. A.1), and we have used them to specify static constraints in the system context to which they apply (Sec. A.3.1). The particular virtues of nets are now exploited to describe dynamic constraints.* Below, we demonstrate by an example how construct transformation constraints have their natural place in a net specification of a system.

Assume that for some predicate `CurrentCon` the following constraints are to be expressed:

static constraint:	the `CurrentCon` construct must be a limping triple
dynamic constraint:	the maximum difference of its components must not increase

The diagram in Fig. A.24 resumes the generic net of Fig. A.4, which models a centralized database. In this, the function DIAMETER is assumed to be defined elsewhere as yielding the maximum difference of triple components.

The places for dynamic constraints are transitions, for static constraints they are state assertions, as in Fig. A.24. It is, however, not always clear from the outset whether a given constraint is inherently static or dynamic. In certain circumstances it may be possible to convert one into the other. Conversion of a dynamic constraint can possibly be done by freezing local before- and after-states for static comparison. Conversion of a static constraint may be performed if all transitions concerned can be specified such that the resulting local states satisfy the static constraint. In the example of Fig. A.24 this could be done by omitting the state assertion and replacing the transition formula with

$$\text{DIAMETER}(db'') \leq \text{DIAMETER}(db') \land db'' \text{ limpingtriple}.$$

---

* Nets are, in fact, capable not only of dealing with construct transformation, but with all aspects of system dynamics, such as coincidence and concurrency.

Appendix B

Algebraic specification of IMC

B.1 General remarks and conventions

Two ways of looking at data structure have been compared in Chap. 1, the compositional and the operational one. IMC is dedicated to the compositional view. In this appendix we want to show that, in principle, compositional structure can also be expressed in an operational way. This is demonstrated for a few typical operations on constructs and spots. The operations on spotsets have also been specified, but these are more complicated and need auxiliary definitions, without contributing much to the demonstration in principle. They have therefore been omitted.

IMC-algebra basically has two sorts: **cstr** (for "construct") and **spot**. In addition, there are two "primeval" sorts, **atom** and **name,** which are assumed to be predefined. They constitute the material from which constructs and spots are ultimately built.

To prevent the algebraic specification from being clogged, a few additional conventions are appropriate. In the following, we introduce descriptional facilities as required. Some of them, which are of a more general character, are described right now.

We assume that there is a four-valued operator if ...=... then ... else ... available, which yields values in the obvious way. To be correct, there should be one such operator for each sort for which conditional expressions are desired. To distinguish these operators syntactically would introduce confusing variety. We therefore use one operator name only (i.e., if ...=... then ... else ...) for all sorts. Note that the equality sign ("=") in the condition is a syntactic delimiter belonging to the name of the if-operator. It is different from that used for expressing term equivalence.

Another descriptional simplification concerns handling "undesirable" terms. Not all syntactically admissible terms of sorts **cstr** and **spot** correspond to constructs and spots in the sense of IMC. IMCL maps all undefined terms to a single entity "undefined". For the algebraic specification it is easier to distinguish between "undefined construct" (Ω_c) and "undefined spot" (Ω_s).

The equations dealing with Ω_c and Ω_s are not dealing with just marginal cases, but are highly important for the resulting structure. Of course, it must also be specified how operators behave on "undefined" entities. IMCL makes it a general rule that any "undefined" entity in a parameter position also renders the result of the operation "undefined" (contamination principle). This can easily be specified by explicit equations, but has been omitted here to avoid rather monotonous arrays of equations which convey little information. The reader is asked to supplement in his mind all equations of the form op(...)=Ω_c or op(...)=Ω_s, where Ω_c or Ω_s appear also in parameter positions for sorts **cstr** or **spot**, respectively. There is one exception to the contamination principle: the result of $\underline{\text{if}}$ ...=... $\underline{\text{then}}$ ... $\underline{\text{else}}$ ... simply disregards the operand which is not selected, even if it is "undefined". In the following, we write Ω when we mean Ω_c or Ω_s, as the case may be.

Further, we want to simplify a type of equation which occurs rather frequently: to comply with the contamination principle, the term on one side of an equation must normally evaluate to Ω if Ω occurs as a parameter on the other side. This does not always work out directly from the term that expresses the heart of the matter, particularly, if a parameter occurs on one side of the equation, but not on the other. For example,

$$\mathsf{T}^{-}(\mathsf{T}^{+}(x,y)) = x$$

is intended to express "T^{-} cancels the effect of T^{+}, no matter what the second parameter of T^{+} is". If however, y evaluates to Ω, the right-hand side should also be Ω. Thus, the equation is more correctly written

$$\mathsf{T}^{-}(\mathsf{T}^{+}(x,y)) = \underline{\text{if}}\ y{=}\Omega\ \underline{\text{then}}\ \Omega\ \underline{\text{else}}\ x.$$

This would, however, make it rather bulky and would distract from the essence of its message. If there are several parameters instead of only one, the protective clause becomes quite voluminous and obscures the sense of the equation. As a remedy, we introduce the convention that equations must generally be read as having a conditional clause after the equal-sign, which says that, if one of the parameter terms on the left-hand side is undefined, the result is also undefined. It is very important to keep this convention in mind when an equation is read. In particular, the fact must be taken into account that, in general, an equation as it stands cannot be reversed.

To support remembrance of the meaning of parameters, a simple rule is observed for their arrangement: if there is more than one construct parameter, the first one specifies the most comprehensive construct. Subsequent construct parameters refer to parts of the construct given by the first construct parameter or to parts of the resulting construct. A spot parameter precedes any construct parameter.

To penetrate an algebraic specification, it is often helpful to develop a pictorial view of how the equations define transformations of terms within an equivalence class. In the following explanations we will therefore sometimes employ a rather figurative style to support intuition. In this we can afford some loose wording, since the precise specification is in the syntax and the equations.

B.2 Constructs

B.2.1 Basic construct operators

Ω_c:		$\rightarrow$ **cstr**	"undefined construct"
E_l:		$\rightarrow$ **cstr**	"empty collection"
E_n:		$\rightarrow$ **cstr**	"empty nomination"
E_t:		$\rightarrow$ **cstr**	"empty catenation"
A:	**atom**	$\rightarrow$ **cstr**	"atom construct"
L^+:	**cstr** $\times$ **cstr**	$\rightarrow$ **cstr**	"collection increase"
L^-:	**cstr** $\times$ **cstr**	$\rightarrow$ **cstr**	"collection decrease"
N^+:	**cstr** $\times$ **cstr** $\times$ **name**	$\rightarrow$ **cstr**	"nomination increase"
N^-:	**cstr** $\times$ **name**	$\rightarrow$ **cstr**	"nomination decrease"
T^+:	**cstr** $\times$ **cstr**	$\rightarrow$ **cstr**	"catenation increase"
T^-:	**cstr**	$\rightarrow$ **cstr**	"catenation decrease"

$$\mathsf{L}^+(\mathsf{L}^+(x,y),y) = \mathsf{L}^+(x,y)$$
$$\mathsf{L}^+(\mathsf{L}^+(x,y),y') = \mathsf{L}^+(\mathsf{L}^+(x,y'),y)$$
$$\mathsf{L}^-(\mathsf{E}_l,x) = \mathsf{E}_l$$
$$\mathsf{L}^-(\mathsf{L}^+(x,y),y') = \underline{\text{if}}\ y{=}y'\ \underline{\text{then}}\ \mathsf{L}^-(x,y')\ \underline{\text{else}}\ \mathsf{L}^+(\mathsf{L}^-(x,y'),y)$$
$$\mathsf{N}^+(\mathsf{N}^+(x,y,n),y',n') = \underline{\text{if}}\ n{=}n'\ \underline{\text{then}}\ \mathsf{N}^+(x,y,n)\ \underline{\text{else}}\ \mathsf{N}^+(\mathsf{N}^+(x,y',n'),y,n)$$
$$\mathsf{N}^-(\mathsf{E}_n,n) = \mathsf{E}_n$$
$$\mathsf{N}^-(\mathsf{N}^+(x,y,n),n') = \underline{\text{if}}\ n{=}n'\ \underline{\text{then}}\ \mathsf{N}^-(x,n')\ \underline{\text{else}}\ \mathsf{N}^+(\mathsf{N}^-(x,n'),y,n)$$
$$\mathsf{T}^-(\mathsf{E}_t) = \mathsf{E}_t$$
$$\mathsf{T}^-(\mathsf{T}^+(x,y)) = x$$

$$\mathsf{L}^+(a,x) = \Omega_c$$
$$\mathsf{L}^-(a,x) = \Omega_c$$
$$\mathsf{L}^+(cn^\circ,x) = \Omega_c$$
$$\mathsf{L}^-(cn^\circ,x) = \Omega_c$$
$$\mathsf{L}^+(ct^\circ,x) = \Omega_c$$
$$\mathsf{L}^-(ct^\circ,x) = \Omega_c$$

$$\mathsf{N}^+(a,x,n) = \Omega_c$$
$$\mathsf{N}^-(a,n) = \Omega_c$$
$$\mathsf{N}^+(cl^\circ,x,n) = \Omega_c$$
$$\mathsf{N}^-(cl^\circ,n) = \Omega_c$$
$$\mathsf{N}^+(ct^\circ,x,n) = \Omega_c$$
$$\mathsf{N}^-(ct^\circ,n) = \Omega_c$$

$$\mathsf{T}^+(a,x) = \Omega_c$$
$$\mathsf{T}^-(a) = \Omega_c$$
$$\mathsf{T}^+(cl^\circ,x) = \Omega_c$$
$$\mathsf{T}^-(cl^\circ) = \Omega_c$$
$$\mathsf{T}^+(cn^\circ,x) = \Omega_c$$
$$\mathsf{T}^-(cn^\circ) = \Omega_c$$

In the equations above, cl°, cn° and ct° appear in parameter positions. For an explanation of these see below towards the end of this section.

The sort **atom** appears in parameter positions only, not as a result sort. Operator A embeds the externally given atoms into the sort **cstr**. The values of A are called "atoms". To simplify terms, we write "a" for A(v), where v stands for an arbitrary variable not occurring in the environment.

Also, the sort **name** appears in parameter positions only. Names need no embedding into an other sort. It is, however, possible to interpret names again as constructs. The formal specification neither requires nor prevents this. Yet, one cannot *use* a construct term directly as a name term, since it is not allowed to appear in a name position. Also, in this algebraic specification, there is no operator that converts a construct term into a name term. If one wishes to use constructs as names, a construct/name conversion operator may additionally be provided.

The equations for collections allow for elimination of duplicates and for arbitrary sequencing of L^+-operations (commutativity). Further, an L^--operation can freely be moved back and forth in a sequence of L^+-operations as long as its parameter is different from that of the operation with which it changes places. When, on its way into the interior of the term, an L^--operator hits on an L^+-operator with the same parameter, the latter just vanishes. When an L^--operator ultimately reaches E_l, it disappears itself. Thus, any collection expression is equivalent to a sequence of L^+-expressions with all different parameters. It can be transformed into any desired permutation of increase operations. These are properties that are characteristic of finite sets.

Nominations are similar to collections. The constructing operator, N^+, obeys a commutative law, too, but only if the commuting operations have different names. If the names are equal, the later (outermost) operation just disappears. This means that a new component assignment for an already used name is rejected. A name can be re-used only after it is first removed by N^-. As in collections, component cancellation by N^-can be propagated into the interior of the term until the operator hits on E_n. On its way, it deletes any N^+-operation with identical name parameter. Any nomination term can be transformed into a sequence of N^+-operations with all different names. It can be transformed to any desired permutation of increase operations. These are properties that are characteristic of finite functions from names to constructs.

Catenation decrease is less selective than collection or nomination decrease. Only the last appended component can be taken away. It is actually a LIFO-mechanism or stack that is specified for catenations. The concepts used are very familiar in list processing languages.

In all, we have five kinds of terms of sort **cstr**: atoms, collections, nominations, catenations and the "undefined" construct Ω_c. They are mutually exclusive.

Above we have mentioned that construct terms can equivalently be transformed into certain special forms. This observation is quite important. To emphasize its importance we state it explicitly:

Proposition

Any construct term is equivalent to

either Ω_c,
or E_l,
or E_n,
or E_t,
or a term beginning with L^+,
or a term beginning with N^+,
or a term beginning with T^+.

Except for terms equivalent to Ω_c, the associated term classes are mutually exclusive.

According to the seven cases of the proposition, we call a construct expression
- an undefined construct term,
- an empty collection term
- an empty nomination term
- an empty catenation term
- a (non-empty) collection term,
- a (non-empty) nomination term or
- a (non-empty) catenation term,

respectively.

The proof of the proposition is straightforward, but note that one has to be very careful not to compromise it by later addition of operators. In principle, the proposition must be re-proved each time a new operator is introduced that yields a construct as a result.

In what follows we will frequently make use of the proposition when we want to talk about term classes. If, for example, we want to state something about all nonempty collections, it is sufficient to claim the property in question for the term $\mathsf{L}^+(u,v)$ with arbitrary variables u and v. For a more concise style, we establish the convention that "cl^+" shall stand for "$\mathsf{L}^+(u,v)$", where u and v must be thought of as being substituted, if necessary, by any variables not in conflict with variables in the context. In any one equation, the same "cl^+" means exactly the same term in all of its occurrences. If we want to include the empty collection, we write "cl°" instead. A statement containing "cl°" actually stands for two statements, one where "cl°" is substituted by "E_l", and one, where "cl°" is substituted by "$\mathsf{L}^+(u,v)$". Similar conventions are assumed for nomination and catenation terms. To sum up, we have

$$\left.\begin{array}{ll} cl^+ & \text{for } \mathsf{L}^+(u,v) \\ cn^+ & \text{for } \mathsf{N}^+(u,v,n) \\ ct^+ & \text{for } \mathsf{T}^+(u,v) \\ cl^\circ & \text{for } \mathsf{E}_l \text{ or } \mathsf{L}^+(u,v) \\ cn^\circ & \text{for } \mathsf{E}_n \text{ or } \mathsf{N}^+(u,v,n) \\ ct^\circ & \text{for } \mathsf{E}_t \text{ or } \mathsf{T}^+(u,v) \end{array}\right\} \text{ with variables appropriately substituted}$$

B.2.2 Additional construct operators

CUTTAIL:	**cstr** × **cstr**	→ **cstr**	"cut tail part of catenation"
CUTTAIL*:	**cstr** × **cstr**	→ **cstr**	"cut tail part of catenation repeatedly"
CUTHEAD:	**cstr** × **cstr**	→ **cstr**	"cut head part of catenation"

CUTTAIL$(ct^{\circ},\mathsf{E}_t)$ $= ct^{\circ}$
CUTTAIL(E_t,ct^{+}) $= \Omega_c$
CUTTAIL$(\mathsf{T}^{+}(x,p),\mathsf{T}^{+}(y,q))$ = if $p=q$ then CUTTAIL(x,y) else Ω_c
CUTTAIL(x,a) $= \Omega_c$
CUTTAIL(a,x) $= \Omega_c$
CUTTAIL(cl°,x) $= \Omega_c$
CUTTAIL(cn°,x) $= \Omega_c$
CUTTAIL(x,cl°) $= \Omega_c$
CUTTAIL(x,cn°) $= \Omega_c$
CUTTAIL*(x,y) = if CUTTAIL$(x,y)=\Omega_c$ then x
else CUTTAIL*(CUTTAIL$(x,y),y)$
CUTHEAD(E_t,y) = if $\mathsf{E}_t=y$ then E_t else Ω_c
CUTHEAD$(\mathsf{T}^{+}(x,y),z)$ = if $\mathsf{T}^{+}(x,y)=z$ then E_t else T^{+}(CUTHEAD$(x,z),y)$
CUTHEAD(a,x) $= \Omega_c$
CUTHEAD(cl°,x) $= \Omega_c$
CUTHEAD(cn°,x) $= \Omega_c$

CUTTAIL is applicable to two catenation arguments, of which the second must be an ending "substring" of the first. It yields the first argument with the trailing substring detached. The third equation allows simultaneous deletion of the last member of each of the arguments. This can be carried on recursively until the second argument is used up or a mismatch is encountered. The latter case makes the term "undefined".

CUTTAIL* repeats application of CUTTAIL as long as possible. Note that CUTTAIL* delivers a defined result even if CUTTAIL is not applicable at all. CUTTAIL* is in fact very liberal, because it is also defined if the arguments are not catenations. In no case is CUTTAIL*(x,y) a catenation ending with y. For any catenation x not ending with y, we have $x=$CUTTAIL*(x,y). Thus, we can use CUTTAIL* to characterize catenations not ending with a given catenation.

CUTHEAD is analogous to CUTTAIL. The second parameter must be an initial substring of the first one. The second parameter moves recursively from right to left over the first parameter until the initial substring is encountered or, if this does not happen, the rest becomes E_t. This then yields the undefined construct. CUTHEAD is more complicated than CUTTAIL, because it runs against the recursive composition of catenation terms.

CONC:	**cstr** × **cstr**	→ **cstr**	"concatenation"
LAST:	**cstr**	→ **cstr**	"last member of catenation"

$$
\begin{aligned}
&\mathsf{CONC}(ct^{\circ},\mathsf{E}_t) &&= ct^{\circ}\\
&\mathsf{CONC}(ct^{\circ},\mathsf{T}^{+}(x,y)) &&= \mathsf{T}^{+}(\mathsf{CONC}(ct^{\circ},x),y)\\
&\mathsf{CONC}(x,a) &&= \Omega_c\\
&\mathsf{CONC}(a,x) &&= \Omega_c\\
&\mathsf{CONC}(x,cl^{\circ}) &&= \Omega_c\\
&\mathsf{CONC}(x,cn^{\circ}) &&= \Omega_c\\
&\mathsf{CONC}(cl^{\circ},x) &&= \Omega_c\\
&\mathsf{CONC}(cn^{\circ},x) &&= \Omega_c\\
&\mathsf{LAST}(\mathsf{E}_t) &&= \Omega_c\\
&\mathsf{LAST}(\mathsf{T}^{+}(x,y)) &&= y\\
&\mathsf{LAST}(a) &&= \Omega_c\\
&\mathsf{LAST}(cl^{+}) &&= \Omega_c\\
&\mathsf{LAST}(cn^{+}) &&= \Omega_c
\end{aligned}
$$

CONC is the obvious operation for stringing catenations together. LAST provides the latest appended member of a catenation.

ICN:	**cstr** × **name**	→ **cstr**	"immediate component under name"
ICT:	**cstr** × **cstr**	→ **cstr**	"immediate component before tail"

$$
\begin{aligned}
&\mathsf{ICN}(\mathsf{E}_n,n) &&= \Omega_c\\
&\mathsf{ICN}(\mathsf{N}^{+}(\mathsf{N}^{-}(x,n),y,n),n') &&= \underline{\text{if}}\ n{=}n'\ \underline{\text{then}}\ y\ \underline{\text{else}}\ \mathsf{ICN}(\mathsf{N}^{-}(x,n),n')\\
&\mathsf{ICN}(a,n) &&= \Omega_c\\
&\mathsf{ICN}(cl^{\circ},n) &&= \Omega_c\\
&\mathsf{ICN}(ct^{\circ},n) &&= \Omega_c\\
&\mathsf{ICT}(x,y) &&= \mathsf{LAST}(\mathsf{CUTTAIL}(x,y))
\end{aligned}
$$

The increase operators L^{+}, N^{+} and T^{+} have their decrease counterparts L^{-}, N^{-} and T^{-}, which take away an immediate component. The component itself is lost. Sometimes, however, one is interested in the immediate component rather than in the rest of the construct. For this, the immediate-component operators ICN and ICT can be used. There is no sense in providing an ICL-operator ("immediate component of collection"), since it would require the desired component to have been already supplied as a parameter. Rather, a predicate IsICL ("is immediate component", equivalent to the "∈" of set theory) would be desirable.

The second equation for ICN may be suspected to be unnecessarily complex because x is first decreased and then increased, both under name n. However, we must make sure that the first argument of N^{+} is in fact a nomination with immediate component y under name n. If x already had name n, then an N^{+}-operation with name n would be ineffectual (see defining equation for N^{+}), that is, we would have $\mathsf{N}^{+}(x,y,n)=x$. With $\mathsf{N}^{-}(x,n)$ exactly those nominations are characterized which do not have the name n.

Note that any nomination having an immediate component y under name n can be given the form $\mathsf{N}^{+}(\mathsf{N}^{-}(x,n),y,n)$.

For ICT, a "position" is specified by a tail part of the catenation. The identified component is the last member of the catenation after the tail is detached. Therefore, if the position parameter (second parameter) of ICT is identical to the first parameter, the result is undefined ($\mathsf{LAST}(\mathsf{CUTTAIL}(ct^{+},ct^{+}))=\mathsf{LAST}(\mathsf{E}_t)=\Omega_c$). For ICT, explicit rules on Ω_c-cases are not necessary, because $\mathsf{LAST}(\mathsf{CUTTAIL}(x,y))$ makes them automatically right.

B.3 Spots

B.3.1 Basic spot operators

Ω_s:		$\rightarrow$ **spot**	"undefined spot"
OWN :	**cstr**	$\rightarrow$ **spot**	"ownspot"
REF :	**spot**	$\rightarrow$ **cstr**	"reference construct"
IML :	**spot** $\times$ **cstr**	$\rightarrow$ **spot**	"embedding spot into collection"
IMN :	**spot** $\times$ **cstr** $\times$ **name**	$\rightarrow$ **spot**	"embedding spot into nomination"
IMT :	**spot** $\times$ **cstr** $\times$ **cstr**	$\rightarrow$ **spot**	"embedding spot into catenation"

$$\mathsf{REF}(\mathsf{OWN}(x)) = x$$
$$\mathsf{REF}(\mathsf{IML}(s,x)) = x$$
$$\mathsf{REF}(\mathsf{IMN}(s,x,n)) = x$$
$$\mathsf{REF}(\mathsf{IMT}(s,x,y)) = x$$
$$\mathsf{IML}(s,\mathsf{L}^{-}(x,\mathsf{REF}(s))) = \Omega_s$$
$$\mathsf{IMN}(s,\mathsf{N}^{-}(x,n),n) = \Omega_s$$
$$\mathsf{IMN}(s,x,n) = \underline{\text{if}}\ \mathsf{REF}(s)=\mathsf{ICN}(x,n)\ \underline{\text{then}}\ \mathsf{IMN}(s,x,n)\ \underline{\text{else}}\ \Omega_s$$
$$\mathsf{IMT}(s,\mathsf{CUTTAIL}^{*}(x,y),y) = \Omega_s$$
$$\mathsf{IMT}(s,x,y) = \underline{\text{if}}\ \mathsf{REF}(s)=\mathsf{ICT}(x,y)\ \underline{\text{then}}\ \mathsf{IMT}(s,x,y)\ \underline{\text{else}}\ \Omega_s$$
$$\mathsf{IMT}(s,x,x) = \Omega_s$$
$$\mathsf{IML}(s,cn^{+}) = \Omega_s$$
$$\mathsf{IML}(s,ct^{+}) = \Omega_s$$
$$\mathsf{IMN}(s,cl^{+},n) = \Omega_s$$
$$\mathsf{IMN}(s,ct^{+},n) = \Omega_s$$
$$\mathsf{IMT}(s,cl^{+},x) = \Omega_s$$
$$\mathsf{IMT}(s,cn^{+},x) = \Omega_s$$

Spots can be constructed "outside in" or "inside out". With "outside in", one starts with the reference construct and repeatedly proceeds to an immediate component of the construct already reached. With "inside out" one starts with the ownspot of the ultimate component and repeatedly embeds the spot already obtained into the extended environment given by the immediately surrounding construct. Here the latter way is chosen, because it is easier for the algebraic specification since it mimics the recursive composition of construct terms.

It may appear rather strange that the equations for **spot** are exclusively concerned with specifying which terms do *not* identify spots (i.e., are equivalent to the "undefined" spot Ω_s). This is, however, not so absurd, bearing in mind that a spot is basically a construct together with a sequence of selection operations leading to some component. Since many selector sequences can be formed which do not match the construct's structure, the main task of specifying spots consists of excluding mismatches.

The most interesting equations for spots (equations 5 through 10) deal with environment constructs which are not appropriate for an intended embedding, though they are of the correct kind:

$\mathsf{L}^{-}(x,y)$ (if defined) is a collection which does not have y as an immediate component. Conversely, any collection x which does not have y as an immediate component can be written $\mathsf{L}^{-}(x,y)$. Thus, $\mathsf{L}^{-}(x,\mathsf{REF}(s))$ denotes any collection not containing $\mathsf{REF}(s)$ as an immediate component. The equation $\mathsf{IML}(s,\mathsf{L}^{-}(x,\mathsf{REF}(s)))=\Omega_s$ says that s cannot be embedded into such a collection.

Similarly, any nomination x not having n as a name is equivalent to $\mathsf{N}^{-}(x,n)$. $\mathsf{IMN}(s,\mathsf{N}^{-}(x,n),n)=\Omega_s$ says that in such a nomination one cannot embed a spot under name n. Nominations and catenations present an additional difficulty: for a nomination not only must the name be available, but also is it necessary that the immediate component under this name is the reference construct of the spot to be embedded. This is the message of the second equation for IMN. A similar consideration applies to catenations and the second equation for IMT. Both equations have a curious pattern: the left-hand term is repeated as part of the right-hand term. This is acceptable from a strictly algebraic point of view, but it poses a problem for practical treatment, since in the "good" case it does not reduce the term. In such a case, a unification algorithm working on algebraic specifications must be on guard not to get trapped in a loop. The issue could be resolved by introducing conditional equations and NOTEQU-operators. This has not been done here, because, for the present purpose, the advantage does not seem to outweigh the preparatory effort needed.

To identify the "bad" cases for catenations, we have to make reference to term classes for catenations not ending with a given catenation. This is possible with CUT-TAIL*, as explained earlier. To embed a spot into a catenation, a position must be identified. As we did for ICT, we identify a position in a catenation by the partial catenation that *follows* (and does not include) the wanted position. This entails that the empty catenation E_t identifies a position (that of the last member), but the entire catenation does not identify a position, since it leaves no remainder. This is expressed by $\mathsf{IMT}(s,x,x)=\Omega_s$.

B.3.2 Additional spot operators

REMOVE: **spot**	$\rightarrow$ **cstr**	"remove component at spot"

REMOVE (OWN (x)) $= \Omega_c$
REMOVE (IML (OWN (x),cl^+)) $=$ L$^-$(cl^+,x)
REMOVE (IMN (OWN (x),cn^+,n)) $=$ N$^-$(cn^+,n)
REMOVE (IMT (OWN (x),ct^+,y)) $=$ CONC (T$^-$(CUTTAIL (ct^+,y)),y)
REMOVE (IML (s,x)) $=$ L$^+$(L$^-$(x,REF (s)),REMOVE (s))
REMOVE (IMN (s,x,n)) $=$ N$^+$(N$^-$(x,n),REMOVE (s),n)
REMOVE (IMT (s,x,y)) $=$ CONC (T$^+$(T$^-$(CUTTAIL (x,y)),REMOVE (s)),y)

In the last three equations, "s" stands for a spot term not beginning with "OWN", that is, a term of the form IML (s',x'), IMN (s',x',n') or IMT (s',x',y'). Thus, 9 equations are actually represented by the three lines.

With REMOVE, we have an example demonstrating how changes in constructs can be specified with the help of the spot concept. REMOVE takes away the component identified by the argument spot. Note that the resulting construct is different from the reference construct of the argument spot, or, in other words, that the given spot is no longer a spot in the resulting construct.

One might expect REMOVE (OWN (x)) to be an empty construct rather then Ω_c, as postulated by the first equation. However, we have also REMOVE (IML (OWN (x), L$^+$(E$_l$,x)))=L$^-$(L$^+$(E$_l$,x),x)=E$_l$. If both equations held, a confusion of aggregation levels would arise, which would certainly cause trouble in various situations.

Since in the REMOVE equations heavy use is made of the convention on undefined parameters occurring in the left-hand side term (see Sec. A.1), it may be appropriate at this point to call this convention to mind. If, for example, in the second equation x is not an immediate component of cl^+, then cl^+=L$^-$(cl^+,x), and therefore, since x=REF (OWN (x)), we have cl^+=L$^-$(cl^+,REF (OWN (x))). We obtain

IML (OWN (x),cl^+)=IML (OWN (x),L$^-$(cl^+,REF (OWN (x)))), which, by virtue of the first equation for IML, is equal to Ω_s. Thus, the REMOVE-parameter on the left-hand side is undefined, but L$^-$(cl^+,x) is not undefined. Without our convention, this would cause a collapse of term classes. The convention forces the right-hand side to be equivalent to the undefined spot Ω_s.

INSRTL:	$\textbf{spot} \times \textbf{cstr} \rightarrow \textbf{cstr}$	"insert inward collection spot"
INSRTN:	$\textbf{spot} \times \textbf{cstr} \times \textbf{name} \rightarrow \textbf{cstr}$	"insert inward nomination spot"
INSRTT:	$\textbf{spot} \times \textbf{cstr} \times \textbf{cstr} \rightarrow \textbf{cstr}$	"insert inward catenation spot"

$$
\begin{aligned}
&\mathsf{INSRTL}\,(\mathsf{OWN}\,(a),x) &&= \Omega_c \\
&\mathsf{INSRTL}\,(\mathsf{OWN}\,(cl^{\circ}),x) &&= \mathsf{L}^{+}(cl^{\circ},x) \\
&\mathsf{INSRTL}\,(\mathsf{OWN}\,(cn^{+}),x) &&= \Omega_c \\
&\mathsf{INSRTL}\,(\mathsf{OWN}\,(ct^{+}),x) &&= \Omega_c \\
&\mathsf{INSRTL}\,(\mathsf{IML}\,(s,x),y) &&= \mathsf{L}^{+}(\mathsf{L}^{-}(x,\mathsf{REF}\,(s)),\mathsf{INSRTL}\,(s,y)) \\
&\mathsf{INSRTL}\,(\mathsf{IMN}\,(s,x,n),y) &&= \mathsf{N}^{+}(\mathsf{N}^{-}(x,n),\mathsf{INSRTL}\,(s,y),n) \\
&\mathsf{INSRTL}\,(\mathsf{IMT}\,(s,x,y),z) &&= \mathsf{CONC}\,(\mathsf{T}^{+}(\mathsf{T}^{-}(\mathsf{CUTTAIL}\,(x,y)),\mathsf{INSRTL}\,(s,z)),y) \\
&\mathsf{INSRTN}\,(\mathsf{OWN}\,(a),x,n) &&= \Omega_c \\
&\mathsf{INSRTN}\,(\mathsf{OWN}\,(cl^{+}),x,n) &&= \Omega_c \\
&\mathsf{INSRTN}\,(\mathsf{OWN}\,(cn^{\circ}),x,n) &&= \mathsf{N}^{+}(cn^{\circ},x,n) \\
&\mathsf{INSRTN}\,(\mathsf{OWN}\,(ct^{+}),x,n) &&= \Omega_c \\
&\mathsf{INSRTN}\,(\mathsf{IML}\,(s,x),y,n) &&= \mathsf{L}^{+}(\mathsf{L}^{-}(x,\mathsf{REF}\,(s)),\mathsf{INSRTN}\,(s,y,n)) \\
&\mathsf{INSRTN}\,(\mathsf{IMN}\,(s,x,n),y,n') &&= \mathsf{N}^{+}(\mathsf{N}^{-}(x,n),\mathsf{INSRTN}\,(s,y,n'),n) \\
&\mathsf{INSRTN}\,(\mathsf{IMT}\,(s,x,y),z,n) &&= \mathsf{CONC}\,(\mathsf{T}^{+}(\mathsf{T}^{-}(\mathsf{CUTTAIL}\,(x,y)),\mathsf{INSRTN}\,(s,z,n)),y) \\
&\mathsf{INSRTT}\,(\mathsf{OWN}\,(a),x,y) &&= \Omega_c \\
&\mathsf{INSRTT}\,(\mathsf{OWN}\,(cl^{+}),x,y) &&= \Omega_c \\
&\mathsf{INSRTT}\,(\mathsf{OWN}\,(cn^{+}),x,y) &&= \Omega_c \\
&\mathsf{INSRTT}\,(\mathsf{OWN}\,(ct^{\circ}),x,y) &&= \mathsf{CONC}\,(\mathsf{T}^{+}(\mathsf{CUTTAIL}\,(ct^{\circ},y),x),y) \\
&\mathsf{INSRTT}\,(\mathsf{IML}\,(s,x),y,z) &&= \mathsf{L}^{+}(\mathsf{L}^{-}(x,\mathsf{REF}\,(s)),\mathsf{INSRTT}\,(s,y,z)) \\
&\mathsf{INSRTT}\,(\mathsf{IMN}\,(s,x,n),y,z) &&= \mathsf{N}^{+}(\mathsf{N}^{-}(x,n),\mathsf{INSRTT}\,(s,y,z),n) \\
&\mathsf{INSRTT}\,(\mathsf{IMT}\,(s,x,y),z,z') &&= \mathsf{CONC}\,(\mathsf{T}^{+}(\mathsf{T}^{-}(\mathsf{CUTTAIL}\,(x,y)),\mathsf{INSRTT}\,(s,z,z')),y)
\end{aligned}
$$

Insertion is the inverse operation to removal. Because insertion affords different specific information for collections, nominations and catenations, we have three different insertion operators.

The set of equations for insertion is relatively bulky because all cases of the three different operators applied to the three different kinds of reference construct have to be considered. Insertion inward an atom spot is impossible. Insertion inward an ownspot is tantamount to augmenting the construct by a new component.

Note that there is an asymmetry between removal and insertion. Removal is done directly at the spot specified. The spot of the component to be inserted does not exist before the insertion has actually been performed. It is therefore better to say that the insertion takes place "inward of" rather than "at" a given spot. Strictly speaking, however, "inwards" is also not really correct. Since the given spot and the spot inward of which the newly created component is are spots in different constructs, they are not directly comparable. Yet we maintain this wording, because it is intuitively clear what is meant.

REPL:	spot × **cstr**	→ **cstr**	"replace component at spot"

REPL (OWN (x),y) $= y$
REPL (IML (s,x),y) = L$^+$(L$^-$(x,REF (s)),REPL (s,y))
REPL (IMN (s,x,n),y) = N$^+$(N$^-$(x,n),REPL (s,y),n)
REPL (IMT (s,x,z),y) = CONC (T$^+$(T$^-$(CUTTAIL (x,z)),REPL (s,y)),z)

In the last three equations, "s" stands for a spot term not beginning with "OWN", that is, a term of the form IML (s',x'), IMN (s',x',n') or IMT (s',x',y'). Thus, 9 equations are actually represented by the three lines.

Component replacement is very similar to component removal. It is in fact simpler because replacement at an ownspot is possible, removal not. Thus, the recursion can start with the ownspot and does not have to distinguish the three cases of IML, IMN and IMT at the next aggregation level, as was necessary for REMOVE.

One might expect that replacement of a component by another construct can be described by removal and subsequent insertion. Though this is true in principle, there is an inherent difficulty in identifying the spot inward of which the insertion is to be made. Note that the spot of removal is no longer available after the component has been removed.

References

[AbFiSc89] Abiteboul, S.; Fischer, P. C.; Schek, H.-J. (eds.): *Nested Relations and Complex Objects in Databases.* Lecture Notes in Computer Science Vol. 361, Springer-Verlag, Berlin Heidelberg, 1989, 323 pages

[AbHu87] Abiteboul, S.; Hull, R.: *IFO: A Formal Semantic Database Model.* ACM Transactions on Database Systems, Vol. 12, No. 4, December 1987, pp. 525–565

[ApCaTe90] Appelt, W.; Carr, R.; Tetteh-Lartey, N.: *Conformance Testing of ODA Documents and ODA Implementations According to ISO 8613 Based on Its Formal Description (FODA).* In Berg, J.L. and Schumny, H. (eds.): An Analysis of the Information Technology Standardization Process. Elsevier (North-Holland), Amsterdam, 1990, pp. 299–309, and Computer Standards & Interfaces 11 (1990), pp. 47–55

[BaBu84] Batory, D. S.; Buchman, A. P.: *Molecular objects, abstract data types and data models: a framework.* In Dayal, U.; Schlageter, G.; Seng, L. M. (eds.): Proc. 10th Int. Conf. on Very Large Data Bases, Singapore, August 1984, pp. 172–184

[BaKh86] Bancilhon, F.; Khoshafian, S.: *A calculus for complex objects.* In [PoDS86], pp. 53–59

[Banc88] Bancilhon, F.: *Object-Oriented Database Systems.* In [PoDS88], pp. 152–162

[Bati89] Batini, C. (ed.): *Entity–Relationship Approach: A Bridge to the User.* North-Holland, Amsterdam, 1989, 526 pages

[BiDePaTh88] Biskup, J.; Demetrovics, J.; Paredaens, J.; Thalheim, B. (eds.): *MFDBS 87.* Lecture Notes in Computer Science, Vol. 305, Springer-Verlag, Berlin Heidelberg, 1988, 247 pages

[BjJo78] Bjørner, D.; Jones, C. B.: *The Vienna Development Method: The Meta-Language.* Lecture Notes in Computer Science, Vol. 61, Springer-Verlag, Berlin Heidelberg, 1978, 382 pages

[BjJo82] Bjørner, D.; Jones, C. B.: *Formal Specification and Software Development.* Prentice-Hall International, London, 1982, 501 pages

[BlBoRuTe90] Blyth, D.; Boldyreff, C.; Ruggles, C.; Tetteh-Lartey, N.: *The case for formal methods in standards.* IEEE Software, September 1990, pp. 65–67

[Bosa62] CODASYL Development Committee (Bosak et al.): *An information algebra.* Phase I Report — Language Structure Group. Communications of the ACM, Vol. 5, No. 4, April 1962, pp. 190–204

[Bour68] Bourbaki, Nicolas: *Elements of mathematics. Theory of sets.* Hermann, Paris, 1968

[Chil68] Childs, D. L.: *Description of a Set-Theoretic Data Structure.* Proc. AFIPS Fall Joint Computer Conference 1968, pp. 557–564

[CODA73a] CODASYL Data Description Language Committee: *Data Description Language Journal of Development.* Report June 1973 (earlier version 1971)

[CODA73b] CODASYL Systems Committee: *Feature analysis of generalized data base management systems.* Systems Journal 12(1), 1973 (earlier version 1971)

[Codd70] Codd, E. F.: *A Relational Model of Data for Large Shared Data Banks.* Communications of the ACM, Vol. 13, No. 6, June 1970, pp. 377–387

[Codd79] Codd, E. F.: *Extending the Relational Database Model to Capture More Meaning.* ACM Transactions on Database Systems, Vol. 4, No. 4, December 1979, pp. 397–434

[Comm91] Committee for Advanced DBMS Function: *Third-generation database system manifesto.* Computer Standards & Interfaces 13 (1991), pp. 41–54

[Date90] Date, C. J.: *An Introduction to Database Systems.* Vol. I, Fifth Edition. Addison-Wesley, Reading, 1990, 854 pages

[Daya87] Dayal, U. et al.: *Simplifying Complex Objects: The PROBE Approach to Modelling and Querying Them.* In [ScSc87], pp. 17–37

[DeTh89] Demetrovics, J.; Thalheim, B. (eds.): *MFDBS 89.* Lecture Notes in Computer Science Vol. 364, Springer-Verlag, Berlin Heidelberg, 1989, 428 pages

[Dijk68] Dijkstra, E. W.: *Go To statement considered harmful.* Comm. ACM, Vol. 11, Nr. 3, March 1968, pp. 147–148

[Dill90] Diller, A.: *Z: An introduction to formal methods.* Wiley, Chichester, 1990, 309 pages

[Ditt90] Dittrich, K. R.: *Object-oriented database systems: the next miles of the marathon.* Information Systems Vol. 15, No. 1, 1990, pp. 161–167

[Durc75] Durchholz, R.: *An analysis of the currency concept.* Angewandte Informatik 17 (6), June 1975

[Durc77] Durchholz, R.: *Types and Related Concepts.* In Morlet, E.; Ribbens, D. (eds.): International Computing Symposium 1977. North-Holland, Amsterdam, 1977, pp. 31–38

[DuRi72] Durchholz, R.; Richter, G.: *Das Datenmodell der 'Feature Analysis of Generalized Data Base Management Systems'.* Angewandte Informatik 12, Dec. 72, pp. 553–568

[DuRi74] Durchholz, R.; Richter, G.: *Concepts for Data Base Management Systems.* In Klimbie, J. W.; Koffeman, K. L.(eds.): Data Base Management. North-Holland, Amsterdam, 1974, pp. 97–122

[DuRi76] Durchholz, R.; Richter, G.: *Information management concepts (IMC) for use with DBMS interfaces.* In Nijssen, G. M. (ed.): Modelling in Data Base Management Systems. North-Holland, Amsterdam, 1976, pp. 49–72

[DuSi83] Durchholz, R.; Simm, H.: *DAGS — Database Management System Generic Support; A Versatile Internal DBMS Interface.* Berichte der GMD, Bericht 142, R. Oldenbourg Verlag, München, 1983, 295 pages

[Earn74] Earnest, C.: *A comparison of the network and relational data structure models.* Computer Science Corporation, November 1973, rev. April 1974

[FaLi89] Falkenberg, E. D.; Lindgreen, P. (eds.): *Information System Concepts: An In-depth Analysis.* Elsevier (North-Holland), Amsterdam, 1989, 357 pages

[GeLa81] Genrich, H. J.; Lautenbach, K.: *System Modelling with High-Level Petri Nets.* Theoretical Computer Science 13, pp. 109–136, 1981

[GoThWaWr75] Goguen, J. A.; Thatcher, J. W.; Wagner, E. G.; Wright, J. B.: *Abstract data types as initial algebras & the correctness of data representations.* In Proceedings of the Conference on Computer Graphics, Pattern Recognition, & Data Structure, IEEE 1975, pp. 89–93

[Grie82] Griethuysen, J. J. (ed.): *Concepts and Terminology for the Conceptual Schema and the Information Base.* Publ. no. ISO/TC97/SC5-N695, ANSI, New York 1982

[GuSc91] Günther, O.; Schek, H.-J. (eds.): *Advances in Spatial Databases.* Lecture Notes in Computer Science Vol. 525, Springer-Verlag, Berlin Heidelberg, 1991, 471 pages

[GyPaGu89] Gyssens, M.; Paredaens, J.; Van Gucht, D.: *A uniform approach toward handling atomic and structured information in the nested relational database model.* Journal of the ACM, Vol. 36, No. 4, October 1989, pp. 790–825

[HaRi89] Hagelstein, J.; Rifault, A.: *A Semantic Analysis of the Collection Concept.* In [Bati89], pp. 149–164

[Hain89] Hainaut, H-L.: *A Generic Entity-Relationship Model.* In [FaLi89], pp. 109–138

[HeRi86] Heuser, C. A.; Richter, G.: *On the relationship between conceptual schemata and integrity constraints on databases.* In Steel Jr., T. B.; Meersman R. (eds.): Database Semantics (DS-1). North-Holland, Amsterdam, 1986, pp. 27–39

[Hoar75] Hoare, C. A. R.: *Recursive Data Structures.* International Journal of Computer and Information Sciences, 4(2), pp. 105–132, 1975

[Hohe90] Hohenstein, U.: *Ein Kalkül für ein erweitertes Entity-Relationship-Modell und seine Übersetzung in einen relationalen Kalkül.* Technical University of Braunschweig, Doctoral Thesis, 1990, 212 pages

[HoUl79] Hopcroft, J. E.; Ullman, J. D.: *Introduction to automata theory, languages and computation.* Addison-Wesley, Reading, 1979

[HuKi87] Hull, R.; King, R.: *Semantic Database Modeling: Survey, Applications, and Research Issues.* ACM Computing Surveys, Vol. 19, No. 3, 1987, pp. 201–260

[Hull89] Hull, R.: *Four Views of Complex Objects: A Sophisticate's Introduction.* In [AbFiSc89], pp. 87–116

[HuSu89] Hull, R.; Su, J.: *Untyped sets, invention, and computable queries.* In [PoDS89], pp. 347–359

[ISO87a] ISO TC97/SC21: *Information Processing Systems — Database Language NDL.* International Standard ISO 8907: 1987

[ISO87b] ISO TC97/SC21: *Information Processing Systems — Database Language SQL.* International Standard ISO 9075: 1987

[ISO91] ISO/IEC JTC 1/SC18: *Information processing — Text and office systems —Office Document Architecture (ODA) and interchange format — Part 10: Formal specifications.* International Standard ISO/IEC 8613-10: 1991

[Jone80] Jones, C. B.: *Software development. A rigorous aproach.* Prentice-Hall International, London, 1980, 382 pages

[Jone86] Jones, S. L. P.: *Parsing Distfix Operators.* Communications of the ACM, Vol. 29, No. 2, February 1986, pp. 118–122

[Kane90] Kanellakis, P. C.: *Elements of Relational Database Theory.* In van Leeuwen, J. (ed.): Handbook of Theoretical Computer Science. Volume B. Elsevier, Amsterdam 1990, pp. 1074–1156

[Kara90] Karam, G. M.: *The FODA Conformance Analyzer.* Computer Standards & Interfaces 10 (1990), pp. 103–116

[KeKlTs77] Kerschberg, L.; Klug, A.; Tsichritzis, D.: *A taxonomy of data models.* In Lockemann, P. C.; Neuhold, E. J. (eds.): Systems for Large Data Bases. North-Holland, Amsterdam, 1977, pp. 43–64

[KhFrCa90] Khoshafian, S.; Franklin, M. J.; Carey, M. J.: *Storage management for persistent complex objects.* Information Systems Vol. 15, No. 3, 1990, pp. 303–320

[Kim90] Kim, W.: *Research Directions in Object-Oriented Database Systems.* In [PoDS90], pp. 1–15

[KiBeGa89] Kim, W.; Bertino, E.; Garza, J. F.: *Composite objects revisited.* Proc. ACM SIGMOD Intl. Conf. on Management of Data, Portland, Oregon, June 1989, pp. 337–347

[Kupe87] Kuper, G. M.: *Logic programming with sets.* In [PoDS87], pp. 11–20

[Lame85] Lamersdorf, W.: *Semantische Repräsentation komplexer Objektstrukturen.* Informatik-Fachberichte Band 100. Springer-Verlag, Berlin Heidelberg, 1985, 187 pages

[LeRi89] Lecluse, C.; Richard, P.: *Modeling Complex Structures in Object-Oriented Databases.* In [PoDS89], pp. 360–368

[Lori91] Lorie, R. A.: *The use of a complex object language in geographic data management.* In [GuSc91], pp. 319–337

[LuLaSt70] Lucas, P.; Lauer, P.; Stigleitner, H.: *Method and notation for the formal definition of programming languages.* Technical Report TR 25.087, June 1968, rev. July 1970, IBM Laboratory Vienna

[Mits88] Mitschang, B.: *Ein Molekül-Atom-Datenmodell für Non-Standard-Anwendungen.* Informatik-Fachberichte Band 185. Springer-Verlag, Berlin Heidelberg, 1988, 230 pages

[Otis91] Otis, A.: *A reference model for object data management.* Computer Standards & Interfaces 13 (1991), pp. 19–32

[PaSp89] Parent, Chr.; Spaccapietra, St.: *About entities, complex objects and object-oriented data models.* In [FaLi89], pp. 193–223

[PeMa88] Peckham, J.; Maryansky, F.: *Semantic Data Models.* ACM Computing Surveys, Vol. 20, No. 3, 1988, pp. 153–189

[PiHe89] Pimenta, M. S.; Heuser, C. A.: *Uma formalização em IMC: o modelo DODM.* Revista Brasileira de Computação, V. 5, N. 2, outubro/dezembro 1989, pp. 11–17

[PiTr86] Pistor, P.; Traunmüller, R.: *A database language for sets, lists, and tables.* Information Systems Vol. 11, No. 4, 1986, pp. 323–336

[PoDS86] ACM SIGACT, SIGMOD (eds.): *Proceedings of the Fifth Symposium on Principles of Database Systems.* ACM, New York, 1986

[PoDS87] ACM SIGACT, SIGMOD, SIGART (eds.): *Proceedings of the Sixth Symposium on Principles of Database Systems.* ACM, New York, 1987, 363 pages

[PoDS88] ACM SIGACT, SIGMOD, SIGART (eds.): *Proceedings of the Seventh Symposium on Principles of Database Systems.* ACM, New York, 1988, 352 pages

[PoDS89] ACM SIGACT, SIGMOD, SIGART (eds.): *Proceedings of the Eighth Symposium on Principles of Database Systems.* ACM, New York, 1989, 401 pages

[PoDS90] ACM SIGACT, SIGMOD, SIGART (eds.): *Proceedings of the Ninth Symposium on Principles of Database Systems.* ACM, New York, 1990, 425 pages

[Rade91] Radermacher, F. J.: *The importance of metaknowledge for environmental information systems.* In [GuSc91], pp. 35–44

[Reis85] Reisig, W.: *Petri Nets. An Introduction.* EATCS Monograph Series on Theoretical Computer Science, Vol. 4, Springer-Verlag, Berlin Heidelberg, 1985, 161 pages

[Rich79] Richter, G.: *Syntax of the Database Operation Language DABOL.* Technical Report IIG.79.214. GMD, Sankt Augustin, 1979, 32 pages

[Rich81a] Richter, G.: *Utilization of data access and manipulation in conceptual schema definitions.* Information Systems Vol. 6, No. 1, 1981, pp. 53–71

[Rich81b] Richter, G.: *IML-inscribed nets for modeling text processing and data(base) management systems.* In Zaniolo, C.; Delobel, C. (eds.): Proc. 7th Intl. Conf. on Very Large Data Bases, Cannes, France, September 1981, pp. 363–375

[Rich84] Richter, G.: *Netzmodelle für die Bürokommunikation. Teil 2.* Informatik-Spektrum 7, 1984, pp. 28–40

[RiDu82] Richter, G.; Durchholz, R.: *IML-inscribed high-level Petri Nets.* In Olle, T. W.; Sol, H. G.; Verrijn-Stuart, A. A. (eds.): Information Systems Design Methodologies: A Comparative Review. North-Holland, Amsterdam, 1982, pp. 335–368

[Rugg90] Ruggles, C. L. N. (ed.): *Formal Methods in Standards. A Report from the BCS Working Group.* Springer-Verlag, Berlin Heidelberg, 1990, 135 pages

[ScDeDuSc86] Schwartz, J. T.; Dewar, R. B. K.; Dubinsky, E.; Schonberg, E.: *Programming with Sets. An Introduction to SETL.* Texts and Monographs in Computer Science, Springer-Verlag, New York Berlin Heidelberg, 1986, 493 pages

[ScSc84] Schek, H.-J.; Scholl, M. H.: *An algebra for the relational model with relation-valued attributes.* Technical University of Darmstadt, Technical Report DVSI-1984-T1, 1984

[ScSc86] Schek, H.-J.; Scholl, M. H.: *The relational model with relation-valued attributes.* Information Systems Vol. 11, No. 2, 1986, pp. 137–147

[ScSc87] Schek, H.-J.; Schlageter, G. (eds.): *Datenbanksysteme in Büro, Technik und Wissenschaft.* Informatik-Fachberichte Band 136. Springer-Verlag, Berlin Heidelberg, 1987, 491 pages

[ScSc89] Schek, H.-J.; Scholl, M. H.: *The two roles of nested relations in the DASDBS project.* In [AbFiSc89], pp. 50–68

[Scio91] Sciore, E.: *An extended universal instance data model.* Information Systems Vol. 16, No. 1, 1991, pp. 21–34

[Seve72] Severance, D. G.: *Some generalized modeling structures for use in design of file organizations.* Doctoral Thesis, The University of Michigan, Ann Arbor 1972, 304 pages

[SiStUl91] Silberschatz, A.; Stonebraker, M.; Ullman, J. (eds.): *Database systems: achievements and opportunities.* Communications of the ACM, Vol. 34, No. 10, October 1991, pp. 110–120

[StHe75] Stonebraker, M.; Held, G.: *Networks, hierarchies, and relations in data base management systems.* Memorandum No. ERL-M504, College of Engineering, University of California, Berkeley, 1975

[Supp57] Suppes, P.: *Introduction to Logic.* D. Van Nostrand Company, Princeton, New Jersey, 1957

[Turs71] Turski, W. M.: *A model for data structures and its application.* Acta Informatica 1, pp. 26–34, 1971

[Ullm87] Ullman, J. D.: *Database Theory: Past and Future.* In [PoDS87], pp. 1–10

[Vian87] Vianu, V.: *Dynamic funtional dependencies and database aging.* Journal of the ACM, 34(1), January 1987, pp. 28–59

[Wegn87] Wegner, P.: *The Object-oriented Classification Paradigm.* In Shriver, B.; Wegner, P. (eds.): Research Directions in Object-Oriented Programming. The MIT Press, Cambridge, MA, 1987, pp. 479–560

[Wolf74] Wolfendale, G. L.: *A system for the definition of the syntax and semantics of data description languages.* In Günther, A. et al. (eds.): International Computing Symposium 1973. North-Holland, Amsterdam, 1974, pp. 517–525

[Zema68] Zemanek, H.: *Abstrakte Objekte.* Elektronische Rechenanlagen 10 (1968), H. 5, pp. 208–217

Index

The index is semi-automatically produced. It contains all words having more than one letter (inclusive of variables, nonstandard constants, catenation words and names), except if specifically excluded. The guideline for excluding a word was to eliminate those that would probably not help in finding a passage. One-letter words and non-technical terms are also retained if they would possibly help in an associative context search. Thus the index is rather comprehensive.

Words are taken as they appear in the text with the following exceptions:
- An initial capital letter of a plain word is converted to lower-case if the rest of the word is lower-case. (For proper names, however, the initial capital letter is retained.)
- Plurals and third person singular present tense forms are converted to their primary forms.

The index does not contain references to the Preface and Appendix B.